**Barnsley
Libraries**

Edition 1.1 – including minor revisions – 2013

Published by Adrian Middleton, 2013
(middlea.jimdo.com)

Paperback edition printed by CreateSpace
(www.createspace.com)

Kindle edition produced using Kindle Direct Publishing
(kdp.amazon.com)

. . . .

Contents

EDITOR'S PREFACE

Adrian Middleton, Sheffield, August 2013

I first encountered The Tour of the Don when researching weather events that had occurred in the Sheffield region for a book of which I was a co-author. Several abstracts appeared in the finished book — "Sheffield's Weather" — published as No. 16 of the Sorby Record Special Series in 2011 (available from the Sorby Natural History Society via their web-site at sorby.org.uk).

The 'Tour' became a bit of an obsession, partly because I couldn't find a copy of volume 2, and partly because so much of it described areas familiar from my childhood — albeit written 116 years before I was born.

I finally discovered a copy of the full two volumes that I could borrow. The copy was fragile and I had too much respect for the old paper to try and scan the pages, so I set up a camera stand and lighting and began a long process of photography, OCR, editing and annotating, correcting errors created by the OCR, and amending the occasional printing error from the original. This formed the basis for the text in this version. Many early 19th century spellings (e.g. 'recal' for 'recall') and phrases remain to irritate and amuse the reader, but the text is hopefully readable. Some licence has been applied in the formatting, particularly of quotations, which have been isolated from the text and indented. Annotations have been added (in { }) where I have found more information — these may appear random, but they reflect my own interests, curiosity and reasons for reading the book rather than any aim for completeness. Binomial species names have generally been amended to show modern capitalisation (*Genus species*) — any further change to species names, in either spelling or naming, is shown in { }. Footnotes from the original have been placed within the flow of the text to simplify the layout as an e-book. Where possible, locations have been identified and annotated with a six-figure Grid Reference — interpretation of these is explained on all Ordnance Survey maps, or they can be typed directly into web-sites such as streetmap.co.uk to pinpoint the location. Latin quotations have been translated, albeit only to the best of my limited ability aided by online translators —

though I have used other translations where they were available. Errors in the annotations are mine! Accept my apologies if you notice them. I would be glad to hear about any errors or any additional comments or information, though I make no promises about there being a revised edition.

Anyone following up the location information may find the following web-sites useful — Streetmap (www.streetmap.co.uk), mentioned above, gives the current OS 1:50,000 and 1:25,000 maps (i.e. the Landranger and Explorer scales); British History Online (www.british-history.ac.uk/map.aspx) allows browsing of the 1:10,560 maps (the old 6 inch) dating from the 1850s (in this area); and the National Library of Scotland (maps.nls.uk) provide browsable copies of the OS 1:25,000 'Provisional Series' dating from 1937-1961, i.e. before many recent developments (they also provide them as a seamless overlay to Google Maps). A useful source for older maps of Sheffield is the 'Picture Sheffield' service (www.picturesheffield.com/maps.php) which provides browsable versions of many historic maps from the last three centuries.

So, how did the 'Tour' come about and who was the author?

The 'Tour' originally appeared as weekly instalments in the Sheffield Mercury newspaper — the date is at the head of each chapter. They appeared anonymously, and only later were they identified as having been written by John Holland. Holland (14 March 1794–28 December 1872) was a native of Sheffield and an editor of the Mercury. A useful summary of his life, and links to other information are available on the internet on Wikipedia under the heading 'John Holland (poet)'.

The 'Tour' reflects Holland's interests. He was a poet — one chapter, on the River Rother, is entirely in verse, and there are many poetic quotes in the text, many of them from his own work. He was also a keen naturalist, with a particular interest in Botany, and at many locations he gives us details of the plants which he found there. His interests also led to him being elected as the curator of the Sheffield Literary and Philosophical Society — the society gets a mention in several chapters.

It also reflects his opinions. As a devout Christian, several chapters discuss related topics, and do sometimes become something of a rant — you will find fewer annotations on these chapters!

Several chapters digress from the ramble along the river to provide outlines of local personalities, and one very strange chapter ('Doncaster and the Doctor', dated 10th December 1836) tells the story of Doctor Daniel Dove of Doncaster, a fictional character and the subject of a rambling novel (for want of a better word) written anonymously over several decades by Robert Southey, the poet laureate. Only a portion would have been published by 1836, and the authorship was a subject of intense discussion in the literary magazines of the time.

Another chapter tells the story of another fictional, or should I say mythical, character — 'The Dragon of Wantley' — which supposedly lived in a cave on Wharncliffe Crags, a location still marked as 'Dragon's Den' or 'Dragon's Well' on 1:25,000 OS maps at SK306959.

The story of the writing of the 'Tour' is perhaps best described by an extract from the "Life of John Holland of Sheffield Park" written in 1874 by William Hudson and shown below — it has been edited to omit some of the more extensive quotes from the text

––––––

From **"Life of John Holland of Sheffield Park: from numerous letters and other documents furnished by his nephew and executor, John Holland Brammall"** by William Hudson, 1874. From Chapter XI. — 1835-1836 — p198ff concerning the writing of "The Tour of the Don".

> "As the year 1835 was drawing near its end, Mr. Holland must have felt himself in command of much leisure, with good opportunities to employ that leisure agreeably and well. Several of his chief literary designs had recently been accomplished; and he was encouraged to seek new employment for his pen. There was one project which had been before his mind for many years, but which had been quite impracticable until the year now under review. That project was, to ramble along the banks of the Yorkshire River

Don, and to write a description of the various portions of its course and especially of that in the neighbourhood of Sheffield. He thought he could trace the desire to do so to the reading of one or two books; and after revolving it in his mind, amidst other literary adventures of twenty years, he at length reached the determination that it should be put into action, and that a series of papers should appear in the pages of the Mercury. There the introductory article was published on the 2nd of January, 1836. The date which it bore was December the 24th; and the writer signed himself "Viator". At the end of the year fifty-three chapters had appeared, and the river had been traced from its source to its confluence with the Ouse. The papers excited considerable interest; their republication was strongly requested; and Mr. Holland, in compliance, sent out, at the beginning of 1837, two volumes forming together nearly five hundred pages, and entitled The Tour of the Don. The explanatory part of the title was, "A series of Extempore Sketches made during a Pedestrian Ramble along the Banks of that River, and its principal Tributaries". For variety, descriptive power, and general interest, this work will most favourably bear comparison with all topographical books known to the present writer. It is now out of print; and he that tries to purchase a copy when it has found its way into the hands of a Sheffield bookseller, learns, and probably marvels to know, how it is valued in the neighbourhood.

The Tourist actually visited the places described. In order to render effectual his efforts to be quite correct in his descriptions of scenery and in his application of local names, he drew section maps of the course of the river, which, however, were not printed. And the tedium of occasional topographical details is hardly felt by the reader, because of the ingenious introduction of notices of eminent men and interesting events, with judiciously selected passages from the poets and occasional original verses.

It would be grateful to the biographer to linger long over The Tour of the Don, the first of Mr. Holland's books that he remembers to have read. It is so comprehensive and so pleasantly written, that it deserves a very prominent place among the productions of its author.

. . . .

The entertaining Tourist lingered long in Sheffield and its vicinity, devoting thereto more than a dozen successive chapters, which appeared in the newspaper during the summer quarter when the reader might, with the greatest pleasure, go out to test the descriptions for himself. Lively topographical essays were interspersed with appreciative, honest, and courteous notices of the principal literary men of Sheffield, and of some other persons known to fame.

For example, Botany received a eulogium in connection with the name of Mr. Jonathan Salt; and Ornithology, the famous works of Audubon, and a memorable interview which Mr. Holland had in Sheffield with that justly celebrated naturalist, had such mention as became a Tourist who was an admiring and successful student of birds and their habits. That interview would be at the house of Mr. Heppenstall, a member of the Society of Friends, who "had his house full of ornithological specimens". The Tourist says: —

> "I shall not soon forget the evening I spent with John James Audubon and Lucy, his wife. He was one of the few men that a lover of natural history, or a lover of mere adventure either, would have gone a great way only to have seen. Truly a fine figure he is, with the eye of an eagle, the limbs of an antelope, and the simplicity of a real child of the forest; yet there was a quiet dignity in his demeanour, and a placid energy in his conversation, which impressed me with the idea of being in the presence of a man whose spirit was with future times, in the assurance that the moderate award of his contemporaries would not be the full measure of his renown."

The sketch of {James} Montgomery proved that love of the country can live and be powerful in a man, and poesy can raise his nature to her great elevation, amid "filthy backyards, black brick walls, shelving roofs, and a grotesque array of red chimney-pots", with a "cluster of substantial obstacles to the common daylight"; and, perhaps, the same sketch brought to some readers their first knowledge of Montgomery's removal from "The Hartshead", the place just described, to "The Mount," a place of residence which most people would deem fit for a poet.

The chapter devoted to Samuel Bailey, a man whose name and works are well known to political and philosophical students, contains some severe but just criticism. Mr. Holland had no sympathy whatever with those religious and political opinions for which Mr. Bailey was distinguished. He paid a just and generous tribute to the philosopher's great ability; but he commended the electors of Sheffield for persistently refusing to send that philosopher to Parliament. Mr. Holland was not a bigot; but he was a staunch orthodox believer; and while he was extremely liberal in matters of mere opinion, he could not bear what he regarded as repudiating the authority of the Word of God.

Ebenezer Elliott, the "Corn-law Rhymer", has frequent mention in The Tour; and the chapter dated August 13th is devoted to him and his poetry.

. . . .

The late Mr, Samuel Roberts, of Park Grange, was the subject of the article for August 27th. It gave an account of some of his numerous literary achievements, awarded him a good share of well-deserved praise for the manifold good work which it had been his happiness to do, and showed that the Tourist was, by no means, in agreement with him as to some questions of historical importance, although his personal character and his literary ability were regarded with great admiration. The two authors were attached friends. It seems very probable that before this time they had talked to each other about the authorship of the Tourist's articles in the Mercury. It was a real pleasure to Mr. Holland to preserve an editorial secret; and his allusions lead to the impression that he had in that respect a special gratification in this instance.

The concealment appears to have been so complete as greatly to puzzle all the literary men of the neighbourhood. Mr. Roberts entered with interest into the speculation; and the biographer has heard Mr. Holland tell the following story as illustrative of his success in an effort to conceal his authorship. During the day on which the article on Mr. Roberts appeared, the Tourist and the subject of his sketch met in the street. "Holland," said Mr. Roberts, brandishing his stick over his head, "now I know who is the author of those papers; for no one but yourself could have given the particulars published this morning about me". A fortnight later the Tourist sketched Mr. Holland himself in such a manner that Mr. Roberts lost all confidence in his former conclusion. Soon the two friends met again, when Mr. Roberts said, "Holland, I must have been in error after all; for you cannot have written what has now been said about yourself".

. . . .

From the Tourist's sketch of himself and his career several things have already been transferred to this volume, which need not be particularly referred to again. The additional sentences, here subjoined are characteristic and very significant : —

. . . .

> "It remains to be added that, for some years past, Mr. Holland has had an official connection with the Sheffield Literary and Philosophical Society; and there he is to be seen, duly and truly, either conversing with some visitor or member of the Institution in the Museum, or seated at his desk in the Council-room, cogitating, it may be presumed, some subject in prose or verse, yea, in the opinion of certain sagacious persons, writing these very papers! I hope neither he nor any other person to whom they may be imputed will think it necessary to deny the authorship."

The Tourist significantly made himself the subject of his last

Sheffield article; and the next following week found him at Attercliffe, whence by weekly rambles he proceeded until he found the Don no more, but stood beside the Ouse. Then his long cherished project was accomplished. Reviewing the process, he wrote that his own name had been withheld out of

> "regard for considerations of obvious propriety, and that the names of others had been introduced, and opinions about them had been honestly expressed, without any unkind personal feeling".

And he was happily able to add: —

> "I do not entertain any such feeling towards any individual living; nor do I believe that I am the subject of any such feeling on the part of others".

It remains to be stated that The Tour of the Don contains a number of original poems and anecdotes, that there is in it much useful information, and that the author appears in it as a very decided Christian, vigorously defending the theory of an Established Church, and yet writing of Nonconformists and their good works in a spirit of great admiration and strong sympathy. The biographer puts the book aside with reluctance and regret, because he feels that it contains most interesting things to which not so much as a reference can be given in the present volume, through want of space."

THE TOUR OF THE DON.

A SERIES OF EXTEMPORE SKETCHES
MADE DURING A PEDESTRIAN
RAMBLE ALONG THE BANKS OF THAT RIVER,
AND ITS PRINCIPAL TRIBUTARIES.

ORIGINALLY PUBLISHED IN THE SHEFFIELD
MERCURY
DURING THE YEAR 1836.

"O thrice, thrice happy he who shuns the cares
Of city troubles and of state affairs;
Who, leading all his life at home in peace,
Always in sight of his own smoke, no seas,
No other seas be knows, no other torrent
Than that which waters, with its silver current,
His native meadows; and that very earth
Shall give him burial which first gave him birth."

Du Bartas

IN TWO VOLUMES

VOL. I.

LONDON:

R. GROOMBRIDGE, PANYER ALLEY, PATERNOSTER
ROW;

AND G. RIDGE, MERCURY OFFICE, SHEFFIELD

1837.

AUTHOR'S PREFACE.

Although the subject matter of the first paper in the following series, is of a character to render anything like a formal Preface in a great measure unnecessary, it would little become the writer to take advantage of that circumstance for the omission of the usual courtesy towards gentle readers. To those persons, therefore, whose perusal of these essays in the newspaper where they first appeared, was followed by the expression of a wish to possess them as they now are, the present tender of a grateful acknowledgment is due; and not less so to those, who may happen to seek and find entertainment or information in a book, of the accumulation of the contents of which they might not previously have heard. To say that a work so unpretending, as that which is now in the reader's hand, might well claim to be exempted from the stern award of literary justice which usually awaits more ambitious performances, were an affectation, only less pardonable than would be the vanity of supposing any great anxiety could exist in high quarters, either to praise or blame in this instance. Having reassured the reader, that the papers comprised in this work were, as intimated in the title page, a series of extempore compositions, written at the times, and under the circumstances implied in the head lines, or in the matter of each article, it may not appear improper to suggest that the reader must neither look for the methodical formality of the topographer on the one hand, nor the consecutive drift of the professed essayist on the other. A knowledge of the fact that many individuals read these sketches with pleasure during their progressive appearance, added to the natural reluctance that even such frail memorials of scenes and circumstances more or less endeared or interesting to so many persons,' should be consigned at once to that oblivion which mostly awaits newspaper literature, induced the publisher to risk their reappearance in the present neat form. The writer has only to add, that he would confess himself disappointed, were he to know that those individuals, "young and old, of either sex", into whose hands this book may fall, would lay it down, without feeling any more interest in the course of the Don, or experiencing any other associations with the places on the line of the river than they did previously to the perusal of the following pages.

Sheffield, Jan. 1, 1837.

TOUR OF THE DON

— — — — — — — —

No. I. — INTRODUCTION.

January 2ⁿᵈ, 1836.

THE idea of a descriptive ramble along the course of the Don, has been entertained from a period almost coeval with the very boyhood of the writer. It probably originated in the perusal of Hutton's (of Birmingham) narrative of a visit to the Roman Wall, down in the north yonder, coincidently with an opportunity of examining an elegant sketch by a lady of the source of the Thames; and, added to these circumstances, the repeated visits paid in hours of youthful leisure, and subsequently, to various portions of the Yorkshire river, especially in the neighbourhood of Sheffield.

The idea, however, thus conceived, lay unexpanded in the author's mind, till much of that vivid freshness with which it was at first presented, had yielded to the ordinary influence of time: but still, what the subject might lose in brilliancy and colour, it seemed to gain in distinctness of exhibition; and amidst a range of rather extensive and diversified literary enterprise, the hope of sometime compiling this little sketch never wholly disappeared.

In the summer of 1834, circumstances not necessary to be particularised here, again led the writer to think of the subject; and conceiving it might not be unacceptable to many of the readers of the *Sheffield Mercury,* he determined to make that paper the medium of his lucubrations, as he wrote them, whenever the prospect of fairly pursuing the river from its source might appear. To say that the present is exactly that moment, might seem presumptuously to calculate upon health and opportunities which Providence alone can furnish: but, on the other hand, to commit himself thus to the subject, as the recurrence of a weekly demand for each section may arrive, will pledge the writer to make a consecutive effort to perform his task. If that which is taken up as a matter of intellectual recreation with the writer, shall prove the source of any gratification to "gentle readers", whether male or female, old or young, a double pleasure must be the result.

It may be necessary further to remark that, whatever effect the lapse of twenty years may have had upon the author's predilection for this subject, the latter half of that period has had a still more important bearing in directing public attention to the river itself. The mighty magician of the North, who, by the potent spell of his pen has given such a charm of interest to many spots in this and the sister kingdom of Scotland, has laid some of the scenes of his celebrated romance of "Ivanhoe" on the banks of the Don; these will be more particularly noticed in a subsequent section. Mr. E. Rhodes, of this town, whose elegant work descriptive of "Peak Scenery" {1818-24} stands unrivalled in its discriminating exhibitions of the chief beauties of that picturesque country to which its details refer, has employed the same powers of delineation in a fragment on "Yorkshire Scenery" {1826}, which touches in some degree on the line of description adopted in the present sketches. It were vain to wish that the pen which inscribes these notices could but be used with the pictorial tact which has enabled the tourist last named, to surpass even the "Author of Waverly" himself in fidelity. But the most local describer remains to be named. The Rev. Joseph Hunter, one of the most learned, elegant, and exact of our living topographical historians, has rendered the district of the Don classical; first, by the publication of his "Hallamshire"{1819}, an elaborate work describing that interesting and diversified tract of which Sheffield is the capital; and, secondly, by a similar history of the "Deanery of Doncaster" {1828/31}, an ecclesiastical section of the great county of York, which comprehends the entire course of the river about to be described.

With works like these before him, an unpretending individual who attempts to pass over any portion of the ground so pre-occupied, with a design of so describing its aspect, as to present any new phase of interest, may hardly hope to escape the charge of temerity, at least. The provinces of the tourist and the topographer, may, indeed, be said to be distinct; but the boundary line between them is often so shadowy, that nothing except want of inclination for passing over it by either party, appears to remind one of its existence. If the writer of this unpretending series of sketches, made in pursuance of a long cherished intention, may venture to flatter himself with the hope that their perusal may not be altogether uninteresting, that hope will certainly be based in no slight degree upon the consideration, that with such a guide as the erudite author last named, it will hardly be possible to blunder egregiously in pursuing the route prescribed. Nor would it be decent here to omit all mention of the fact that the Don — a "thrice and four times" honoured flood! — has received other and later, albeit briefer greeting from the pen of the garrulous, erudite, and philosophical — pedantic and fantastical some will say — biographer of "Doctor Daniel Dove", formerly of Doncaster {the subject of Chapter L in Volume 2 of 'The Tour'}. With this entertaining scribe we shall probably more than once exchange salutations in the course of this fluvial peregrination: meanwhile, to shew that our author is worthy of the distinction here accorded — listen, gentle reader, to what he says of his hero and friend: — "The feeling of local attachment was preserved by Daniel Dove in the highest degree — he had as much satisfaction in being acquainted with the windings of a brook, from its springs to the place where it fell into the Don, as he could have felt in knowing that the sources of the Nile had been explored, or the course and termination of the Niger."

No. II. — HISTORICAL NOTICES.

January 9th, 1836.

"The river flowing quick as ink from pen
Of learned scribe; like that hath often left
Strong trace indelible, or record clear
Of its own early state, or things that were
In bygone ages witnessed on its banks."

"THERE is no end", says a clever writer, "to the interest Rivers excite. They may be considered physically, geographically, historically, politically, commercially, mathematically, poetically, pictorily, morally, and even religiously". In each of these points of view, might the river Don be regarded — in most, if not in all of them, it will be considered in the course of the present rambles. Meanwhile, that we may proceed with something like order, let us, in conformity with established usage, afford some insight as to the name and reputation of our River, as furnished by elder writers on British Topography. The appellations *Don* or *Danus,* which, with several others of like form, have long been applied to this beautiful River, are derived, by Camden {1607}, from *Dan,* an ancient British word, implying a deep or low channel; and by Whitaker from *D'Avon* a word of the same people signifying "The Water;" while both these etymons may be doubted, we have the fact that one of the great Northern European rivers bears the same name. Our river has not only had the luck of bearing an appellation which has puzzled the antiquaries, but likewise of having been characterized by two epithets, both remarkable for their inappropriateness: it is by Milton designated the "gulphie Dun", and by Harrison {in Hollinshed's Chronicle (1587)}, the "swift Done". A river of the same size, more free from any thing resembling gulphs, it would not probably be easy to find; and although when swollen with rains, its various tributaries render its torrent impetuous enough, yet under ordinary circumstances, the progress of the stream is by no means remarkably rapid in any part of its line.

The celebrated Roger Dodsworth {1584-1654}, whose immense collections on all matters relative to Yorkshire topography, have afforded such an exhaustless mine of information to local historians, observes that "the river Dune riseth in the upper part of Pennystone [and runneth] thence to Bolderstone by Midhop; — leaving Wharncliffe Chase (stored with roebucks, which are decayed since the great frost), on the north, belonging to Sir Francis Wortley, where he hath great iron works. The said Wharncliffe affordeth two hundred dozen of coals for ever to his said works. In the chase he had red and fallow deer and does; and leaveth Bethuns, a chase and tower of the Earl of Salop, on the south side. By Wortley to Wadsley, where in times past, Everingham of Stainbro' had a park, now disparked. Thence to Sheffield, and washeth the Castle walls, keepeth its course to Attercliffe, where is an iron forge of the Earl of Salop; from thence to Wincobank, Kymberworth, and Eccles, where it entertaineth the Rother, coming presently to Rotherham, then to Aldwark Hall, the Fitzwilliam's ancient possessions; then to Thriberg Park, the seat of Reresbys, knights; then to Mexbrough, where hath been a castle, thence to Conisbrough Park and Castle of the Earl of Warrens, where there is a place called Horsa's tomb. From thence to Sprotbrough, the ancient seat of the famous family of the Fitzwilliams, who have flourished ever since the conquest. Thence by Newton unto Doncaster, Wheatley and Kirk-Sandal, to Barnby-Dunn, by Bramwith and Stainforth, to Fishlake, thence to Turnbridge, a porte town, serving indifferently for all the west parts where he pays his tribute to the Aire."

This account of the progress of the Don, is on the whole tolerably correct, allowing for some looseness of connection with certain places named, and the easy mistake of a stranger concerning the Midhope river, which will be adverted to more particularly hereafter. It may be mentioned, too, in this place, that although the embochure of the river was originally as Dodsworth describes it, an important alteration has long since taken place in this respect. From the time of the general drainage of "the Levels", the waters of the Don have forsaken the lower part of their bed, and now pour themselves into the Ouse near Goole. Previously to this event, the Don, on its arrival at Thorne, divided itself into two branches or channels; one of these communicated with the Aire, as above described, while the other emptied itself into the Trent, a little previous to its junction with the

Ouse. This branch of the Don constituted the boundary line of the county of York, and the southern extremity of the kingdom of the Brigantes.

Drayton {Michael Drayton, 1563-1631} in his elaborate topographical poem, entitled, "Poly-Olbion"; and in the 28th song {published in 1622}, where he

> "Makes the three Ridings in their stories
> Each severally to show their glories",

introduces the muse of the West Riding as thus addressing the Don: —

> "Thou first of all my floods, whose banks do bound my south,
> And offer'st up thy stream to mighty Humber's mouth;
> Of yew and climbing elm, that crown'd with many a spray,
> From thy clear fountain first through many a mead dost play,
> Till Rother, whence the name of Rotherham first begun,
> At that her christened town doth lose her in my Don,
> Which proud of her resource tow'ard Doncaster doth drive,
> Her great'st and chiefest town, the name that doth derive
> From Don's near bordering banks, when holding on her race,
> She, dancing in and out indenteth Hatfield Chase,
> Whose bravery hourly adds new honours to her bank.
> When Sherwood sends her in slow Iddle that makes rank
> With her profuse excess, she largely it bestows
> On Marshland, whose swol'n womb with such abundance flows,
> As that her batt'ning breast, her fatlings sooner feeds,
> And with more lavish waste, than oft the grazier needs:
> Whose soil, as some report, that be her borderer's note,
> With th' water under earth, undoubtedly doth float;
> For when the waters rise, it risen doth remain
> High, whilst the floods are high, and when they fall again,
> It falleth; but at last, when as my lively Don
> Along by Marshlands' side, her lusty course hath run,
> The little wand'ring Went, won by the loud report
> Of the magnific state, and height of Humber's court,
> Draws on to meet with Don, at her approach to live {*}."

{* Note that this is an error in the quote given in the original. It should read 'at her approach to Aire' (p187 of 1876 reprint).}

It is remarkable in the two preceding extracts that neither Drayton nor Dodsworth, whom the poet evidently follows, mention any of the several rivers which flow into the Don above the Rother: also, that the poet does not so much as name Sheffield; which place, it might have been expected, would have afforded good matter for a line.

Rivers — especially those of vast volume, are estimated as being among the most important causes of modification of the earth's surface; their age, origin, and effects, involve questions of the highest consequence to the geologist, as those upon which the solution of so many problems affecting the physical history of the globe depend. Probably those persons only who have read the elaborate volumes of Mr. Lyell — the most full of information relative to what is termed "Tertiary geology", can at all conceive of the prodigious effects attributed to large rivers, as comprising a portion of those "causes still in operation", to which the learned investigator is inclined to refer so enormous an agency in the raising of hills, the scooping of vales, and especially in the deposition of the matter of diluvial plains. It is not of the theories of Mr. Lyell, but of his collections of facts, that I accord this commendation.

The antiquity of rivers, as just intimated, is remarkable — Who ever heard of the birth of a great river? Often have they, indeed, like other great ones, been diverted for evil or for good, from their natural courses. In some instances too, waters which were undoubtedly once of considerable volume, have shrunk into streamlets — or, perhaps, have been lost altogether: but for the most part, rivers are among the oldest recognized coevals of the actions of mankind; and of which actions in subsequent ages, they have become the authorical vouchers, or the poetical accessories.

It is thus, we perceive, that rivers become important aids in the identification of historical events: the general unchangeableness of their courses rendering them at the same time of not less consequence in determining great geographical problems, or in affording memorials of long established local divisions. The writer of a clever essay "On the Natural Boundaries of Empires" {John Finch, ?1833}, in adverting to one class of them remarks that, in the first ages of man, rivers are a true boundary; they prevent the passage of armies. They are now used as a boundary, chiefly because they afford a definite line, about which there can be no dispute. Europe, Asia, Australia, Africa, America, present numerous examples. A singular fact takes place in regard to them: — a small stream is considered a better division between nations than a large one — the Rubicon and not the Po, was the boundary of ancient Rome. The Pruth would not form a line of demarcation between Russia and Turkey, but there is a scanty population on its banks. — France has fought to obtain the boundary of the Rhine: she must now either advance to the mountains beyond, or retire to the next range of hills in her present territory.

The reason of this law is obvious;

> "the fertile banks of large rivers", says our author, "are usually peopled by numerous tribes of men; the calm and tranquil surface of the river invites them to pass over; the interests of commerce keep up a continual intercourse; the river is easily passed, and both banks will speedily unite under one government."

That which takes on the large scale with respect to kingdoms, typically occurs with regard to towns: — the Thames did not push its way through London — the inhabitants congregated on its opposite banks: mutual convenience built the bridges. So of Sheffield — and of fifty other places.

Never have the Ganges, the Nile, the Danube, or the Rhine, seen hostile nations with firm possession of their opposite shores. The small stream which divides Spain and Portugal, is a more lasting boundary than the Tagus would be, if it flowed in the same direction.

> "Where Lusitania and her sister meet,
> Deem ye what bounds the rival realms divide ?
> Or ere the jealous queen of nations greet,
> Doth Tayo interpose his mighty tide ?
> Or dark Sierras rise in craggy pride ?
> Or fence of art, like China's vasty wall? —
> No barrier wall! no river deep and wide!
> No horrid craggs! nor mountains dark and tall!
> Rise like the rocks which part Hispania's land from Gaul!
> But there between a silver streamlet glides,
> And scarce a name distinguisheth the brook,
> Though rival kingdoms press its verdant sides."

According to the authority above quoted,

> "there is no opinion more general, and more erroneous, than that of large rivers forming a boundary to nations. It is wrong to vex a peaceful river with armed garrisons upon its banks: it is no less wrong in a political point of view; numerous forces will be stationed on the shores by either party, and collisions must necessarily ensue."

The Don, could it "utter oral history", might tell something of such conflicts: — at present a quiet river, flowing within a single section of a single county — yea, within one ecclesiastical division of that section — it was once a line separating between hostile kingdoms. Mr. Hunter {in 'Hallamshire' 1819, p4} mentions a certain Latin poem, entitled "*Reliquiae Eboracenses*", by a Dr. Dering, Dean of Ripon {1743, by Dr Heneage Dering, 1701-1750}, in which

> "the Don is made to relate the great war which the Brigantes waged with the invaders; and in conformity with Camden's description, he is depicted
>
> > *Cinetus arundinibus crinem, et frondibus alni.*
>
> [With sedges girdled and with alder crowned.]

> "Sheffield is feigned with due regard to historic probability to be the place from which the Brigantes were supplied with arms; and her industrious artizans are represented hanging up before them armour taken from the foe, as patterns by which to fabricate their own.
>
> > *'Mille ardet Sephihea focis. Fomace liquescit*
> > *Montibus effossi vicinis massa metalli;*
> > *Et longe resonat glomeratis ictibus incus :*
> > *Nec limce aut cotis cessat labor. Insuper arma*
> > *Ante ocidos fabri ponunt Romana; notantque*
> > *Mutandum siquid; seu tint exempla sequenda.'*
>
> [Where busy Sheffield dims the vale below,
> A thousand hearths at once intensely glow;
> Drawn from the bowels of the hills around,
> Huge piles of ironstone press the caverned ground;
> By these the roaring furnace is supplied,
> Till from rich ores the molten currents glide:

Next, aided by the slowly labouring wheel,
They on the ringing anvil vex the steel;
Each ponderous hammer while the mass it beats,
Awakening Echo in her lone retreats.
Nor less the file, and grindstone swift, demand
The skilful pliance of each active hand.
Meanwhile, the smiths, ingenious to discern
Vulcanian artistry, and prompt to learn,
Before their eyes old Roman armour place,
Mark its fit fashion, its firm substance trace;
With such rare patterns, joined to long-tried skill,
Brigantian artists their bold task fulfil;
The breastplate shines — the spear is tempered well,
And round the glittering arms proud partial bosoms
swell.]

"When father Don", adds Mr. Hunter, "has concluded his narrative, he invites the hero of the poem and his companions to an entertainment he is about to give in his hall to his brother rivers: and much of a poetic imagination is discovered in the description of the hall and its icy ornaments. — What principally engaged the attention of the visitors were certain vases of crystal, each containing the perfect image of some celebrated personage who had been born or had lived upon this river's banks. They recognize the founders of the nobility of Wentworth and Osborne, and a more eminent character of earlier time —

> *'Gallorum terror, Sephilseus heros.'*
> [Sheffield's hero — terror of the Gaul!]

the great John Talbot, first Earl of Shrewsbury.

> "This work is little known. The classical reader will find that he needs not the aid of local attachment to receive much pleasure from its perusal."

With such gems has the historian of Hallamshire beautifully inlaid one of the most perfect of topographical works. The concluding compliment to the classicality of Dering's Hexameters, may well startle the presumption which has dictated the paraphrase placed between brackets.

No. III. — GENERAL REMARKS.

January 16th, 1836.

"Wide o'er the brim, with many a torrent swell'd,
And the mixed ruin of its banks o'erspread,
At last the raised-up river pours along:
Resistless, roaring, dreadful down it comes,
From the rude mountain and the mossy wild."

THOMSON.

A FEW words more will suffice to complete the brief introductory sketch necessary for our purpose; the filling up, or carrying out of which will furnish the matter of subsequent chapters. In the first place, then, it may not be uninteresting here, briefly to enumerate, in the order of their succession, the more important of the solid strata occurring upon the immediate line of the river. As the beds about to be named dip, generally speaking, from west to east, we come upon the basset edges or lines of outbreak, first of those that are lowest in the series, and successively upon those of the superior masses, as we travel downward with the stream of the Don. It will be seen from this, as well as from what follows, that rocks the highest in relation to the level of the sea, or other line, may be, and indeed frequently are, lowest in geological position — elevated mountain ranges of primitive character, appearing either to have protruded through the incumbent strata, leaving the latter inclined upon their flanks; or some powerful external agency has swept away the more elevated investiture of modern strata, the edges of which successively "come to day", within the circuit of denudation phenomena, indicative of both these causes occur.

The names and order of the rocks in our course, are derived from the delineations on the beautiful coloured geological Map of Yorkshire, published by Mr. W. Smith {1821, in a series of County Maps} — a name venerable in the annals of modern Geology. It may be necessary farther to premise, concerning the basset edges or surface selvages of the strata spoken of, that they must not be supposed to present themselves in any thing like straight lines, or even gentle curves; on the contrary, the surface indication, is often as zigzag in its bearings as can well be imagined: neither must it be assumed that the definable outlines of these last inclining suits of strata extend to equal distances — much less that they all run right through the county; though eight or ten of them do, in fact, preserve for about fifty miles something like parallelism relatively to a line drawn between Sheffield and Bradford; while two or three of the beds are traceable through nearly twice that distance.

The elevated range of hills west of Sheffield, and which form the horizon boundary to the view in that direction, and extending northwardly far beyond the point where the Don rises, consist of what is called Moorstone, or with reference to some of its beds, millstone grit. It reposes upon the metalliferous or mountain limestone, which, however, does not appear in this part of Yorkshire; though from Clitheroe on the S.S.W. to Bernard Castle on the N.W., it protrudes throughout the moorstone district in vast mountainous ranges, containing the rich veins of lead, calamine, &c. worked in the mining districts: it is the limestone, mostly so conspicuous in the bold and romantic scenery of the Peak. The moorstone, including the millstone grit, so called from the siliceous nature of its constituent particles, is in some places of immense thickness, having been proved in several situations in Derbyshire to the depth of 120 yards.

In the heights of this Moorstone, as already stated, the Don has its rise, and down gullies of which, its feeders flow, until, having passed a tract of clay, the river comes to the Flagstone rock upon which Penistone {~SE246033} stands: it then runs between the edges of the last named, and what is called the Wortley rock, crossing the latter at Sheffield. Between Tinsley {~SK396903} and the Holmes {~SK414923}, the river passes over a strip of the Bradgate rock, a fine grained freestone, of the grit character, like the preceding — it then enters upon that striking coloured stratum called, from the town built upon it, the Rotherham red rock. It then passes successively between Mexbrough {~SK480996} and Sprotbrough {~SE541017}, through three series of rocks, denominated from Chevet {~SE340154}, Ackworth {~SE440179}, and Pontefract {~SE461223}; the middle one being a free workable grit, wrought for grindstones and other purposes. The above named strata, from the millstone grit series to the Pontefract rock inclusive, comprehend what are usually termed the coal measures, the seams or beds of combustible matter lying between the several rocks, or, to speak with reference to the whole, alternating with them: the coal seams in each case being enclosed between, or divided by layers of shale, or indurated clay of different descriptions.

Between Sprotbrough {~SE541017} and Balby {~SE557016} the channel of the Don intersects for somewhat more than a mile, a portion of what Mr. Smith terms the "Redland Limestone", consisting, first, of the variety denominated from one of its constituent ingredients, magnesian; secondly, red clay and gypsum; and, thirdly, the Knottingly limestone, a hard, blueish white, thin bedded rock, which yields the lime celebrated for agricultural purposes. Below Doncaster {~SE567037}, we enter the red marl district, the character of which, is in immense tracts, deeply obscured by diluvial gravel, or by the turf investiture of Hatfield Chase {~SE714100}. The foregoing is only intended as a slight and general sketch of the strata occurring in the line of the river: it will, however, serve as a key in some sort, to the geological character of the district about to be traversed.

The Don, from the point at which its stream becomes sufficiently considerable, is used, as we shall afterwards perceive, for giving motion to various works by means of water wheels. At Tinsley {SK400914}, three miles below Sheffield, it becomes implicated with arrangements for navigation, by means of which its waters are rendered of vast importance, as connecting, by the Humber, the mercantile operations of Sheffield, and those of an extensive adjacent district, with the German Ocean. The historical particulars of this subjection or appropriation of the river, being rather matters of commercial than of pictorial interest, may be almost altogether omitted in this sketch. Less uninteresting, however, to the tourist, are many of the details illustrative of that noble and successful scheme of drainage, which so totally changed the aspect of that "Marshland" tract, through which the river flows immediately before it falls into the Ouse {SE749229}.

As might be expected, in so extended a course, as that pursued by the Don, the geological formations encountered are, as we have seen, sufficiently various; nevertheless, thus much may be said generally, that whatever may be the substratum exposed in its channel, the reputation for fertility and good husbandry of the lands along its banks, almost from its source to its termination, could scarcely be surpassed — it flows, indeed, for a considerable space through what may literally and emphatically be called a *corn country.*

The distance between the mouth of the Don in conjunction with the Ouse {SE749229}, and its source, in the moors above Thurlstone {~SE133028}, measured in a direct line, is about forty miles; while the actual length from the former to the latter point, cannot be less than seventy miles. From this statement, it will be inferred that it pursues either a very circuitous or a very flexuous route — and in fact it does both: a line drawn in the direction first intimated, would pass through Silkstone {SE290058}, which place is about thirteen miles from Sheffield {SK350877}, the most southerly deflexion of the river: the amount of the smaller tortuosities on its line can only be conceived of by an inspection of the Map, or by an actual traversing of the banks.

Such numerous deviations from a strait course, in the current of a river so liable to be suddenly swollen with any considerable fall of rain on the hills west of Sheffield, renders the occurrence of injurious floods comparatively frequent. Of these casualties, various records have been preserved. Not to mention earlier or inconsiderable overflows, it may be remarked that, in 1755, and again in 1768, we have notices of great floods; the former washed away several bridges; in the latter year the torrent of the Sheaf, was so impetuous at the place of its junction with the Don at Sheffield, that it carried down the houses forming the north side of Talbot's Hospital {SK358875}, and drowned five of the pensioners: this occurred in the month of November. But the former was a Summer flood, and committed its ravages on the 5th of August; and on the 17th of the corresponding month, 42 years afterward, both the rivers were swelled to an "amazing height". By a still more remarkable coincidence of dates, on the 17th of August, 1799, the Don and Sheaf again overflowed their banks, inundating houses, and doing considerable damage to corn fields in their course. One of the highest floods probably ever remembered at the time, was that of the 16th of January, 1806; though that was more than equalled by the one of July, 1834. On both these occasions, the level space between the Bridgehouses and the Wicker, in the northern suburb of Sheffield, was completely laid under water; in the latter instance, the tops of the posts carrying the "white rails" along the river side, being only just visible {'White Rails' (~SK356880) are mentioned and shown in a number of paintings as along Nursery Street, or the opposite bank of the river} . In Rotherham {~SK427930}, the lower parts of the town were, in like manner, flooded: and so unexpected and sudden was the inundation, that happening as it did during the night, many persons, who had retired to rest in small dwellings situate in low situations, were with difficulty aroused to a sense of their peril, and rescued from the water. Of course, a vast variety of matters came down with the torrent, including timber, hay, domestic animals, &c.: many of these were stranded in the low level fields, over which the waters lay like a sea, or were detained by various obstacles; while the salvage of others was effected under circumstances of "jetsom" and "flotsam", by individuals disposed to exert themselves in the labour.

No. IV. — THE MOORS.

January 13th, 1836.

"My soul this vast horizon fills,
Within whose undulating line,
Thick stand the multitude of hills,
And clear the waters shine."

{From 'The Peak Mountains'} MONTGOMERY.

It was a beautiful morning at the beginning of August, when I found myself, after one of the most delightful rides I ever enjoyed, standing on that high table land of the English Appenines, in which so many important streams have their origin — streams, which, after rising within short distances of each other, and flowing in widely different directions, become rivers of consequence, carrying the waters, collected during their progress through several counties, to those great ocean receptacles which wash the northern and western shores of our island.

The scenery, by which I was surrounded, was of a most interesting character — for with all its amplitude and want of cultivation, there was nothing of savageness — nothing that could properly be called dreary; for the absence of rugged rocks precluded the idea of the former characteristic; while the rich purple tinge caused by the heath in flower, forbade that impression of sterility which seems essential to the latter appellation, — at all events in this country, and when the mind is in tune to enjoy nature. The exclamation, which I felt most inclined to indulge on the spot was "majestic!" followed by the chastened ejaculation of the Poet: —

"Ah, who can look on nature's face,
And feel unholy passions move ?
Her forms of majesty and grace,
I cannot choose but love."

PEAK MOUNTAINS. {by James Montgomery}

But, how much are the emotions with which even such an impressive expanse of swelling hills and sweeping vales — such "forms of majesty and grace" — are regarded, modified by the immediate pursuits, no less than the mental constitution of the beholder! We are told that

> "Petrarch had long wished to climb the summit of Mount Vernose {Ventoux}; a mountain presenting a wider range of prospect, than any among the Alps or Pyrenees. With much difficulty he ascended. Arrived at the summit, the scene presented to his sight was unequalled! After taking a long view of the various objects, which lay stretched below, be took from his pocket a volume of St. Augustine's Confessions; and opening the leaves at random, the first period, that caught his eye, was the following passage: —
>
>> 'Men travel far to climb high mountains; to observe the majesty of the ocean; to trace the sources of the rivers; but they neglect themselves'. Admirable reasoning, conveying as admirable a lesson! Instantly applying the passage to himself, Petrarch closed the book; and falling into profound meditation, 'If,' thought he, 'I have undergone so much labour, in climbing this mountain, that my body might be the nearer heaven, what ought I not to do, in order that my soul may be received into its immortal regions.' "
>> {~1350, from Petrarch's Letters}

To numbers, less pious or less poetical than Petrarch, who are daily whirled over the sublime elevation on which I stand — these "heights of England", as they are truly and significantly called by the country people hereabouts, the stupendous array, hardly suffices to divert for a moment, the thoughts of business which engross the mind: the *road to or from Manchester* being, with not a few persons, the only object of importance. To the sportsman, these extended tracts of unsubjugated moorland, appear chiefly interesting as the haunts of great numbers of grouse; and to the shepherd valuable, as affording sustenance to his flock. A member of this ancient fraternity, I noticed at a distance, not exactly like one of Virgil's buccolic pastors, *"sub tegmine fagi recubans"* {Reclining under beech}, but sitting on a large stone under the hill side, while a number of sheep were grazing before him; the picture being altogether, maugre the absence of "oaten pipe" and other classic accompaniments, one of the most pastoral I almost ever met with — except in books. I did not go up to the man; to whom I, therefore, gave the advantage of passing with me for a very sentimental personage; as, for aught I know to the contrary, might also be an individual who was following a flock of geese with much apparent gravity and satisfaction, along the road. But, whatever taste the shepherd might have for the beautiful, or the gozzard {gooseherd} for the sublime of nature, with which they were surrounded; and, however loth I might have been to have purchased those opportunities of contemplation which both undoubtedly possessed, on the terms of being compelled to pursue the monotonous calling of either, I dare say they would have considered my project of coming so far merely to look at the region including the sources of the Don, as not a whit more dignified. Wishing, however, my chance companions on the coach "good speed", and leaving the Strephon and Tityrus just alluded to,

> "Each in his way of life to cheer himself,"

I plunged amidst the heather, and soon found that, however deliciously cool the morning air might feel while ascending the eminence above Board Hill {? Bord Hill ~SE172009, Border Hill in 1854 OS 1:10560 map}, it was at least warm enough when, after having walked for a few minutes over an adjacent tract called Windleden Car {Windleden Carr ~SE147012 in 1854 OS 1:10560 map}, I paused to enjoy *in situ,* the effect of the following lines: —

> "The Moors — all hail! — ye changeless, ye sublime,
> That seldom hear a voice, save that of Heaven!
> Scorners of chance, and fate, and death, and time,
> But not of Him, whose viewless hand hath riven
> The chasm, through which the mountain stream is driven?
> How like a prostrate giant — not in sleep,
> But listening to his beating heart — ye lie!
> With winds and clouds dread harmony ye keep;
> Ye seem alone beneath the boundless sky;
> Ye speak, are mute — and there is no reply!
> Here all is sapphire light, and gloomy land,
> Blue, brilliant sky, above a sable sea
> Of hills, like chaos, ere the first command,
> 'Let there be light!' bade light and beauty be.
> But thou art here, thou rarest cloud-berry!
> Oh, health-restorer! did he know thy worth,

The bilious townsman would for thee resign
His wall-grown peach, well pleased. In moorland earth
Thee would he plant, thou more than nectarine!
Thou better grape! and, in thy fruit divine,
Quaff strength and beauty from the living bough."

VILLAGE PATRIARCH. {by Ebenezer Elliott}

The cloud-berry *(Rubus chamaemorus)* mentioned in the foregoing lines, whatever claims it may possess to the virtues attributed by the poet, is very rarely found — if indeed it be found at all — on the moors hereabout; though it may be met with at no great distance, particularly about Fidler Green {SE155002}, at which place I found a neighbouring hillsman had been digging up a quantity of these *club-berries,* as he called them, to send to Manchester, at the desire of a gardener, who wished to try the effect of cultivation upon them. The cranberry, *(Vaccinium oxycoccus {V. oxycoccos}),* is more common, though not so plentiful as the cowberry or clusterberry (*V. vitis Idaea. {V. vitis-idaea}).* Intermixed with the heath, we frequently notice too, the graceful stem of the crowberry, (*Empetrum niger)* the small black fruit of which affords sustenance to various birds. The quantity of these "fruits of the moor", however, taken collectively, is trifling compared with that of the common bilberry (*V. myrtillus.)* In the months of July and August, hundreds of children, and women too, may sometimes be seen on different parts of these moors, busily engaged in gathering these minute berries, which, possessing a subacid flavour, are often mixed with gooseberries in tarts: for the latter purpose, considerable quantities are sent to Sheffield every market day during the season. Bilberries are likewise used in some of the preparations of the Manchester dyehouses, — the children from Holmfirth constantly collecting them for that purpose.

The tract of uncultivated ground now under description, appears to have had its poet in the person of Mr. Godfrey Bosville {?1717-1784}, who about 1740, composed a piece in couplets, entitled "The Moors". This poem was never published — nor have I ever seen any other extract from it than one given by Mr. Hunter. The following lines are in keeping with the scenery: —

"In this deep solitude and brown domain,
Where silence holds her melancholy reign,

— 35 —

High on the hills and in the middle air,
The watchful shepherd tends his fleecy care;
A lonely trade! Yet in the summer's heat,
On some high cliff the distant brethren meet,
Where stones unweildly, piled by Saxon hands,
An uncouth work of ancient prowess stands,
To tell their future race of battles won:
That race sits heedless on the unlettered stone."

Bosville is a name otherwise associated with literary recollections:
of two sons of the author of the lines above alluded to, the elder lived
and died amidst the friendship of men of genius in the metropolis:
the second fell in his country's cause before Lincelles {? Battle of
Lincelles, 1793}, and his memory was embalmed in an early
production by a poet whose name was destined to become "Fame's
cynosure" to Sheffield. The following lines recal a touching
circumstance connected with the fate of the soldier: — the lady who
had to

"   Bosville's arms
Consigned the virgin treasure of her charms,
Ere twice the inconstant moon renewed her horn,
Saw the gay bridegroom from her bosom torn;
From weeping love, at glory's call he fled,
And made a soldier's grave his nuptial bed."

PRISON AMUSEMENTS. {by James Montgomery}

But to return — the most abundant material of the vegetable covering
of these vast moors, and that to which they are indebted for much of
their pleasing effect upon the eye, is the common ling, *(Calluna
vulgaris)*. Nor must the praise of this excellent little shrub be
confined to its appearance — it has other claims upon our attention;
for, besides affording, as it does, such an admirable covert for the
grouse, which here so abound, it yields abundance of honey to the
bees which delight to feed upon it; and also an economical substitute
for the common brush, the making of which affords a livelihood to a
number of individuals. At the season when the ling is in bloom, it is
common with many persons at a distance, to carry their bees for a
time, into these regions of plenty; and scores of hives may
sometimes be seen in rows under the walls in the vicinity of

inhabited spots, or stuck half buried in the slope of the hills. The writer noticed a number of stocks so placed in the hill-side just below the habitation called Snailsden House {? SE143031} — indeed, this snug mountain apiary strongly recalled that secluded ravine in the Pentland Hills of Scotland, in which the ingenious author of the "Revolt of the Bees", has placed the locale of his fiction; because, it seems, a shepherd resides there, who,

> "Besides tending his flocks, receives, during July and August, the bee-hives of the neighbouring inhabitants beyond the mountains, for the purpose of enabling the bees to gather honey from the hether — he has generally more than a hundred hives."

The Scotch locality is still more memorable in poetic records, as that where about Allan Ramsay laid the scene of his "Gentle Shepherd", and whose dainty description of the spot it is by no means out of keeping with *our* scene also to recal: —

> "＿＿＿＿＿＿Farer up the burn to Haby's howe,
> Where a' the sweets o' spring and simmer grow:
> Between twa birks out o'er a little lin
> The water fa's, and mak's a singin' din:
> A pool breast deep, beneath as clear as glass,
> Kisses wi' rosy whirls the bord'ring grass."

These moorland hives, towards the end of autumn, often acquire an astonishing increase of weight. Honey gathered from ling, has a peculiar bitterish flavour, which renders it less acceptable in some markets; though this is not everywhere the case.

Intermingled in its growth with the ling, is that very pretty shrub, the fine leaved heath *(Erica cinerea) {Bell Heather}*. These plants, so analogous in general structure, were until lately, comprised by botanists in the same genus. Mr. Salisbury, however, has separated them.

> "To avoid", says Sir J. E. Smith, "the inconvenience of giving a new generic appellation to the hundreds of plants, familiar to every body as *Erica,* or heaths, he has judiciously called our common ling, *Calluna,* from χαλλυνω {'to sweep up'}; which is doubly suitable, whether with Mr. Salisbury and Dr. Hall, we take it to express a *cleansing* property, brooms being

made of ling; or whether we adopt the more common sense of the word to *ornament* or *adorn,* which is very applicable to the flowers. Gaertner indeed was so struck with the peculiar construction of the *capsule,* that he adds a mark of admiration to his description."

There is no species of true heath found growing wild in America.

Amidst scenery, thus interesting in outline and adornment, we find the springs of that important river, whose course it is our object to trace.

No. V. — DON WELL.

January 20th, 1836.

"   Beside that brook
The mountains have all opened out themselves,
And made a hidden valley of their own:
No habitation there is seen; but such
As journey thither find themselves alone
With a few sheep, with rocks and stones, and kites
That overhead are sailing in the sky:
It is in truth an utter solitude,
Nor should I have made mention of this dell
But for one object which you might pass by,
Might see and notice not."

WORDSWORTH {from 'Michael'}.

"WHAT", asks an elegant compiler — "what can be more gratifying to a proud and inquisitive spirit, than tracing rivers to their sources; and pursuing them through long tracts of country, where sweep the Don" — to name the other rivers enumerated in the original passage, would be to disclose that the great European namesake of our Yorkshire Don is referred to; — but no matter: the gratification must exist in its degree, whatever the size or importance of the river.

Who, then, has not heard of the river Don? — *our* river Don — every adult individual, surely, from the Humber to the Mersey. But who has heard of "Don Well?" Not perhaps ten persons in ten thousand, even of those who know something of Yorkshire topographically. Let an individual, however, examine any good map of the county, and surely as he finds the lines indicative of the river, may he trace them up to a point inscribed as above: it will, indeed, be found by no means equally easy, even with the map in hand, to trace up the gallant stream to this distinguished fountain. If, however, the reader chooses to take a fine summer's day for the experiment, let him mount one of the morning coaches from Sheffield to Manchester, via Deepcar; let him ride about sixteen miles, or till he finds himself fairly on the "backbone" of England; and then let him throw off in quest of adventures. If his spirit be in tune with Nature's harmonies, he will not be disappointed: the pleasure of breathing the pure mountain air, inhaling the fragrance of the heath while plunging through its masses — even should the rambler get lost for an hour or two, will only be a pleasant affair. In high summer it may be so; but in winter — the snow thick and driving as it fell yesterday! — aye, even in autumn — it is a very different thing. I was once there on a visit to the well, in November; and a pretty plashy progress it was! While striding from tussock to tussock — sometimes missing the foothold upon the slippery grass, and sinking nearly up to the knees in an insidious "plash", — I said to myself, "I wonder whether ever a lady encountered a ramble on this *dead edge* ?" Never in winter, surely, thought I; and why should she, unless the fountain of the Don, like the fabled Arethusa, had the power of forming youth to beauty! Well, that sleety day is not without its pleasing remembrances — gone as it is with past years; and here I am again:

> " 'Tis years since I, beholding the deep swell,
> Don! of thy river, rolling in its course,
> Wished oft to travel upward to thy source, —
> And now I stand beside thy parent Well:
> Forth from the rock, see how the water gushes,
> And to the stream hard by, its oozy way
> Pursues — now hid, now glittering to the day,
> 'Midst moss, and matted grass, and scattered rushes :
> Green is the sluice — green amidst winter's snow,
> And summer's scorching heat; for this clear spring
> Doth no cessation of its issuing know,
> Whatever season may its changes bring.
> Long, long bright fount! thus full and freely flow,
> While future bards, perchance, may better praise bestow.

To stand — especially in the morning of life, and at the beginning of a new year — beside the fountain — source of a great river, must be a tripartite circumstance surely sufficient to excite some peculiar reflections even in the mind of the least susceptible individual. The comparison of life in its progress to the course of a stream, has been ingeniously pursued by many a poet, and by many a proser too: indeed, the idea is so natural and obvious, that we sometimes hardly recognise a figurative form of expression. Fancy suggests a recondite similarity. It has been confidently alleged by physical, and eagerly taken up by metaphysical writers, that such is the constant passing off of old, and accessions of new, particles of matter in the human body, that the man of twenty is a different person, as regards his materiality, to the man in whom inheres the mental consciousness of both at forty. This apparently puzzling remora, with which some authors have hampered the question of personal identity, is forcibly brought to mind by the manner in which we speak of a river. The Don, for example, we should say, has flowed in its present course for a thousand years; and there is a loose, and indeed a strict, sense in which this is significant enough: but on looking at the actual meaning of the terms, we do not fail to perceive in a moment their want of exact conformity to the fact — that the present river, so far as the water is concerned, is no more the same as that which bore the appellation at the Conquest, or even yesterday, than the grass on the hill yonder is the same that grew there a quarter of a century ago, because it has all along during the interval presented the same verdant appearance, and been called "Green Moor".

The comparison of human life to a river, was an idea which at one time took strong and abiding hold upon the imaginative faculty of one of the most singularly original minds which this age has known — that of the poet COLERIDGE. This remarkable man had, it seems, considered it a fault in Cowper's "Task" {published 1785}, that the subject which gives the title to the work was not, and indeed could not be, carried on beyond the three or four first pages; and that throughout the poem the connections are frequently awkward, and the transitions abrupt and arbitrary — as indeed they must almost necessarily be in a work of such excursive character. Coleridge, looking for a subject that should give equal room and freedom for description, incident, and impression, fixed upon "The Brook" as best calculated to illustrate, by its description and associations, ideas of the origin, progress, vicissitudes, and termination of human life.

> "I sought", he says, "for a subject that should give equal room and freedom for description, incident, and impassioned reflections on man, nature, and society, yet supply in itself a natural connexion to the parts, and unity to the whole. Such a subject I conceived myself to have found in a stream, traced from its source in the hills among the yellow-red moss and conical glass-shaped tufts of bent, to the first break or fall, where its drops become audible, and it begins to form a channel; thence to the peat and turf barn, itself built of the

dark squares as it sheltered; to the sheepfold; to the first cultivated plot of ground; to the lonely cottage and its bleak garden won from the heath; to the hamlet, the villages, the market town, the manufactories, and the seaport. My walks, therefore, were almost daily on the top of Quantock, and among its sloping coombs. With my pencil and memorandum book in my hand, I was *making studies,* as the artists call them, and often moulding my thoughts into verse, with the objects and imagery immediately before my senses. Many circumstances, evil and good, intervened to prevent the completion of the poem, which was to have been entitled, *The Brook.*"

"Would that the Brook had been written by Coleridge", exclaims one of the enthusiastic admirers of the metaphysical poet. The idea has been in some sort adopted, and avowedly so, by Wordsworth in his "River Duddon". Fine, however, as that series of sonnets is, Coleridge's poem, it is conceived, would have been much finer: but the work was *not* written; and in a retired cottage at the foot of Quantock, the enthusiast soon devoted himself to other and widely different studies, namely, "the foundations of Religion and Morality". *How* these all-important topics were discussed, need not be described here; neither does the present writer mean to attempt to moralise formally either in prose or verse, *a la Coleridge,* upon the Yorkshire Don,

> "Hasting to pay his tribute to the sea,
> Like mortal life to meet eternity."

It need not, however, be supposed that all allusion to passing seasons and circumstances will be directly avoided. Commencing our progress at once with the river and the year, it would be extremely unlikely, in a ramble like this, to shudder while encountering the wintry blast on these hills, and not be allowed to speak about the cold; to greet the verdant blush of reviving Spring in the budding beauty of Wharncliffe, and not be expected to associate with the enjoyment of the spot, the praise of genial influences; — as impossible would it be but why go farther in this style? — the reader, especially if a "gentle reader", will cheerfully take what comes, if presented in the spirit of kindness.

"But *where is* the Well?" enquires the impatient and ungentle reader.

This question shall certainly be answered in due time: meanwhile, it surely cannot be a very serious disappointment not to find the Well in this chapter, when the writer recollects once having spent a long summer's day in a fruitless search for it in the Moors!

No. VI. — THE SOURCES OF THE RIVER.

February 6th, 1836.

"_____The streams
Descending from the regions of the clouds,
And starting from the hollows of the earth
More multitudinous every moment, rend
Their way before them. What a joy to roam
An equal amongst mightiest energies."

EXCURSION.

Although very distinct prominence has, in the preceding section, been given to the DON WELL, both because it is so particularly indicated on all good maps of the county {SE133028}, and because it is really an interesting object on several accounts, we shall presently find that it is neither the exclusive fountain of the infant river, nor even the only striking orifice from which its waters immediately arise.

A person standing upon almost any point of the "Alpes Peninos", or elevated region alluded to in a former chapter, can hardly fail to perceive that his station forms in reality a sort of "dead edge", as it is significantly called on the maps — an irregular summit line, which runs between the anticlinal slopes of counties stretching, with various undulations of surface toward the north-east and south-west. Over the entire space commanded by the eye, may be discerned numerous denes or gorges, down some of which streams are seen to meander, while others are too distant, too deep, or at too considerable angles with the line of vision, to allow of more than an obscure indication of their uses. For instance, if a person stand at the foot of Snailsden, he sees the lower part of that mountain embraced by two of the more important of those feeders, which presently coalesce with others to form the infant river.

Snailsden is a long and magnificent mountain, commencing a little above Carlecoates {SE177035} (hereafter to be mentioned), and terminating, about three miles westwards, in a bold and rounded promontory called its *Pike* {SE132033} — a term applied with no more propriety than it would be to Brentland Edge {? Britland Edge Hill ~ SE106026}, another bold swelling hill beyond, in the direction of Mottram, which latter place can be distinctly seen from the moors above Don Well, when the weather is fine. Although by the term Snailsden, be commonly understood the mountain, it refers in strictness to the little valley adjacent — *den,* or *dene,* signifying a valley; and being in numerous instances used as a suffix in that sense, hereabout.

On the north side of Snailsden — and, properly speaking, down the ravine of that name — a considerable stream descends, which is locally known as the Swinehul Cleugh {? Swiner Clough ~ SE128029}. On the southerly side of the mountain, we have what is called the Dearden Water {?SE142018}, and running into which, at some distance above its union with the Swinehul, are two gullies called grains — a common Scottish appellation for small bifurcate water-courses, and no doubt introduced among these hills by the shepherds from the "north countree". It is upon the higher of these grains, that we find the celebrated DON WELL {SE133028} it is a hole in the bank side, apparently about twenty inches in diameter, and a dozen yards from the channel of the stream, with which its beautifully pellucid water quietly mingles, after flowing down a slope deeply matted with long grass and the well-known bog-moss *(Sphagnum).*

> "You see the glimmer of the stream beneath,
> But hear no murmuring: it flows silently
> O'er its soft bed of verdure."

The lower grain is also replenished by the water of an adjacent well, the volume of whose supply is not at all inferior to that above-mentioned; but it is not *the* Don Well. If, however, this spring lack the patronymic celebrity of its neighbour, it is not without distinction of another sort — namely, as being the most delightful water in the world when mixed with brandy! This compliment rests on the competent testimony of sportsmen who frequent these moors: and a delicious spot of velvetty grass hard by, exhibits several stakes driven into the ground, the original intent of which might almost as much puzzle a person who had never heard of black cocks, percussion caps, or Joe Mantons, to make out, as the stupendous circle of big grey stones on Salisbury Plain has puzzled the antiquaries: a shooter would at once recognise in this "Oasis of the desert" the station of last season's encampment, where had bivouacked his brethren of the trigger. A little below the junction of the two principal streams above named, their united water is augmented by a third, called the Harding, or Harden Cleugh {Harden Clough SE143038}; and afterwards by a fourth, the Smoden *(small dene ?)* {?Smallden Clough ~SE144014}.

These streams do not differ much in the character of their banks or channels: their beds are, for the most part, composed of masses of a coarse uneven slate; these stones are in many instances, scattered confusedly about; sometimes, however, they lie so as to form natural steps or terraces, over which the water falls in sparkling cascades. Other stones, of a different character, plentifully occur; and after a flood, considerable masses of shale or black indurated clay are laid bare; these, from the action of the air and water, presently decompose, and lie scattered in the water courses. Fragments of casts of stems, indented in the manner of various tropical plants of the cactoid tribe, are not uncommon; the writer met with an exceedingly handsome and ponderous specimen of this class of petrifactions in the Smoden, when crossing the trough of that stream, August 9th, 1834.

To an individual who, like myself, happens to be no sportsman, the solitude of these valleys is greatly relieved by the frequent rising of grouse — sometimes singly, but often several together; and, after a sort of surly note, as if angry at the disturbance, alighting at a short distance among the heath: at such indications, the emotions and calculations of a true gunner would doubtless be very different from mine. During my excursion on the day above named, considerable numbers of these highly prized and beautiful birds rose and settled around me; and I must confess I felt no satisfaction in the reflection, that before three days should pass over, many a strong wing which was then clapping so vigorously would be broken, and many a dappled bosom at that moment bright and plump in the sunshine, would be ruffled and bloody through the arts of the fowler!

Snailsden, which I had seen in early autumn, rising high above the surrounding eminences, in colour like the rich purple bloom of a full ripe plum, appeared now of a velvetty black — the intervening moorland space falling in shade from a deep dark tinge — through a russet brown, until it terminated in the withered bracken at my feet — some plots of which lay in swath, having been mown for drying as winter bedding for cattle. The sheep, which in summer so prettily dapple these hills, were no longer to be seen: but five or six fine

Highland goats, the property of ___ Stanhope, Esq., of Cannon Hall {SE272083}, which appeared by starts to nibble the pruinose herbage, and then lift up their heads to gaze at an intruder on their domain, gave rather a picturesque appearance to the sequestered slope of the Dearden dell {Dearden Clough SE142018}.

On looking at the general physiognomy of this hilly region, and at the same time suffering one's mind to wander for a moment into the maze of physical cause and effect, it becomes difficult to repel the intrusive question — whence originated these deep and variously intersecting valleys? Did the earth receive, in the process of its original formation, these vast hollowings of its surface? Were they produced by what are termed "secondary causes" — the operation of submarine currents, when ocean lorded it over these heights? Are they some of the mighty furrows made by the watery ploughshare of the Noachian Deluge? Or have they been eroded by the long — continued action of post-diluvian rivers, of which the present lightsome streams are the shrunken representatives?

Each of these theories has had its supporters —

> "But see, the storm is coming! Snailsden fades;
> Each vale, each rock grows white."

Last Saturday morning, the moorland valleys — in fact, the whole region about the sources of the Don wore a resplendent aspect: during the preceding day, driving flaky showers fell with few and brief intermissions from morning until night: the storm, it is true, did not exactly

> "   curl up the crumpling floods,"
> Nor "perriwig with snow the bald-pate woods;" —

the former flowing on, somewhat augmented by the profuse deposition; the latter standing out on the pure white grounds in dark and bold relief. The night was frosty; and the sun rose in a firmament of cloudless blue, bending over an undulating expanse of most glistening whiteness.

There is in the outline of the moors, when enveloped with snow, as they were last — and indeed during the present week, a peculiar and chastened beauty, which persons are in general too much chilled to appreciate. Covered by such a mantle, almost every asperity of surface, and generally every harsh tone of colour, are obscured; there appears something like a process of magical assimilation to have taken place; and "the mind in the eye" glides, as it were, over the glistening whiteness, with a facility and velocity far surpassing the powers of the most skilful sleigher that ever drove over its surface with dogs or deer. It is true, the scene presently becomes monotonous; but still, *it* is beautiful. And then, when the fall has been gentle, and the quantity not too great, how surprisingly distinct does it often render the more prominent features of a landscape! — trees, fences, buildings, and almost every other conspicuous object, appearing of uniform dark colour, give to the snow-covered expanse some of the effect of an uncoloured engraving, or delicate pencil-sketch of the scenery presented; and so distinct are sometimes these inimitable pieces of Nature's delineation, that places are clearly descried under the influence of a chilly blue winter's sky, that had been unnoticed amid the splendours of summer.

Another interesting, but less obvious — or rather, often less striking — effect, is the revelation which a slight snowfall makes of the movements of whatever creature has ventured to walk abroad, especially during the night. While the ground is bare, thousands of animals run to and fro, leaving, for the most part, no visible traces of their movements to the prying curiosity or destructive propensities of man: but let there only fall a few inches depth of snow, and after its cessation for a night, you may trace the fox to his covert in the wood; the well-known foot of the hare is recognised, where her presence had scarcely been suspected; the foumart {polecat} is traced to the sough, and the weasel to the wall; and even the mouse, light as it is, is yet not so light as the snow, — but, in common with the airiest birds, the wren and the titmouse, its "little footsteps lightly print" the snow. In the case of a person neither urged by hunger nor stimulated by the strong motives for extirpating noxious animals, there appears something cowardly — not to say cruel — in the taking advantage of a timid creature's involuntary evidence against itself, to effect its destruction, which is often practised. I like well enough to detect these nocturnal expatiatings of living things upon the pure white snow, just as I like to discover birds' nests in the green bushes; but neither the former nor the latter have any thing to fear in me, from

> "Guns or gins, or dogs or nets,
> Lime twigs, or ruthless hands."

Do you, gentle reader, like snow and ice — in their place and season? If you do — or fancy you do, — take the following quotation: —

"is there any one", enquires the intrepid Captain Ross, when frozen fast in the Arctic regions, — "is there any one who loves the sight of ice and snow? I imagine now, that I always doubted this: I am quite sure of it at present. The thought of ice may possibly suggest agreeable sensations in a hot July day; the sight of a Swiss glacier, in the same weather, is 'refreshing', I doubt not. This also is picturesque, I admit, as are the frozen summits of the Alps, particularly under the rosy tints of a rising or a setting sun. These and more are beauties; and they are not the less beautiful that they are, to some, rarities; while they are also characteristic, and are portions of a general landscape, to which they give a new and peculiar interest, as they add to its varieties. In the present days, it is not also a little in the praise of ice, that the traveller can say, I have visited Switzerland, I have scrambled across a glacier, I have seen the sun rise on Mont Blanc while the earth below was still in shade, I have ascended it — I, even I, the fearless and enterprising, have ascended the father of mountains, yea even when the guides hung back in fear. Even thus is ice beautiful, regaling, acceptable. Thus, too, is snow the delight of schoolboys: have we not all hailed the falling feathers, because we should now make snowballs, and pelt each other, and erect a statue of heaven knows who, a colossus of snow to melt away, like the palace of the great female Autocrat, before the sun? Is it not, too, the emblem of virgin purity and innocence; and might not much more be said in praise and admiration of snow? It is an evil, however, to balance against this, that it deforms all landscape, destroys all 'keeping', by confounding distances, and with that proportions, and with that, too, more and worse than all else, the harmony of colouring; giving us a motley patchwork of black and white, in place of those sweet gradations and combinations of colour which Nature produces, in her summer mood, even amid the most deformed and harsh of landscapes. These are the objections to a snow landscape, which even the experience of a day may furnish: how much more, when, for more than half the year, all the element above head is snow, — when the gale is a gale of snow — the fog, a fog of snow, — when the sun shines but to glitter on the snow which is, yet does not fall, — when the breath of the mouth is snow, — when snow settles on the hair, the dress, the eye-lashes, — where snow falls around us and fills our chambers, our beds, our dishes, should we open a door, should the external air get access to our 'penetralia', — where the 'crystal stream', in which we must quench our thirst, is a kettle of snow with a lamp of oil, — where our sofas are of snow, and our houses of snow, — when snow was our decks, snow our awnings, snow our observatories, snow our larders, snow our salt, — and when all the other uses of snow should be at last of no avail, our coffins and our graves were to be coffins and graves of snow! Is not this", enquires the gallant Captain, "more than enough of snow that suffices for admiration ?"

No. VII. — SUPPLIES OF WATER.

February 13th, 1836.

"The evening mists, with ceaseless change,
Now clothe the mountain's lofty range,
  Now leave their foreheads bare,
And round the skirts their mantle furl,
Or on the sable waters curl,
Or on the eddying breezes whirl,
  Dispersed in middle air.
And oft, condensed, at once they lower,
When, brief and fierce, the mountain shower
  Pours like a torrent down;
And when return the sun's glad beams,
Whitened with foam, a thousand streams
Leap from the mountain's crown."

{From 'Lake Coriskin'} SCOTT.

THE sustentation of the before mentioned, and several other streams, may be referred to three sources — first, the moisture imbibed immediately from dense clouds or fogs; secondly, to springs; and, thirdly, to rain and snow. It may possibly be thought by some persons gratuitous or absurd, to reckon the aqueous precipitation from, or rather, perhaps, it might be termed imbibition from contact of the clouds which frequently roll over these heights in such majestic volumes, among the instruments by which the ground is saturated — but that it *is* a cause, however inconsiderable, will hardly be doubted by any person who has been long out in one of the fogs alluded to — when the "Scotch mist", or *griming,* as it is called, is sufficiently dense and humid to saturate thoroughly the clothes of an exposed individual in a very short time. The collective quantity of water drained by the capillary attraction of millions of stems, from an atmosphere surcharged with moisture, must obviously be considerable; indeed a moment's examination of the drenched moss, heather, &c. will corroborate the fact. It is true, evaporation goes on rapidly at certain seasons in so exposed a situation; but still — to say nothing of the excess of misty days — the surface vegetation, which seems so admirably adapted to collect the moisture, serves equally well to prevent its too easy dissipation by the action of the sun. To a person altogether unaccustomed to the meterological phenomena common to regions like these, few appearances can be more striking than those frequently presented by clouds and mists. At some times the heath-clad summits not only seem to, but in reality do pierce the clouds, or rather, the latter often so repose upon and overhang the former, that it seems difficult to say where the line of separation lies. Under such circumstances, a person enveloped in the vapour not only presently becomes wet to the skin, but sometimes also, especially if a stranger, completely bewildered and lost in the "palpable obscure" — instances of this often occur — some of them of a fatal character. Such a fog Dante appears to have had in mind, when he composed the following lines: —

> "Call to remembrance, reader, if thou e'er
> Hast on an Alpine height been ta'en by cloud,
> Through which thou saw'st no better than the mole
> Doth through opacious membrane; then, whene'er
> The watry vapours dense began to melt
> Into thin air, how faintly the sun's sphere
> Seemed wading through them: so thy nimble thought
> May image, how at first I rebeheld
> The sun, that bedward now his couch oerhung."

PURG. {PURGATORY} CANTO, XXII.

It is commonly, however, when the clouds hang in dense well defined masses upon the distant mountain slopes, or slowly roll over them, that ideas of grandeur are most natural excited; especially, when, as may sometimes happen, the body of vapour assumes the appearance of an inclined series of vast subrotund masses stretching as it were from earth to heaven. Nor are the effects of the more transient and insubstantial mists at times less striking, whether stratified in parallel lines with stripes of moorland scenery; deposited so tranquilly in the depth of certain vallies as to impress the conviction that immense lakes are there reposing; or even when merely stretching their filmy tissue, rainbow-tinted perhaps, over the purple promontories. To return.

Of springs, more or less considerable, there are several; indeed, with some limitation, we may designate the moorland tract under consideration, in the language of the sacred writer, as — "a land of brooks of water; of fountains and depths springing out of the hills".

The greater part, however, of these springs, instead of gushing forth as at Don Well and the fraternal fountain, already mentioned, rather ooze out in the midst of small rushy swamps, as at the head of Windledon Car {SE147012 on OS 1854}, or steal forth obscurely, under a covering of moss and bracken — their direction for some distance being sometimes merely indicated by the superior greenness of the saturated ground.

But the most important agent in the replenishing of these mountain streams, is, of course, the melting of snow or the prevalence of rains, which fall more frequently and abundantly in these elevated regions, than in the country below. The low temperature of these heights, as compared with that of less exposed grounds, leads to the former being frequently whitened over with snow, at an earlier period than the latter: for a similar cause, the snow often accumulates in prodigious quantities during the winter months. The skeleton of the storm — or at least some "snow bones", as the country people call them, often remaining late in the spring. It is on the sudden breaking up of a frost that has for some time been piling up liquid stores in a solid shape, that many of the gullies down which the summer streamlet only perceptibly ran, become the collectors of impetuous torrents, all uniting below, and not seldom overflowing the prescribed bounds of the river, and doing serious mischief. On the other hand, it is commonly to the suddenly dissolving of those massive clouds, which appear to be attracted or arrested by the lofty summits, that we have to attribute the ordinary summer freshes of the river, and especially those violent floods which are often more unexpected, alarming and destructive, than those which occur from the breaking up of a storm in the winter. One striking effect of the showers which sometimes descend with such violence on these moors, is that deep furrows are often ploughed by the coalescing torrents in the soft peaty soil before they reach the rivulets. These gullies are, in some places, seen ramified over a large surface of ground, and look, during a storm, not unlike incipient rivers themselves: they bear in fact, the same relation to the various established streams which flow down the vallies, that these do to the main river.

Abundant, however, as, at times, is the supply of water, that supply is no less precarious and irregular; and there have been at least three projects for making reservoirs in the vicinity of the sources of the

Don, with the view of turning to account the surplus water of the river. The first project, agitated in 1785 {quoting from Hunter's 'Hallamshire' (1819) p127 re William Jessop of Newark, founder of Butterley Iron Works, and builder of Cromford Canal}, had reference to laying up the water which came down in winter, for the summer use of the grinding wheels on the river: to this end, the engineer recommended the construction of a reservoir at a place called Deadman's ford {*location not identified*}, a few miles above Penistone, on the south side of the Don. Here, about thirty acres of water, of the average depth of three yards, were to be dammed up: eight or nine smaller receptacles were likewise to be formed on the branches of the river higher up. The scheme, however, though plausible, never took effect. A similar project, relative to storing the water, was subsequently entertained, with reference to supplying a contemplated canal. And, within the last four or five years, when a new Water Company was proposed in Sheffield, the sources of the Don were looked to, as likely to afford a constant supply of water.

To level mountains and fill up vallies, in the literal sense of the terms, might seem, at first thought, hardly to belong to man; but if he have not often achieved either the one or the other of those objects — and he has *sometimes* done both — his ingenuity has not seldom enabled him to achieve no less effective conquests over difficulties; he has bridged the vale, and bored the rock, carrying his artificial lines of transit, often with little or no rise or fall, through the rugged magnificence of Nature. The hills on which we now stand, interposing, as they do, so serious an impediment to certain modes of heavy or rapid conveyance between the eastern and western districts, have again and again tempted the spirit of stupendous speculation, in connection with that potentate of lines and levels, the "civil engineer", to visit their summits.

> "The year 1825", says Mr. Hunter, "a year which will be long remembered as a time when the country was overwhelmed with projects of vast magnitude, presented a still grander scheme, [than the making of a canal from Tinsley.] Towering as are the hills of grit and limestone to the north-west of Sheffield, the project was seriously entertained, and a costly survey made, of boring through the hills, and making a water communication with the Mersey. The report of the engineer is full of curious information, and his recommendation on it

is, that, if an attempt shall be made to execute the project, it will best be accomplished by following the line of the Don."

In 1825, the mania of speculation was in favour of canal: ten years brought a change — and the year 1835 saw projectors rail-road mad. To cut a canal where there was no navigable river, appeared, so far as the water and the canal were concerned, a sort of co-operation of Art with Nature — the former not superseding, but directing the latter. A railroad, on the other hand, is a thoroughly artificial affair: the line, the rails, the engines, are exquisitely foreign to nature — and even the few buckets full of what may, perhaps, be called water, is so tortured, to effect its conversion into a motive pabulum, that it is rendered at least 1,800 times unlike itself: indeed, like the luminous matter of a comet's tail, which Newton considered of such extreme tenuity, that thousands of miles of it might be compressed into a cubic inch, and still not be more dense than our atmosphere, so a volume of rarified aqueous vapour, that rushes with incredible velocity and energy through miles and miles of cast iron piping, lies, when condensed, a few quarts of quiet cold water in a boiler or a bucket.

Ten years have wrought a change: we heard *then* of a canal — we hear *now* of a railroad; a public meeting having been only a few weeks since held in Sheffield, to hear the report of an engineer relative to the practicability and advantages of flying over these mountains by steam power. Nor is this the first project of the kind, any more than the canal scheme mentioned by Mr. Hunter, the only one that has been contemplated on that line. Pending the success of the latest transmontane railroad scheme, a project has just been published by Mr. J. T. Fairbank, of Sheffield, *(vide Mercury, 30th ult.)* which challenges for that venerable motive agent, the water wheel, an available and economical superiority over the steam engine itself in railroad communication: and certainly, judging from the simplicity and apparent feasibility of the idea, the subject seems entitled to more consideration than it has obtained.

The intention of the Sheffield and Manchester railroad projectors appears to be to proceed along the north-east side of the Don, to its source, which is reached at about twenty one miles from the town first-above named, with an average rise of between forty and fifty feet per mile. Mr. Fairbank asserts, that a thirty-horse engine will only be able to draw five tons of effective weight, — i.e. over and above the locomotive apparatus itself, — on an ascending incline having the unusual gradient above-mentioned. The object of the writer, therefore, is, to suggest the employment of water power to draw, by means of ropes and winders, the loaded train up the steepest parts of the railway, in the manner long practised by means of fixed engines in various places.

The moving power, being water, would, it is remarked, cost nothing; and it is added, that, if a reservoir or reservoirs of one hundred acres or upwards were constructed, at an expense of from forty to fifty thousand pounds, to dam up the flood water, so far from injuring the mill owners on the river below, it would greatly benefit them, as they would then have water in dry seasons.

No. VIII. — DON-FORD BRIDGE.

February 20th, 1836.

"In wild and lonely mood,
I've seen the winter floods their gambols play
Through this stone arch, that trembled while I stood
Bent o'er its wall to watch the dashing spray,
As its old stations would be washed away."

{From 'The Flood'} CLARE

THE tributary streams named in a preceding section, including also
the Windledon, are collected above Townhead {SE165028}, at a
place the original character of which is still suggested by the name of
Don-ford Bridge {Dunford Bridge SE157024}, a modern stone
structure of a single arch, over which the Salterbrook road passes to
Penistone. This bridge is the first that occurs on the Don, which here
enters a cultivated region by a shallow valley, having a few trees on
one side. The cradle of the river is not remarkably interesting:
nevertheless, on account of the stunted alders which overhang the
spot, it is liable to be regarded as pretty by a person just escaping
from the comparative nakedness of the moors.

Just below the bridge, on the right hand side of the river, there is a
patch of cultivated ground — and which, when I saw it last
November {1835}, included a very fine field of turnips; and this at a
season when in many apparently much more favoured situations the
crops had utterly failed. There is something exceedingly interesting
in the appearance of these little farm plots, won from the waste by
which they are sometimes surrounded — but more commonly lying
at the extreme verge of cultivation on the one hand, and of
barrenness on the other — a sort of "land debateable", where
agricultural prowess, aided by ingenuity and implements, appears to
have attacked and subdued the native genius of the waste. At the
sight of these moorland enclosures, one feels inclined to ask — Why
not carried farther? Or why carried so far? Such questions more
naturally obtrude themselves here, where the soil appears rich, and
easily available, as compared with the stony character of the moors
about Baslow and elsewhere.

One easy and beneficial mode of improving mountain land, is the planting it with trees: of late years hundreds of acres of waste on the moors west of Sheffield have been thus appropriated, either by companies or individuals — and plantations, in various stages of growth, now adorn what had otherwise been wide and treeless wastes. A considerable piece of ground sloping to the Windledon has recently been planted with larches and also with forest trees. Of course, it will be several years before even those that grow most rapidly, can be expected to yield any profit — and still much longer before those designed for timber will become valuable: but forest trees generally yield a sure though distant return; and perhaps planting, under almost any circumstances, is the least selfish of tastes, even if it should run into prodigality; and it is one of which, at all events, the posterity of the party indulging it, has rarely cause to regret — so true is the quaint couplet —

> "He who delights to sow and set,
> Makes after ages in his debt."

At what period, or whether ever these mountainous tracts may have been distinguished by the presence of trees, we have no means of ascertaining — the moors considerably to the south of these have undoubtedly at some remote era produced the birch, and probably some other of the lighter wooded trees, its remains being frequently found buried in the soil. The probability, indeed, that this description of tree did anciently flourish on these hills, seems to be greatly strengthened by the frequent occurrence of the term *Birch,* as a prefix in the denomination of places hereabout.

Sometimes, during the spring and autumn seasons, these and the neighbouring moors present a singular appearance in consequence of large tracts of old ling being set on fire, in order that the shrub may spring up fresh and tender, in which state it is eaten by cattle and sheep.

> "I have found", says a certain author, "that if heath be cut when young and in bloom, and the finer parts infused in a tea-pot, it produces a pleasant liquid, not only grateful to the taste and well flavoured, but extremely wholesome, and, in many points of view, preferable to the tea that comes from China."

Will any notable housewife be found curious enough to verify this statement?

There is one phenomenon of vegetation so curious, and so frequently exhibited in moorland situations, that the mention of it here will hardly be deemed out of place. I allude to the springing up of white clover wherever the ground is newly broken up: under such circumstances, this valuable trefoil, *(Trifolium repens)* is "one of the first spontaneous productions". How to account for the original deposition of the seeds, the preservation of their germinating force through an indefinitely long period, and other matters connected with the appearance of the plants, appears next to impossible: the fact, however, is undeniable as regards the spontaneous exhibition of a crop of white clover, wherever the ancient waste is pared and burned for tillage. This striking peculiarity is not confined to Trefoil; botanists have remarked it in reference to certain other plants: thus, after the great fire of London in 1667, the entire surface of the destroyed city, was in spring covered with such a vast profusion of a species of a common cruciferous plant, the *Sisymbrium irio* of Linnæus {London Rocket}, that it was calculated the whole of Europe could not contain so many plants of it: in the opinion of some writers it almost invariably springs up where a house has been burnt down, if the ground be suffered to lie waste for a season. It is also known that if a spring of salt water makes its appearance in a spot, even at a great distance from the sea, the neighbourhood is soon covered with plants peculiar to a maritime locality, which plants were previously entire strangers to the country. When certain marshes in Zealand were drained, the *Carex cyperoides* {? now *C. bohemica*}, we are told was observed in abundance; now this sedge is not at all a Danish plant, but belongs to the south of Europe. The almost invisible dust by means of which some — indeed most of the minuter species of cryptogamous plants are reproduced, is so light, that one can well conceive how it may be carried to considerable distances — still the following instance just published appears extraordinary: —

> "In a work upon the useful mosses, by M. de Brebisson, this botanist states that a pond in the neighbourhood of Falain having been rendered dry during many weeks in the height of summer, the mud in drying was immediately and entirely covered to the extent of many square yards by minute compact green turf, formed of an imperceptible moss, the *Phaseum axillare,* the stalks of which were so close to each other, that upon a square inch of this new soil, might be

counted more than five thousand individuals of this minute plant, which had never previously been observed in the country."

A botanical fact of an opposite character, may not be unacceptable, after the mention of the preceding phenomenon. Few persons can have rambled over these moorland tracts early in the summer season, without noticing an elegant plant — the cotton-grass *(Eryophorum {Eriophorum — ? E.angustifolium})* hanging out its white flower-spikes, like silken tassels to the breeze. Several species are natives of Britain; and one of these may be noted as an instance of a plant — extremely local to be sure, in the first place — having, it is probable, perished from the Flora of these Islands: — *E. alpina {now Trichophorum alpinum},* of which specimens exist in several collections, was originally gathered in the Moss of Restenet, near Forfar, in Scotland; the bog has long been drained, and it is believed its once local Eriophorum is quite extinct. A recent number of the "Florigraphia Britannica" {Vol 1, Fig 84 and p57} presents a figure of this interesting plant, stated to be from a drawing of a specimen "in the collection of the Sheffield Literary and Philosophical Society, which appears to have been sent by Mr. Brown (the original discoverer of the species) to the late Mr. Salt, who left this valuable and excellent collection". {I understand that Salt's herbarium sheet for *E. alpina* is now missing from the SLPS herbarium (held by Museums Sheffield).}

To allow the imagination to turn to vegetable phenomena, may for the moment, beguile the mind of the fact that, the spot we are now passing, presents at this season of the year a peculiarly dreary and cheerless aspect — and it must be something particular that would induce a person to linger about Don-ford Bridge on a bitter day in the month of February, — especially with a double edged north-easter cutting its way up the valley, as the frosty wind on Wednesday morning. At such a season, the "gathering of the waters", in the broken but roomy bottom whence the "Don proper", may be said really to commence his course, is an affair of dashing and splashing and dinning that excites neither poetical nor pleasing associations. In summer it is different: mark you those rugged and somewhat dilapidated enclosures? Guess you their use? Here, in the month of July may — or might have been witnessed immediately before the operation of sheep-shearing, the lustral process so graphically described by the author of "The Fleece:" —

> "＿＿＿＿＿to the double fold, upon the brim
> Of a clear river, gently drive the flock,
> And plunge them one by one into the flood:
> Plung'd in the flood, not long the struggler sinks,
> With his white flakes, that glisten through the tide;
> The sturdy rustic, in the middle wave,
> Awaits to seize him rising; one arm bears
> His lifted head above the limpid stream,
> While the full clammy fleece the other laves
> Around, laborious, with repeated toil;
> And then resigns him to the sunny bank,
> Where, bleating loud, he shakes his dripping locks."

It may be noted that the waters here, are not always orderly or beneficent, even in the midst of winter: the writer recollects that near the latter end of July, 1834, when he happened to walk up here, a heavy fall of rain had so swelled the river that its channel became too contracted for the quantity of water sent down from the moors: the consequence was such an overflowing of the banks hereabouts, as well as lower down, that many score roods of stone walling were destroyed; while from several fields on the line of the torrent, the crops and soil were washed away together. Looking over the battlements of the second bridge lower down, it was impressive to notice how —

> "White foam, brown crested with the russet soil,
> As washed from new ploughed lands, would dart beneath,
> Then round and round in thousand eddies boil
> On t'other side; — then pause, as if for breath,
> One minute — then engulphed — like life in death."

At Carlecoates, two miles below Don-ford Bridge, the river is overlooked by a somewhat singular eminence called the "Castle Hill" {SE178029}, which, surmounted by a solitary tree, is a striking object for several miles lower down. Below Carlecoates, and opposite Sofly {Soughley on modern maps, Softy in early OS. SE186029}, the Don, "encreased to youthful strength", receives the tribute of the Wogden {Wogden Clough, SE175016}, which rises near Board Hill; and, coming from the opposite direction, the stream called the Crowbrook {Town Brook, SE184032}: while about three quarters of a mile lower down, the Sledbrook {Sledbrook Dyke, SE195036} enters at Hazlehead. Having thence proceeded about a mile, the river has become sufficiently considerable to give motion to the water-wheel of a corn mill at Bullhouses {SE212030}: and here, it may be interesting to remark, that this is the first work the water is made to perform.

No. IX. — THURLSTONE.

February 27th, 1836.

"A mountain hamlet, on a ridge exposed,
O'erlooks the hasty stream: how bleak and cold
Its winter aspect! and yet, surely there,
Warm hearts and generous feelings occupy
Some bosoms, and keep up thy sympathies
Humanity! about are these cottage hearths."

ANON.

For two or three miles after quitting Don-ford Bridge, the river pursues its course along the bottom of a shallow valley, presenting little that is immediately interesting in scenery or association. Above Townhead, the road affords some good views of bold undulating hills to the right: while lower down, on the opposite side, and overlooking the river at Carlecotes, rises a striking conical eminence called the "Castle Hill" {SE178029}, and which, from having on its summit, a solitary tree, is conspicuous from a considerable distance. Just above Hazlehead, the road from Sheffield to Huddersfield crosses the Don by means of a capital stone structure called Wear Bridge {Wares Bridge in OS First Series 1 inch, Hazlehead Bridge elsewhere. SE194030}: it were pleasant to linger for an hour hereabouts, on a fine summer evening — but we must hasten to the place named at the head of this chapter.

Thurlstone {~SE232035} is a somewhat poor looking and scattered village, or rather hamlet, consisting of stone houses built, for the most part, on the left bank of the Don, which here flows through a deep contracted valley: the Salterbrook road passes along the edge of the valley on the same side as that on which the buildings are mainly situate, the plantations on the opposite slope, having a pleasing effect during the summer season when the trees are in foliage; while in winter the place looks excessively cheerless and dreary. In the village there are three or four mills, for grinding corn or for other purposes — and in former years, before canal and railway facilities had so quickened the pace of competition in all kinds of business, considerable quantities of flour were made here. The miller attended the market at Wakefield to purchase grain, which he carried home, ground it into flour, and then distributed it to various customers who were scattered, somewhat extensively, about the moors: the expensiveness of fetching the corn from such a distance to the mill, as compared with the facilities by which the water borne flour itself is now more cheaply distributed from a nearer point, is said greatly to have depreciated the value of these mills.

At what period the streams in this neighbourhood, and their common receptacle the river below, were first taken advantage of for the purpose of working machinery, does not appear. Ancient, however, as undoubtedly may be considered the model of some of the cutlery grinding wheels lower down upon the Don, and elsewhere upon its romantic tributaries, the adaptation of the water wheel to give motion to horizontal stones for grinding corn, is probably of still higher antiquity. At all events, machinery of this kind has existed in this country from the times of the Saxons; as the repeated entries of *mol.* or *sit. mol.* having reference to the fact in Doomsday Book, sufficiently evince: indeed, these "mill seats", necessarily of importance to our ancestors, are not only frequently recognised in conventual charters, but are, in very many instances, it is interesting to remark, retained even at the present time. The steps by which the old hand quern, the most ancient form of mill known in this or other countries, was superseded by stones made to revolve by means of a water wheel, have not been pointed out.

I know not how it is, but I never enter an old flour mill, especially one of the ruder construction, without peculiar sensations — there is something soothing in the sounds within — something primitive in the construction and uses of the machinery — a sort of gravity or decorum, so to speak, in its movements — none of the rattling, dashing, dizzy rapidity — the confounding complexity of your modern spinning and weaving mechanism, amongst which one walks in a sort of bewilderment, half doubting whether the living or the inanimate motions be the more astonishing: nor is there any of that noisy tearing that accompanies the patent substitute for the flail: the "sharp threshing instrument having teeth" — for the scriptural description is literally applicable. There is commonly too, a quietness of character about the rural miller, exceedingly in harmony with his vocation: it is true, he acts in conjunction with machinery — but he runs no race with it — it seems to be an obedient and orderly agent, whose wants he leisurely supplies, and upon whose operations he looks without handhold or anxiety. Such is the water flour-mill — the steam mill is another thing.

I am aware that this character was formerly, as indeed in some places he may be still, held in but moderate estimation; in times when money was scare, and the multure {toll} of grain commonly paid for in kind, to say nothing of customary perquisites, the "toll-dish" was not always honestly used. In the old ballad of "The King and Miller of Mansfield", the latter is represented as helping himself to something besides flour, in a way by no means uncommon some centuries ago, with persons of his class dwelling in the vicinity of well–stocked deer chases: the stranger, (King Henry II., as he turns out to be), having drank pretty freely with his host of "nappy ale" {strong ale};

> "Wife, quoth the Miller, fetch ye forth lightfoote,
> And of his sweetness a little we'll taste:
> A fair ven'son pastye brought she out presently,
> Eate, quoth the Miller, but sir make no waste:
> Here's dainte lightfoote! In faith said the King,
> I never before eate so daintye a thing.
> Quoth the Miller's son, no daintye at all it is,
> For we do eat of it every day. —
> In what place, say'd our King, may be bought like to this ?
> We never pay pennye for it, by may pay {*}:
> From merry Sherwood we fetch it home here:
> Now and then we make bold with our King's deer."

> {* 'by may pay' should probably read 'by my fey' (? 'by my faith') – as in 'The Book of Brave Old Ballads' (date and author unknown) available on Project Gutenberg.}

Few millers now-a-days it may be presumed regale themselves on purloined venison — probably about as many as happen to entertain kings *incog:* the Miller of Thurlstone, I trow, does neither the one nor the other.

Leaving the flour mills and the village, we might now pass over the bridge; but the *genius loci,* even of Thurlstone, suggests at least *one* interesting association. In a cottage about a hundred yards from the road, was born the celebrated Dr. Nicholas Sanderson, who, although he lost his sight before he was two years old, displayed such a talent for the acquisition of mathematical knowledge, as to rise to eminence in the science, and ultimately to become Lucasion Professor of Mathematics in the University of Cambridge, where he died in 1739, having fulfilled the duties of his Chair with increasing reputation for twenty-eight years. Mr. Hunter considers Dr. Sanderson as the most distinguished person in science produced in this part of the kingdom.

Popular tradition ascribes the attainment of a knowledge of letters by the blind boy, to his habit of passing his fingers over the inscriptions on the grave-stones in the church-yard of Penistone: it might be so — the distance is trifling, and it were almost a pity to disturb so picturesque a story; but when one looks at the grave-stones at present in that enclosure, how few are there, if any, that bear dates coeval with the boyhood of the blind mathematician?

It will naturally be asked, whether the cottage in which this celebrated man was born, be still standing? I am sorry to say, it is not: having become dilapidated, it was taken down, and a coach house, or something of that sort, erected on the spot. The owner of the site, however, Gamaliel Milner, Esq., who resides hard by, has considerately identified the locality, by causing the following record to be cut conspicuously upon a stone in the gable of the new building: —

Hic natus est
DR. NICHOLAS SANDERSON,
1682.

Not far from the bridge there is a small Wesleyan Chapel — this being the first place of religious worship that had occurred on the line of the Don, was regarded by the writer with a little more interest on that account: as one of the advanced posts of a people who have gone out not only into the "highways and hedges", but into the moral desert wherever spread, in order to compel sinners "to come in", and enjoy the blessings and privileges of the Gospel, it was really interesting to a person concerned for the spread of religion: but there was another reason why I viewed with interest this little and comparatively obscure place of worship — the river, on leaving the chapel, whence it flows a short mile, bordered with trees, to Penistone, has become of considerable volume, and it was impossible, after having accompanied it thus far from its source, repeatedly stepping across its shallows, at once to recollect its insignificance above, and witness how commodiously the summer bathers might disport in its flood at this place, without thinking of the following striking passage in the Prophesy of Ezekiel:

> "Then brought he me out of the way of the gate northward, and led me about the way without unto the other gate, by the way that looked eastward; and, behold, there ran out waters on the right side. And when the man that had the line in his hand went forth eastward, he measured a thousand cubits, and he brought me through the waters; the waters were to the ancles. Again he measured a thousand, and brought me through the waters; the waters were to the knees. Again he measured a thousand, and brought me through: the waters were to the loins. Afterwards he measured a thousand; and it was a river that I could not pass over: for the waters were risen, waters to swim in, a river that could not be passed over. And he said unto me, Son of Man, hast thou seen this? Then he brought me, and caused me to return to the brink of the river. Now when I had returned, behold at the bank of the river were very many trees on the one side and on the other. Then said he unto me — these waters issue out toward the east country, and go down into the desert, and go into the sea".

— EZEKIEL, XLVII. 2-8.

A much more conspicuous object than the little place of worship last mentioned, is a chapel built about fifty years ago by the Independent denomination; it stands near the Huddersfield road side, on the hill, a few hundred yards from Penistone bridge. It was in this humble building — in this out of-the-way place, that the celebrated Rev. W. Thorpe, who died a few years since at Bristol, commenced his Ministerial career. Here, he more than gave promise of those powerful pulpit talents, for which he became afterwards so greatly distinguished; nor were the first fruits of his superior talent unappreciated by his mountain audience — those who remain of that audience, describe with evident delight the effect of his preaching upon their own minds and feelings, and the appearance of the crowds which were wont to congregate on the Sabbath, to hear the eloquent preacher at Bridge-end Chapel. William Thorpe was a giant among his brethren: it is true, the mace of his eloquence was sometimes knotty, but it was wielded with a hearty — ought I not to add — a

heavenly purpose: he bore within him too, a brave Protestant heart
— his loyalty was still more remarkable — peace to his memory!

No. X. — PENISTONE.

March 5th, 1836.

——— "Those slow-descending showers.
Those hovering fogs, that bathe our growing vales
In deep November (loath'd by trifling Gaul
Effeminate), are gifts the Pleiad's shed,
Britannia's handmaids — as the beverage falls,
Her hills rejoice, her vallies laugh and sing."

{From 'The Fleece'} DYER.

On leaving the bridge last mentioned in the preceding section, and
over which pass the roads diverging in the directions of Huddersfield
and Doncaster — the Scaut dyke {Scout Dyke, SE239044} from
Ingbirchworth, falling into the Don just here — we ascend the hill for
a few hundred yards to reach Penistone — the river rounding toward
the north, the base of the eminence which is strikingly surmounted
by the church. Penistone will appear to the casual passenger
somewhat like Thurlstone on an enlarged scale: it claims, however,
the distinction of being a market town — the charter having been
granted about 130 years ago. The number of inhabitants in the
township, is stated in the late census to be 703, not half so many as in
the contiguous township of Thurlstone, which numbers 1,599.
Penistone has often been called in joke, "the finished town" — not
from the perfection of its plan, its streets, or its buildings — but from
the fact that no additions appear to be made — no new buildings
erected: in short, the laying of one stone upon another in the way of
architecture, however humble the erection, is quite a wonder.

The stationary amount of the population may be taken as
significantly indicative of the *statu quo* condition of this "market
town" — Penistone having added to the number of its inhabitants
fifty-eight souls in ten years!

There is nothing in the buildings or their accessories to arrest the
curiosity of the tourist — unless, indeed, Water Hall {SE246037}, at
the foot of the hill, beside the river, may be regarded as an exception
to this remark — from a family seated at this place so early as the
time of Edward III., and formerly residing at the house just named,
descended

> "the two brothers, whose names are so highly distinguished in the literature of the present times, Dr. William Wordsworth, master of Trinity College, Cambridge, and William Wordsworth, the poet."

The situation of Penistone is peculiarly bleak and exposed; and the cultivated tract by which the town is surrounded, was formerly remarkable, not more for the paucity of its produce, than for the lateness of the period at which the crops commonly yielded to the influence of the gentler seasons. Of late years, the agricultural aspect of the neighbourhood appears to have undergone a striking change for the better: so that the character of the land, while not comparable to much of warmer and richer descriptions below, is by no means what it once was: nor like what is still the character of some of the higher ground of the adjacent valley, especially about Langsett, where oats might have been seen standing in stooks upon the field, late in the month of November last year.

Allusion has been already made to the saturating character of the moorland mists: the writer of this notice walked from Midhope to Penistone, on the morning of the seventh of December, 1835, which, it may be remembered, was remarkable for the densest fog which had occurred during the season: never, surely did any one before go out on such a day in search of the picturesque! As I traversed the three-mile long lane, encaged, as it were, in a moving lantern of chilly light, it was some amusement to notice the appearance of the various lichens which encrusted the walls, and which appeared to derive distinctness of outline and depth of tint from the peculiar atmosphere in which those minute vegetables and their admirer, were enveloped. It would just have been the morning and the occasion, to have engendered in some minds peevishness and melancholy — but why should it have such effect? —

> "In nature there is nothing melancholy,"
> And he whose harp of feeling — whose tuned heart
> Doth not respond to each and every part
> Of the four season's change — hideth some folly,
> Or some weakness — is, perchance, unholy,
> Selfish of ease, or of brave exercise
> Too sparing — or most like, the evil lies
> In want of health: t' enjoy creation wholly —
> Spring's blandest airs, the summer's proudest heats:

Autumn's deep changes, and stern winter's cold;
Is the prerogative of him who greets
In every change, more precious far than gold,
God's blessed motion for the good of all —
Men, brutes, birds, trees, that crowd the earthy ball.

Onward I wended, until in due time, the tower of Penistone Church {SE246033}, made its appearance, looming through the mist like a gigantic apparition. I love to come upon a rural Church under any conditions of atmosphere. Dull as the morning undoubtedly was, I was struck on approaching the Churchyard, to perceive that all was not dullness even there — a cheerful gaily dressed wedding party of six or eight persons being just issuing from the porch, scattering as they passed along a quantity of halfpence among a lot of merry children whom the twelve o'clock bell had most seasonably liberated from school in time to obtain the bridal largess. Well, thought I — after smiling what I had not the courage to speak — "may happiness be yours, ye wedded pair" — the misty obscurity of this day, is strikingly significant of the unseen future of matrimonial experience: I know of a certainty that this mist will be dissipated; that the sun will again shine, and display those features of the landscape, which at present are looked for in vain — equally confident no doubt are these sanguine young people that, although perhaps they do not see very far beyond the present hour, that if gloom sometimes obscure their providential path, the sunshine of life will again break out and the scenery of domestic joy display itself in renewed beauty.

In the preceding chapter allusion is made to the tradition that the poor blind Thurlstone boy, who afterwards became the celebrated Dr. Sanderson, taught himself to read by feeling with his fingers over the gravestones in Penistone church-yard: be this as it might, it is interesting that in that sacred enclosure may be seen the memorial of John Sanderson, his father, who, as he did not die until the year 1725, must have had the gratification of knowing the elevated position to which uncommon talents had raised his son. How little had that father foreseen that his blind child was destined to fill the situation which had been so recently vacated by Sir Isaac Newton! — if indeed this illustrious name had then found its way among the yeoman of Thurlstone. As little, probably, did the master of the Grammar School at Penistone, under whose care young Sanderson was placed, or Mr. West, his generous and intelligent patron think, as they might see the summer rainbow spanning with its arch of beauty the adjacent vales, that to their studious elevé, from whose "sightless orbs", every scene of external nature was absolutely shut out, would be confided the duty of explaining the phenomena of

"Even light itself, which every thing displays;"

And this from the very seat, previously occupied by, and according to the theory of the great master discoverer, Newton; he whose

> "——— brighter mind
> Untwisted all the shining robe of day;
> And from the whitening undistinguised blaze
> Collecting every ray into his kind,
> To the charmed eye reduced the gorgeous train
> Of parent colours."

Near the Church, on the road-side, stands a neat building having upon it a tablet with the following inscription: —

FEMALE NATIONAL SCHOOL.
Endowed by
Mr. Joseph Camm, of Beverley.
M.D.CCC.XXII.

{? N side of church SE246033, refurbished in 2009 as 'Busy Bees Daycare and Nursery'}

The individual whose good work is thus recorded went from this neighbourhood — namely Rough Birchworth {SE262015}. The writer of this paper has been a zealous but humble advocate for the religious education of the children of the poor, and sincerely has he rejoiced in the success of any scheme for giving more extended and beneficial effect to agencies having that object. Pleasant, therefore, was it to find on this bleak elevation, and on the dull morning in question, a National School for Girls; more cheerless than the fields — duller than the weather must have been the sensibilities of the man who could look upon the children in that seminary without yearnings of hope and confidence as to the result of the teachings upon the scholars. When it is recollected how important a part a woman has to take in whatever station of society she may be placed — how large a proportion of the good or the evil of the sphere in which she moves, is commonly attributable to her influence — the early inculcation of sound moral principles is a matter of vast importance. If, therefore, the servants and sisters — the wives and mothers of the present and future generations of the inhabitants of Penistone and the neighbourhood be not greatly the better for the advantages they have enjoyed in this free school, the fault must surely lie with themselves — it is pleasant at least to indulge the reasonable hope, that here as well as in other places the expectations of the charitable founders of these institutions will be realized.

Let it not be supposed that Penistone is always, or commonly indeed, enveloped in such a blanket of mist, as on the morning above alluded to — no such thing. And when the weather is fine, the tower of the Church, as seen from various points at a distance, is a very pleasing object. Long may it stand thus conspicuous; long be the index of high and hallowed associations. — .

> "May ne'er
> That true succession fail of English hearts,
> That can perceive, not less than heretofore
> Our ancestors did feelingly perceive,
> What in these holy structures doth exist
> Of ornamental interest, and the charm
> Of pious sentiment diffused afar,
> And human charity, and social love.
> Thus never shall the indignities of time
> Approach their reverend graces unopposed:
> Nor shall the elements be free to hurt
> Their fair proportions; nor the blinder rage
> Of bigot zeal madly to overturn."

No. XI. — THE CHURCH.

March 12ᵗʰ, 1336.

"Long be our Father's temple ours,
    Woe to the hand by which it falls;
A thousand spirits watch its towers,
    A cloud of angels guard its walls :
And be their shield by us possessed,
    Lord, rear around this blest abode,
The buttress of a holy breast,
    The rampart of a present God — "

{From 'The Village Church'} CUNNINGHAM.

I LOVE to see the village church tower, or spire — as it may happen to be — rising up at intervals, and not seldom embosomed in trees, as one rambles through almost any part of happy, cultivated, flourishing Christian England. It has ever been with me, an object of peculiar respect, — I had almost said reverence; sanctifying, as it were the beauty of the landscape in which it often forms so conspicuous and harmonious a feature.

Apart from the character of the incumbent (though I am fully sensible of the importance of such character), these, and a thousand other associations hardly ever fail to start up in my mind, at the sight of any one of those monuments of the pious wisdom of our ancestors. "Wisdom of our ancestors!" methinks I hear responded with something like a flippant sneer; "and will any person having the modern 'Schoolmaster' before his eyes, venture to use, in such connection, so proscribed a phrase?" Aye, indeed, and with all sincerity too: the writer, in the present instance, just means by it, that our ancestors were at once pious and wise — and liberal as well as foresighted to boot, in making such provision as they did make, for the religious instruction of all ranks of society; and in saying this, far distant is the wish to be, in the least degree understood as undervaluing, much less of disparaging anything which for the promotion of goodness, the benevolent spirit of modern times has done for the people of this or other countries.

"What, then, the tourist is a Churchman, an out-and-out advocate for a religious Establishment in connection with the State?" But the tourist is *not* a churchman, in the churchman's sense — i.e. he does not statedly worship in the parochial or any other church: at the same time he *is* a decided advocate for a religious establishment in connection with the state: and strange as it may appear, he never yet met with an *honesty* and at the same time *religious man* of frankness, intelligence, and candour, who, whatever his denomination, did not in reality, hold a very similar sentiment.

This is certainly no place to discuss the question: but the writer cannot help thinking — and saying, that one capital source of opposition to an establishment — apart, of course, from all those obvious motives of selfishness, to one or other of which opposition to the Church of England may so often be traced — is the infidel notion that civil government is a something necessarily distinct from and independent of religion; an error not greater than that which should maintain that the religion of an individual ought not to have any influence upon his views and conduct as a citizen — a modern doctrine which some are indeed found to contend for and act upon, but which the stoutest stickler for what is conveniently called "liberty of conscience", if he be *a religious* man, will hardly be daring enough to defend.

Surely, to a professor of religion, unless steeped to the eyes in the lees of old controversy, nothing can be more clear than the fact, that it is the duty of a Christian Government to make provision for the instruction of its subjects in Christianity — and this, whether said subjects wish it or not; just on the same grounds that it is the duty of Christian Churches to send missionaries to the heathen, or into the dark places of our own land, whether the parties who may be "sitting in darkness and under the shadow of death", wish for instruction or not. Indeed, it is a remarkable fact, that the missionaries sent out among the heathen by those the sects, members of which are commonly the sturdiest sticklers about what they may happen to consider as an interference with their "rights of conscience", are never so very scrupulous about consulting the consciences of those to whom they address themselves abroad. The London Missionary Society, for example, sends preachers to the South Seas: they address the natives: the Word is clothed with power: numbers are converted: "Kings become", in a literal sense, "nursing fathers, and queens nursing mothers", to the infant Church: — in short, almost without a figure might a nation be said "to be born in a day".

In such a state of things, did the missionaries shrink from availing themselves of the *civil* influence of a *religiously* disposed king, to promote the increase and ensure the stability of Christianity in the islands? Did they not actually crown the young king Pomare III., amidst an elaborate ceremonial, pursuing even to minute details its resemblance to the gorgeous coronation of our British monarchs in Westminster Abbey? Did they not concur in the promulgation of a code of general laws, avowedly based upon Bible precepts? Did they not by those *laws* ordain the observance of a Christian Sabbath? — aye, and witness punishments by civil mulcture {? toll} for breaches of its religious observance? And did they not do this *nolens volens* {willing or unwilling} the opinions of those islanders who did not concur at all in the matter — those who stood out as Tahitean Independent Dissenters; and who probably thought themselves well off that they got repealed an outstanding penalty against tatooing? They did all this — and they acted piously, scripturally, naturally, and honestly; so also, but under transcendently less favourable circumstances, did the founders of the English Church and Monarchy. It were beside the question here to talk of abuses: the principle of the thing is all that is contended for.

One great and palpable evil is, that in religious controversies men are usually driven upon deciding or defending extreme cases. If a churchman happen to say any thing in behalf of the established system of religious worship in this country, the Dissenter at once calls upon him to say whether or not he thinks their Right Reverences the Bishops can by possibility be supposed to be the legitimate successors of the apostolical fishermen of Galilee? Now this certainly seems to be a very cunning and cutting question — but is it *the question ?* There are gentle and learned, and luxuriously housed Doctors among the Independents, who are surely almost as little to be compared with the poor fishermen aforesaid, as the Prelates themselves. It will, to be sure, be said that the emoluments of the one are derived from voluntary offerings, while the other are supported by compulsory payments. This is no place to discuss such a question; but even if the allegations be admitted, it does not materially mend the matter. The facts are these: there is no rule of christianity acted upon I presume, by any one body of professors of religion, which compels a Minister of the Gospel to be the poorest man in his church — there is none (among the Independents at all events), to prevent him from being the richest: common sense, sound expediency, and may we not add, the scriptural rule point out a medium position, as that which in the present state of society is most beneficial.

Much, very much has been said about the danger and evils of the exercise of secular influence in the Church, especially by individuals belonging to some of the smaller and feebler denominations — this is an exceeding delicate point: to contend for the tolerance even to the slightest extent of such influence in round terms, would be monstrously anti-christian; to point out any religious society in which it does not now prevail, would be to exhibit

"That faultless monster which the world ne'er saw".

In the matter of personal salvation — of Christian morals, the Word of God contains rules which can rarely be mistaken by sincere and good men. In questions of abstract doctrine, and more particularly in reference to forms of government, the case is widely different surely; and it is to be feared that while, on the one hand, a temporising state policy has but too often, and too easily, converted the Church into an engine of civil government — ministers of religion interchanging with ministers of state unhallowed favours, — it has not seldom occurred, on the other hand, that a querulous, captious, techno-theological spirit has prevented the doing a vast amount of practical good, because some small, or it might be considerable, portion of human infirmity mingled with the proposed endeavour.

Transcendental doctrines — so fascinating in ethical science — are liable to be turned to very dangerous use, no less in the Church than in the State. There are political writers who seem to anticipate — some of them honestly perhaps — the possibility of bringing about a sort of civil millenium; while their polemical compeers are with equal zeal asserting the necessity of discovering or forming a religious Utopia: both parties evidently forget, or disregard, the Scriptural doctrine of man's fallen nature. It is very true that the disciples of Christ are exhorted to be "not of the world", but still they are, and while they live they must be *in* the world: *there,* the righteous and the wicked must have many things and many duties in common: the "wheat and the tares must grow together until the harvest". Great and lamentable indeed have been the evils inflicted upon mankind, by parties aiming, by means of the secular arm, to "compel them to come in" — to the Christian fold; but scarcely less deplorable have been the effects of cavils which, ostensibly aiming to keep the world out of the Church, have awfully tended to keep the Church out of the world.

"But would the Tourist compel those to support an Established Church, who conscientiously object to its doctrines?" Undoubtedly he would, so far as pecuniary support goes; just as he would compel a man to support, in that way, any form of government under which he might happen to live, while at the same time he differed individually from that government. Let it be here kept in mind, that this would be in reality no coercion of *conscience* — it would be the *purse* alone that would be affected: and it is upon the acknowledged right of any Government to tax the people for the maintenance of the State — upon whatever considerations that right may be based, — that a *Christian* Government must rest its claim to be supported in the establishment and sustentation of religious worship. There would be no end to allowing "liberty of conscience" in money matters; and, generally speaking, the expression is greatly abused in its application. Allow the freest scope to conscientiousness in all that pertains to religious opinion and worship; but let not a man plead his conscience to save his purse. Every Government will find itself compelled to distinguish between a religiously enlightened and a pecuniary conscience.

"Must persons, then, be compelled to subscribe to doctrines, and worship according to forms, which they disapprove?" Certainly not, in any case whatever, *except* as Governors; and surely a Christian Government ought no more to admit into its councils anti- or avowedly non-Christian men, than the members of a monarchical Government should indifferently co-operate with persons who are openly or undoubtedly the abettors of democracy or anarchy. No small portion of the mistakes into which good men fall in reference to these high questions, arises from the operation of a lax sentiment relative to *allowing fair play to opinion,* as if pushing religion in such a way as to jostle infidelity or indifference, forsooth, were a high crime and misdemeanour! Many small talkers, whose motto is *Magna est Veritas, et preval{e}bit {Truth is great, and will prevail},* — not a Scriptural sentence, by the way, — seem not to perceive, that, however *Truth* may finally prevail, *Error* is every moment making conquests. It seems utterly forgotten, even by some persons calling themselves Christians, that fallen human nature is wholly on the side of evil; and, therefore, that *the fair play* to be expected from such a source can only be decided opposition to Christianity. With reference to the differing peculiarities of the *really religious* sects, the present writer regards them as so trivial, compared with the great doctrines upon which they substantially agree, that he is disposed to say from his heart — would that all mankind formed one family of "United Brethren", as Moravians; that they were a "Society of Friends", as the Quakers; that they all, professing repentance, had come "up out of the water", as Baptists; were obedient to one holy "Synod", as Presbyterians; had enrolled themselves members of a "voluntary Church", as Independents; that they weekly met for the promotion of their spiritual improvement in "class meetings", as Methodists; or, as including the greater part of the excellencies of all the above systems, they were one and all "Churchmen", in the best and highest sense of the word! Every man has undoubtedly a right to worship God according to the dictates of his own conscience, and in this country, at all events, he enjoys that right freely and fully; and, in reference to this glorious privilege, the individual who writes this sentence would devoutly say — *Esto Perpetua {? Let it remain so}.*

What a dissertation! Who could have foreseen that the sight of a country church would have led to such a sentimental parenthesis in our narrative? And, meanwhile, where is the river Don? Smoothly and quietly pursuing its umbrageous course at the foot of the fields down the gentle valley below Penistone.

No. XII. — THE MAY FLOOD.

March 19th, 1836.

"The rain came heavily, and fell in floods."

{From 'Resolution and Independence'} WORDSWORTH.

The tourist, immediately on quitting Penistone, perceives from the stone by the road-side, that he is exactly thirteen miles from Sheffield, — the moors, however, are now fairly left behind, though not the mountain influences; and he who would breathe the keen healthful breezes from the west, or wish to sport with the biting frost — winds from the north, need, as previously stated, ascend no higher ground than this point.

The Don, as will already have been perceived, is indebted for much of its immediate beauty, in many parts of its progress to the fine alders, which not merely fringe its banks, but in some instances, present an upright altitude of stem, and a luxuriant divergence of branches, not witnessed in situations less favourable to the growth of the tree. Clumps of the alder, *(Alnus glutinosa),* have, it has been remarked, the colour and effect of oaks, in wet boggy situations, where the latter will not thrive; and certainly no observant person could walk along the road pursued by the writer in reference to this chapter, without being struck by the pleasing circumstance of the presence of these trees, whether unaccompanied by others, or sparingly intermingled in their ramifications with the characteristic foliage of the oak, the ash, or the sycamore.

Below Penistone, the river enters upon a course so considerably sequestered, as to be at times hardly distinguishable from the road which runs at a short distance above the right bank. This remark refers to the seasons when the bankside trees are in full foliage: in winter, the line of the stream is conspicuous enough at most points.

The fields on both sides of the river, appear to be pretty well cultivated; and, as already intimated, to be repaying the labour and expense bestowed upon them: many of the nearer enclosures are bounded by fences of hawthorn — these contrast pleasingly with the appearance of various tracts of recently reclaimed land hereabout, the generally treeless aspect, and formal stone fences of which, suggest the idea of trigonometrical diagrams laid down on a large scale.

Adjacent to the road, however, the boundary lines, even when consisting of rough gray walls, were at the period of one of my summer visits, enlivened by prodigious quantities of foxglove flowers, which seemed to flourish here as rightful denizens by ancient prescription, of a soil scarcely yet entirely subjugated to the plough. To fancy's eye, these fine, hardy, and aboriginal tribes of Flora, appeared a sort of "red Indians", which the march of cultivation had not yet succeeded in extirpating, or driving from their ancient soil beyond the frontiers of this "far-west" extension of the influence of modern enclosure acts. These features of the scene appear the more grateful, as they are succeeded by a comparatively naked tract — the river course, however, soon re-assumes the umbrageous character before adverted to.

About a mile and a half from Penistone, the road is crossed by a toll-gate, from which the river is still seen urging its tranquil way at the bottom of the fields, perhaps increasingly shaded by alders and other trees, and presenting here and there a pretty combination; as for example, with Willowbridge {Footbridge at SE267026, marked as Willow Bridge on OS 1:25k}, a raised picturesque arch, belonging to a cross-road; and below which is Rollins's Flour Mill in the township of Oxspring {Mill pond shown by river at SE271021 on 1855 OS 1:10560, present Mill Farm estate, but 'Corn Mill' shown to SW away from river nearer Sheffield Road}: here is a good bridge, over which the road goes to Barnsley. "And what of Rollins's Mill?" enquired I of a friend, who seemed to associate with the plain substantial structure some circumstance that compensated its want of beauty — "O", he replied, "that mill has long been noted in this neighbourhood, for the production of super-excellent flour, the combined result, as is stated, of great skill in the purchase of wheat, perfect grinding, and especially the operation of dressing machinery of exceeding fineness". Be it so; such commendation is something. In connection with this incidental mention of "fine flour;" which, by the way, it is gratifying to recollect, was never produced in any other country of superior quality, nor at any period even in England, more generally consumed than at this time — it may be observed that oatmeal cakes are still a good deal eaten at some places in this district. This bread differs, however, considerably from the thick, soft, sour cakes of Lancashire and Derbyshire, as well as from the light, white, and commonly sweet oaten bread of many parts of Yorkshire.

When a person enters the inn, at which the coaches stop at Midhope Stones {SK234995}, the first thing that strikes his eye, especially if he be hungry, is a sort of rack suspended on the joists of the ceiling of the kitchen, and overlaid with some scores of thin oat-cakes, or, as the batch is called, *reed bread;* having been placed on the rails of the rack in its flaccid state, the manner in which each cake is warped, first by hanging over at the edges, and secondly by drying, gives it a curious appearance to a stranger. When eaten, it is found to be just so tenderly crisp, and withal so sweet, added to its undoubted wholesomeness, that many persons are extremely fond of it. It owes its appearance and texture to the method of baking the leaven, which, instead of being taken at once from the tub and poured upon the bake-stone, as is commonly done in Sheffield, is in the first place, spread upon a light thin wooden spatula or shovel, large enough to receive the cake: upon this board, the leaven is shaken so as to distribute it in the form of the intended cake; *dry meal,* being repeatedly riddled or scattered with the hand upon it, at intervals during the operation; this gives to the bread that singularly rough crackled surface, as well as produces that dry and open character for which it is remarkable. It is baked nearly in the ordinary manner, on a smooth compact slab called a *crow-stone.* Should any apology be thought necessary for this digression from a description of the course of the river, to the method of preparing oat-cakes by certain of the inhabitants in its vicinity, the reader may be assured that no apology would be needful to the pedestrian, before whom a tray of this crumpet bread accompanied by a pat of Penistone butter should be placed, after several hours' rambling in the midst of a hot summer's day.

A little below the flour-mill above-mentioned, a bold projecting headland obstructs, and changes the straightforward direction of the Don, which, by an abrupt angle is transferred from the left to the right hand of the tourist, flowing under a bridge at the bend, over which the road from Penistone to Wortley passes {Thurgoland Bridge SE277017}. Here the river flows through pleasant pasturage lands, often of no great breadth, but commonly of a good depth of soil. These alluvial selvages of the valley water courses consist, for the most part of sandy loam, which appears to have been deposited by the river in the course of ages. In some instances, they are, as previously stated, little more than mere marginal stripes of level cultivatable soil; in others they are wider, and occasionally they become amplified into beautiful meadows — in either case, it is frequently apparent that the water loaded with sediment must not only have innumerable times overflowed the new ground, but that its volume must have formerly greatly exceeded that now adapted to the dimensions of the present channel.

Here, indeed, floods are common, as well in summer as in winter — when not only the soil and the crops, but occasionally live stock will be carried away. The fickleness of the climate of this country is proverbial; from our insular situation, this must always have been the case: nevertheless, the occurrence of a case of extremely unseasonable weather, rarely fails to call forth a repetition of the trite remark, that such deviation had not occurred before "in the memory of the oldest persons". The prevalence of heavy falls of rain in these elevated situations has already been adverted to; it may be interesting to add, that in the level parts of the kingdom, and in the neighbourhood of the metropolis, the mean annual rain is about nineteen or twenty inches; — Dr. Dalton remarks, that the six months of most rain are those beginning with September. In the year 1806, the quantity of rain which fell in the neighbourhood of Sheffield was considered unusual, having been 19.85 inches.

In the last week of April, 1807, occurred one of the greatest transitions from cold to heat that was ever recollected in England: within four and twenty hours the thermometer rose from the temperature of Christmas to that of Midsummer! During the first few days of the succeeding month, the oppressive heat of the weather was moderated by heavy storms of thunder and lightning, while the earth, refreshed with rains, poured out of her lap in welcome profusion the verdure and beauty of May; as if — to use the words of an elegant describer of the transition, — "Nature had been suddenly awakened from the death-sleep of winter, and started up in a moment in all the loveliness, life, and luxuriance of spring". Two circumstances, far different in character, rendered memorable, the frosty close of the former, and the fervid opening of the latter of these vernal months.

Snowy as the last week in April happened to be, it did not so alarm a couple at Sheffield, who had made up their minds to be married, but that they proceeded to the church: the road from the bride's residence was steep — the causeway was slippery — the bride, shame on the negligence of the groom's man! stumbled and fell —

but the parties reached the church: the nuptial ceremony was duly performed by the priest. * * * * * * Let the reader fill up the space occupied by these asterisks according to his taste: but the happy couple, having added to the intended matrimonial ceremony, the unexpected solemnity of a baptism, bore from the church with them — or rather, from the church was borne, with the "blushing bride", an infant daughter!

On Saturday evening, the 2nd of May, the day before having been characterized by thunder and lightning, accompanied by large bullets of icy hail, in various places — dark lowering clouds gathered over these hills with a most portentous aspect. At length, the rain, which at first fell heavily, descended in torrents such as had never been witnessed before, by any person living — a mass of clouds having, as it is termed, "burst", over the range of hills from Bradfield to Silkstone. The suddenly descending deluge tore up the ground on Green Moor {~SK281993}, and the adjacent eminences, in a singular manner and to a great depth: the impetuosity of the torrent carrying the soil into the valleys in such quantities that it required a long time to cart it away. The rivers at Loxley, Rivelin, Midhope, and Penistone, pouring their accumulated waters into the Don, effected unprecedented desolation on its banks, not only carrying away great quantities of the arable soil, but trees, utensils of husbandry, cattle, &c. Unhappily, this was not the extent of the calamity; in one house at Silkstone, a woman and her four children were seated together, when the flood came rushing in, and swelled to the height of the chamber so rapidly, that though the mother succeeded in getting three of her children up stairs, the fourth, a girl of seven years of age, perished. In an adjoining house, a woman and two of her grandchildren were also drowned: on some of the low grounds the water rose five yards in about five minutes! No wonder that a storm, the effects of which were so fatally terrible, and the traces of which are not yet obliterated on the hills, should be strongly remembered by many, who describe it emphatically as "the May flood".

No. XIII. — WORTLEY MILLS.

March 26th, 1836.

"Look where you may, a tranquilising soul
Breathes forth a lite-like pleasure o'er the whole.
The shadows settling on the mountain's breast,
Recline, as conscious of the hour of rest;
Steadfast, as objects in a peaceful dream,
The sleepy trees are bending o'er the stream;
The stream half-veiled in snowy vapour, flows
With sound like silence, motion like repose."

From the bridge mentioned in the preceding paper, the road runs along the southern side of the adjacent hill, overlooking the Don, which flows down "the bottoms" {? Cheese Bottom SE280011}, in summer with the tranquillity indicated by the foregoing lines, and rarely with turbulence at any season. Near the point of highest elevation of the road, stands a finger-post pointing the way from Penistone to Wortley in a right line; and to Barnsley and Hoyland Swaine, by diverging ways: here {~SE285012}, let the rambler turn round, and look back towards the south-west {?error should read 'north-west'}, and he has a fine view of Penistone in the distance, — and beyond that, stretching along the horizon, the bleak and elevated line of country called High Flatts (SE211074): on the brow of the nearer hill, are scattered the houses forming the hamlet of Rough Birchworth {SE262015}; while far beyond them, the moors are seen boldly defined in their outline on the clear blue sky, or apparently mingling with the heavens, when clouds obscure the vista. A little higher, in the direction of Barnsley, a still prouder observation-post is attained {?~SE288014}, commanding an extensive prospect towards the north-east, and from which, according to local report, York Minster, though distant nearly forty miles, — and, as some add, Lincoln Cathedral also, may occasionally be discerned with the unassisted eye.

The river bank may be regained, either by pursuing the Wortley road to Thurgoland, or by turning down Roper-lane {? Roper House Lane, SE283010}, immediately from the finger-post abovementioned; the latter will be the pleasantest course, provided the ground be dry, — if otherwise, it will be next to impossible to get any thing like "dry-shod", along this "miry lane full ankle deep in clay". Roper House {SE284012}, close to the road side here, is remarkable for the great number of the nests of the house martin, *(Hirundo urbica)* which are plastered up under the eaves. Shakspeare, it will be recollected, has remarked that

> "————————this guest of summer,
> The temple — haunting martlet, does approve
> By his lov'd mansionry, that the heaven's breath
> Smells wooingly here. No jutting frieze,
> Buttress, nor coigne of vantage, but this bird
> Hath made his pendant bed and procreant cradle:
> Where they most breed and haunt, I have observed
> The air is delicate."

The building in question has an eastern aspect, and although certainly somewhat sheltered, can hardly be said to stand in a remarkably genial situation: the original adoption of this retired spot by the birds for their nesting place, may have been accidental; while their attachment to, and occupancy of it during successive seasons, is probably due, in great part, to the circumstance of their being unmolested; for the number of these "procreant cradles" has considerably increased of late years. A similar colony of hirundines, selects a summer location under the eaves of the Methodist chapel in the adjacent hamlet of Thurgoland.

Descending by Roper-lane, a few hundred yards brings us to a cluster of deserted tumble-down smithies, adjoining a block of lowly dwelling-houses, — this is the "old wire mill" {Old Mill Lane, SE278005}, so called to distinguish it from two or three other and similar establishments a little lower down. At what period, or by whom the art of wire-drawing was introduced into this country does not appear: it is said, however, that all the wire manufactured in England was wrought throughout by hand till 1565, when the art of drawing with mills was introduced by foreigners. A couple of centuries later, the business of wire-drawing flourished considerably in this secluded valley of the Don; while at Barnsley and its neighbourhood, immense quantities of it were used in the making by hand of the old fashioned cards used in the teasing of wool. This description of employment, however, has long been given up; no private individuals, at this time of day, spinning wool as our grandmothers did, at their own "high wheels", consequently not requiring the hand cards; while the circular cards used in the mills are pricked and wired by machinery of the most ingenious and complicated description.

A person who has never witnessed the method by which rods of iron are reduced, and, as it were spun out into the finest wire, could not fail to be gratified by a visit to these mills. In one of them the old practice of what is called "rumpling", originally derived from Germany, is still retained, and exhibits a simple but peculiar contrivance for catching at, and pulling the rods of iron by means of peculiar nippers, through holes drilled in what are called the "draw-plates".

From a point a little above the old wire-mill, the river, after passing through a pleasant meadow-bosomed dell, enters a deep defile, the sides of which, especially on the right hand, have a broken tumbled appearance, as if they had formerly been ransacked for mineral treasures. The road and the river run nearly together down the sequestered vale from the wire-mills to Wortley forges {SK294998}.

The iron-works situated in this capacious glen belong to Vincent Corbett, Esq., and are of considerable antiquity, Wharncliffe Chase having, as we have previously seen, supplied them with charcoal fuel about the time of Queen Elizabeth. On coming upon these vulcanian establishments unexpectedly, as a person may do by following the stream, and when the hammers are not at work, the first feeling experienced is almost an involuntary one of repugnance at the manner in which the retirement of nature appears to have been outraged by the intrusion of such dull, smoky, fiery, and withal noisy nuisances as these forges. And, — but that it has been no voluntary surrender of sylvan pre-eminence on the part of the *genius loci,* we might exclaim in the language of a fair poetess: —

> "_____ blush, Oh blush,
> Thou venal genius of these outrag'd groves,
> And thy apostate head with thy soil'd wings
> Veil! who hast thus thy beauteous charge resign'd
> To habitants ill suited; hast allowed
> Their rattling forges, and their hammer's din,
> And hoarse rude throats, to fright the gentle train,
> Dryads and fair haired Naiades; — the song
> Once loud and sweet of the wild woodland choir,

To silence."

SEWARD.

After all, however, although these works have confessedly

"Scared the quiet of this solitude",

it is still a spot where a summer's day might be rustically spent:
there are some pretty snatches of walks along the margins of the
watercourses and dams; some joyous clambering up the rough gorse
covered banks, or embowered pathways by the river side at the foot
or under the trees mantling the Tin-mill rocher {SK293989}, — even
down to the still more sequestered margin of Cockshut's great dam,
as it used to be called{? Tin Mill Dam, SE295989 (a burial in 1774
refers to 'Mr CockShut's Tin Mill Dam')}. The expansions,
undulations, and convolutions of the light smoke, as sometimes seen
ascending in this dell on a still autumnal morning, appear to
represent, as distinctly as smoke can do it, the following words used
by a Latin author, (Lambinus) as descriptive of a similar incident: —

"Cum trepido seu tremulo motu sursum feruntur. Rotantes,
torquentes, glomerantes, rotarum in morem volventes."
{?~ With hurried and trembling upward motion. Rolling,
twisting, collecting, like wheels moving.}

Ten years ago, I spent with two or three friends a pleasant holiday at
this place, — one of the party was a lovely young female, then in the
heighday of hope, — such hope as is the child of love, when love
itself is rendered lovelier by confiding in pledges of affection
interchanged under circumstances of peculiar trial. "Many waters
cannot quench love", says the wise man; and the truth of the maxim
was illustrated in this case, — my fair friend was with us on the
embowered margin of the Don at Wortley mills, — her lover was on
the banks of the Delaware: "her heart was here, — his far away, —
the Atlantic roll'd between". But the parties faithfully met, —
married, — and saw their sons rise up around them, — she died in
the prime of womanhood; and let me, while passing Wortley Forges,
weave a simple sonnet to her memory: —

Here, while all lonely, I repass this spot,
    Where, once, in bygone years I stray'd with thee;
    In friendly wise our thoughts exchanging free,
And hopes of him afar, whom we did not
To pray for fail; and heaven confirmed the lot

Your love had cast: I saw thee meekly stand,
    Wife, — mother, — saint, — thy ever cordial hand
Held forth to greet me still: art thou forgot,
Now dead? No: surely still do many bear
    Thy memory kindly written on their hearts;
And though long since, for thee, the mourner's tear
    Fell, — stirred, at seasons, recollection starts;
Each chord of feeling owns the impulse true,
And sympathies long hush'd their tones once more renew.

After leaving the Low forge {SK291995}, and when dropping down towards the Flour mill {?SK297990}, a very pretty view of the church and village of Wortley is obtained, as they appear cresting the opposite hill, at the distance of about half-a-mile. The flour mill is placed just upon an elbow of the Don, where the river makes an abrupt turn to the right; becoming almost obscured from view when the summer foliage adorns the trees embosoming the old Tin mill {SK294988}. When, however, I was this way two or three days since, although the air had the genial temperature of May, the umbrageous beauty of the scene lay, for the most part, folded in bud, — the buds, indeed, showed green at the tips, the honeysuckle leaves were unfolding, and the willow-catkins, golden-yellow or silver-white, suggested that Palm Sunday was at hand, — PALM SUNDAY! how pleasing the sound, how rural the association; — verily, our forefathers showed themselves poetical as well as pious in the denomination of these high festivals of their church: never may the iron hoof of infidelity, however speciously gilded, be allowed to trample these red letter days out of the calender. Close by the flour mill abovementioned, the Don is crossed by means of a series of little stone piers placed upon the bed of the river, and called *leapings* {? Ford on OS 1:25k at SK297991}. This simple and convenient description of traject is very common in Derbyshire, where, by the way, the blocks of stone are rarely either of so equal an height, or placed at such regular and short intervals as in the case before us; indeed, the High-Peakers, are often required literally to *leap,* — not step merely, from one rugged and slippery foothold to another. Leaving the Tin mill on the right, and passing over the stone bridge {? Soughley Bridge SK292986}, we instantly get a glimpse of one of the most interesting objects of our tour, — Wharncliffe. But we must here leave the Don for a moment, to pay our passing respects to one of its more important tributaries.

No. XIV. — THE LITTLE DON.

April 2nd, 1836.

"———————— The weary traveller descries
Still deeper cliffs and mightier mountains rise:
To find the shepherd's cot he urges on
With anxious heart, and finds not that alone:
A cultivated vale his eyes shall bless —
Midhope, a garden in a wilderness.
Like fair Bermuda's isles, that southward run,
Those isles the favourites of the radiant sun."

THE MOORS.

It will be seen, on turning to No. II. {'Historical Notes'} that Dodsworth describes the Don as running "by Midhope", although he had previously stated, correctly enough, that the river had its rise in the hills above Penistone, in conformity with our description of its source in a previous paper. It is more remarkable that Mr. Hunter, whose general accuracy is so surprising, should, in one instance, appear for a moment to have forgotten the preference claimed by the Penistone River. Having in the "Hallamshire", when speaking of the capital river, mentioned with so much exactness that "the head of the principal brooklet which forms this river is about four miles above Penistone, and near the springs of the Mersey", we are surprised, when in the introduction to his Deanery of Doncaster {1828/31}, he says of the Don — "its spring is near Lady Cross, at the extreme point of the deanery westward". He adds, with no less of fidelity than of elegance — "its long and sinuous course lies wholly in this district, and it is by so much more considerable than any other stream by which this rich and fertile country is watered, that the whole region might without much impropriety, be spoken of as the great valley of the Don."

{Lady Cross – 'remains of' on old Turnpike Road ~SK148997, or possibly at building at SE141000}

The "Little Don" — as in courtesy, it seems we must designate the Midhope stream — has its origin on the same "dead edge" with, and not much more than a mile distant from, the source of the capital river. It does not, however, like the latter, burst from any distinct spring or fountain — but is rather collected in the first instance from a swampy tract in the neighbourhood of Lady Cross; — "and what, and where is *Lady Cross?*" enquires the reader. *What* it may have been originally, is difficult to say; possibly a mere shaft or land-mark — more probably, however, as the name imports, an actual but rude cruciform structure similar to those which the piety of past ages scattered so plentifully over the bleak moor, as well as in the secluded vale, or beside the monastic pile: in the present instance, the shaft and transverse piece, supposing the latter ever to have existed, are gone; but the foot of the former, firmly set in a stout basement stone, still remains beside the old Salterbrook road, about six miles above Midhope Stones. Several fragments, or local appellations indicative of the former existence of these objects are met with on the moors, or recognised in recorded perambulations. Windledon Cross is mentioned in old maps {? ~SE140005}, though now no longer existing; as is also Boardhill {? ~SE172009}, and various other crosses on these hills. From the frequent mention of these crosses, in ancient perambulations, they, no doubt, served important uses in the indication of the boundaries of adjacent lordships: their appellation, if not their form, generally securing for them that respect which might not have been paid to land-marks entirely divested of association with the doctrines of Christianity. It is no less true that in our day, and to a people from whose minds religious associations with these memorials has been almost banished — the appellations "Lady Cross", "Stanedge Pole", and "Boulder Stone", suggest nearly similar ideas: in olden times, the case must have been very different — the packhorse driver, or the still more solitary wanderer over these dreary heights, must not only frequently have been indebted to these conspicuous objects for a knowledge of his track, but have felt recalled to his mind sensations previously excited in connexion with the more splendid crucifix, and its attendant ceremonies in his local chapel. Such, at least, it is pleasant to imagine may have been the fact — but was it so?

The stream, having collected itself from a number of small tributaries upon and below the bleak and open tract of Langsett High Moors, approaches the Manchester road near Langsett {SE212004}, and accompanies it to the termination of the valley. In this valley, mischiefs from freshes in the river are quite as sudden and considerable as in the vale beyond: a striking instance of this kind occurred in 1834.

It was a fine autumnal afternoon — there had been no rain — or, at all events, none of consequence, when the passengers by the Manchester coach to Sheffield, dismounted a few minutes at the well-known inn, at Woodhead {Angel Inn SK096999}, on the western side of the "Appeninos:" after a few moments the bonny landlady ran in exclaiming, that such a flood as she never saw was coming down: and sure enough it was coming, bearing down before it both crops and soil! On the coach gaining "the heights", it was found that a cloud had burst, the distribution of its waters westward, being the torrent just mentioned, while the deluge eastward was rolling down the vales of Midhope and Penistone; just above Oughtibridge the coach passed the leading swell of the flood, which resembled the elevated tide wave called *Eagre* {Tidal wave or 'bore'}; its height above the subjacent current of the Don appearing to be scarcely less than about four feet!

The country about Langsett, has a dreary aspect at almost all seasons, except during high summer: this appears more particularly the case at the fall of the year, when from the lateness of the harvest the idea of desolation is very powerfully impressed — especially in the minds of casual passengers. The writer has already mentioned, that he noticed a crop of oats set up in a field, in the month of November last year: and if any credit be due to the validity of an ancient tenure which has been published as belonging to this place, one might infer that formerly the inhabitants of this vale, not only often witnessed the ungenial phenomenon of "Winter, lingering on the lap of May" but on the lap of June too: — the tradition alluded to states that certain lands were held by the tenure of the occupier presenting to the lord of the manor a red rose at Christmas, and a snow-ball on Midsummer-day!

Whatever may be thought of the state of local agriculture, as indicated by such a quit rent as that just mentioned, it does appear, on better authority, that this valley was not always so quiet as at present. About a mile, before we reach Midhope Stones, from Langsett, and just over a plantation behind Husker House {? Uskers SE227002}, on the left hand side of the road, there is a bold eminence called "Alderman's Head" {SE229007}, — why so called, does not appear — but the spot is rendered interesting from a local tradition, not unsupported by historical evidence: there are two versions of the story, one in prose, the other in rhyme: the former may be seen in the elegant page of Hunter — the latter is here presented to the reader: —

THE YEW TREE OF PENISAL.

De Midhope, of Langsett, as chronicles sing,
Was lord, when our Edward the First rul'd as King :
Broad lands, on each side of this well-watered vale,
Had swell'd his rich rent-rolls from heirship and sale.

In woodland and pasture he summered his flocks,
And chased the wild deer o'er the heath-skirted rocks;
While to Kirkstead he paid tythe of all he possessed,
He bravely and freely rejoiced in the rest.

For Penisal, whither his serfs might repair,
He purchased the grant of a market and fair;
Where weekly came vendors with basket and beast,
And clothiers each year, at Saint Barnabas' feast.

Ere long, and — he planted a beautiful yew,
Which flourished through ages, so slowly it grew .
On a plot of rich greensward around this fair tree,
Met buyer and seller, in bargaining free.

Hither came with stout ellwand {*}, the webster whose pack
Of linseys and woolseys was strapped on his back:
He, on the wide yew, keen with tenter-hooks made,
From bough-end to bough-end his fabrics displayed.

{* a measuring rod an 'ell' long}

Hither came too, the pedlar, with glittering things, —
Sharp whittles, gay girdles, hooks, buckles and rings :
And far o'er yon moorlands bleak, purple, and high,
Came mother and daughter to gossip and buy.

Tradition, unchronicled History's page,
Tells what houses rose here in a subsequent age;
How the Yew Tree, thrice honoured, in growing renown,'
Stood green in the midst of old Penisal town!

How in its broad shadow might yearly be seen,
De Midhope's retainers on Alderman-green :
Each paying obstreperous, or sullen or mute,

To the lord of the manor his service and suit.

But ages have left not a trace of that town;
And its fair and its market alike are unknown :
While the Yew — the brave Yew! long survivor of these,
Shewed how much faster Time levelled houses than trees.

Yea, it stood but three lustres {#} since on yon green knoll,
When twenty-five feet was the girth of its bole;
And round it with many a strange legend and tale,
Oft lingered the greybeards and youth of the vale.

{# a 'lustrum' – a period of five years}

It stood — and perchance had been standing this day,
Had not a lone fisherman rambled that way:
He thoughtless, or reckless, to warm his chill'd hands,
Lit up in its hollow a bonfire of brands!

'Twas April — and moonless the night of Saint Mark:
O'er the neighbourhood flicker'd strange gleams in the dark;
'Twas the Yew Tree aflame! its green beauty was gone;
At the ravage affrighted the rustics look'd on.

Five days and five nights shone the red glow around,
Ere the time-honoured tree was burnt close to the ground;
Few years marked the spot — but men died and grass grew,
And left to tradition the Penisal Yew.

A little below Alderman's Head, there stands, in a field by the road-side, a very ancient mouldering yew tree: probably it may have been coeval with the one mentioned in the foregoing verses. At Midhope Stones {SK235995} there is a good inn, at which the coaches stop; a capital stone bridge over the river; and on the hill-side rises the little rustic stone chapel, within its narrow grave-ground. From this point to Deepcar, the vale is mostly cultivated on both sides of the stream: and although the propriety of the appellation — "a garden in a wilderness", may not be very striking to all persons, its applicability will seldom be questioned by any one coming down here from the moors, especially during the summer season.

I have hardly ever walked down this vale, without having my attention particularly arrested by the vast profusion of vegetable exuviae embedded in the gannister, which lay in heaps beside my path, ready to be broken up for mending the road. To the cheap and apparently inexhaustible supplies of this hard, fine grained, siliceous stone, which are mostly drawn from this neighbourhood, the trustees of many of the hardworn roads about Sheffield are greatly indebted; indeed, but for this economical material, and the slag, or vitreous masses derived from the matters used in fluxing the iron ores at the blast furnaces, many of the roads would be with difficulty kept in a passable state. It is less, however, for its uses, important as these may be — than as the matrix of such a multitude of fossil stems, that the gannister always appears so interesting to me. Thousands of persons, no doubt, have been in the habit of passing these inexplicable remains of a former world without expending upon them even a momentary thought — many would certainly do so, if these reliquia were of a greatly superior order of organization, like the testaceae, &c. of the mountain limestone of Derbyshire — nay, doubtless, there would not be wanting those who would incuriously pass by those casts, or lapidified fragments of the higher classes of animals whose remains do frequently occur in a fossil state. To an individual, whose attention is once directed to the subject, the difficulty is that of withdrawing his observation, lest he may miss some specimen, which, by being more perfect than the rest, might throw a ray of light upon their character — the difficulty of such an individual "leaving the black stones alone", will often be experienced here.

This stone, which is chiefly quarried about Stannington {List of Mines show ganister mining at High Matlock from 1910 (SK310892) and Woodend from 1902 (?~SK321891) (NMRS web site)}, and to some extent also in the sides of this vale, is associated with the lower coal — indeed with the second seams of Farey, or those immediately above, or enveloped in the moorstone. Hence, while some portions of the stone beds are of a beautiful saccharoid whiteness, others are deeply tinged with oxide of iron, but more are dark or even black, as though colouring matter had flowed from the coal with which the gannister is often in immediate contact. The vegetable remains consist of stems and branches, or leaves — the former, sometimes of inconsiderable diameter, but frequently the thickness of one's arm or even thicker: they are commonly more or less flattened, and dotted all over with depressed tubercles: they are almost invariably coated with a carbonaceous crust, sometimes merely a black film or powder — the bark or outside of the original vegetable having obviously been converted into coal, while the inner part, which was probably of a succulent nature decayed, its place becoming occupied by infiltration of stony particles until the result was a perfect cast of the stem, such as we find it. The leaves, or perhaps branches of the plant, which now appear long and ribbon-like, have likewise been changed into coal, and are seen like black stripes intersecting the stone in every direction. *What* were these vegetables? *where, when,* and *how* did they grow? and by what means did they become enveloped, so as to be preserved to after ages in the flinty substance above named? These, and various other questions must present themselves to every enquiring mind, at the sight of these gannister fossils: but who will answer them? Messrs. Lindley and Hutton, who in their beautiful "Fossil Flora" {published in parts between 1835 and 1840}, have given several engravings of this class of stems, are of opinion that *Stigmaria ficoides,* the vegetable in question, was a prostrate land plant, the branches of which radiated regularly from a common centre, and finally became forked: that it was dicotyledonous: of a succulent nature; and that the tubercles upon the stem are the places, from which the leaves, which are supposed to have been cylindrical, have fallen off.

At the lower part of Midhope Dale, just before it opens upon Deepcar, coal is obtained by drifts excavated to a considerable depth in the sides of the valley: from these narrow thurles {? Tunnel, from **Þurlen**, *v.* to pierce, drill or bore. Middle English} is likewise obtained fire-brick clay, and the gannister just mentioned. It may be noticed too, as a somewhat uncommon occurrence, that recently an ample vein of lead ore has been discovered protruding through the thill {Thill – Underclay or Seat-earth of Coal Seams – ref. Arkell and Tomkieff, English Rock Terms, 1953} or floor of the mine, and running horizontally under the coal seam. The coal is mostly burnt into cokes in the open air, near the road side, and carted to Sheffield for the use of the furnaces. The nocturnal appearance of these extended fires, and the grimy aspect of the men in attendance upon them, sometimes forms rather a striking picture. The coal, some of which belongs to the lowest beds, having formerly been worked even at Stanedge Pole, is mostly of the second and third beds, namely those connected with the gannister previously noticed: it is excavated from Hunshelf Bank {SK275991}, and some other places hereabout: for household purposes it is generally very indifferent, being of a tender, dirty smouldering quality. Its character may be inferred from the following anecdote which is locally current as descriptive of the "Stannington coal" — namely, that an individual having occasion to go from that neighbourhood to London, made up his fire in the grate when he set out, and found it burning on his return!

No. XV. — WHARNCLIFFE

April 9th, 1836.

"In all their pride still wave the Wharncliffe woods,
　　Still o'er their bowers the summer dews descend;
In freshness flow the Don's translucent floods,
　　High o'er whose banks the rifted rocks ascend;
　　Still all his hidden brooklets rippling wend
Through mossy banks, and murmur as they flow
　　Where pensile flowers, like bashful virgins bend,
To see their beauties in the waves below,
That kiss their perfumed lips, and in their blushes glow."

　　　　　　　　　　　　　　W. H. STERNDALE

READER, we are at Deepcar {SK290979}. Now turn your back on
the westering sun — that superb burst of sylvan grandeur, rising
from the river to the sky, is Wharncliffe! And who has not heard of
Wharncliffe? Wharncliffe poetically — Wharncliffe pictorially — or
Wharncliffe politically? Indeed, in approaching this interesting
portion of our subject, it is impossible not to be at once struck with
the magnificent aspect of the scene before us, and the disheartening
consideration, that it will be next to impossible to introduce a single
new element into the description of a spot to which so many gifted
pens have done honour.

Elliot, who has sung of "Wharncliffe and the Demons", has a striking
expression in reference to the rugged outline of these "billowy
heights", which

　　"——————————— ascend, —
　　Surges eternal, silent, motionless,
　　As if the Almighty's hand had still'd and fix'd
　　The waves of chaos in their wildest swell!"

Our author has elsewhere repeated the idea, designating the mountain
masses as the "——— billows of a granite sea".

Perhaps the poet will pardon the hypercritical remark that "granite"
no more occurs on Locksley Edge, than it forms the crest of
Wharncliffe — indeed, the "young mechanic" who would indulge his
"Sabbath morning" contemplations sitting in a "granite chair", must

travel far beyond the precincts of Hallamshire. Less surprising, however, is it, that the poet should have bestowed upon gritstone rocks the appellation of granite, than that the topographer should have assigned a calcareous character to the elevation before us, — yet Mr. Hunter thus writes: — "The slope of a mass of *mountain limestone,* at the foot of which runs the Don, is nearly covered with wood, forming, perhaps, one of the finest native forests in the kingdom". The nearest Yorkshire locality exhibiting the protrusion of rocks having the geological character implied by the foregoing terms, would probably be Skipton, distant from Wharncliffe between thirty and forty miles.

The Don, as already mentioned in a preceding chapter, enters this wooded region at Deepcar, a point, which as it is also coincident with the approach of the Manchester road to the river which it afterwards accompanies, affords to persons riding on the coach towards Sheffield, the advantage of coming suddenly and unexpectedly on the scene.

Having fairly entered the defile down which the river flows from Deepcar, the prospect for a while, especially on the left, is nearly altogether sylvan; and a person might almost fancy himself for a moment, as fully sequestered from the world in this umbrageous dell, as if he were in the depth of an American forest — with this difference, however, even amidst his momentary indulgence of the idea of solitude, that the road is so beautifully smooth, in summer at least, as to remind him that civilisation and its accessories are, though here shut out, not distant; and that the next passing minute, or the nearest turn of the road, may dissipate his reverie by the exhibition of that very antithesis of solitude — a well loaded bundling stage-coach! To an eye unaccustomed to such a sight, there is something peculiarly impressive in the appearance of a lofty and long extended slope, covered, as this is, with beautiful if not with majestic timber; and presenting, along with the boldest undulations of surface, the deep green colour of the summer foliage. In addition to that diversified aspect, as to general form, which this sea of wood at such a season presents, the characters of the trees themselves, particularly during a high wind, lend an interest to the scene which cannot be disregarded, nor easily described. Under such circumstances, the dark massive billows of the oak, the more broken waves of the ash, and the foam-like lightness of the birch, overtopping, as it does, the other trees in many places, give to this ocean of "leafy verdure" an aspect of magnificence, the effect of which is materially heightened by the bold ridge of broken rocks, which crests the summit towards Wortley: while beyond this "munition of rocks", and on the same elevated line, Wharncliffe Lodge {SK305956} appears, to keep up our simile, not unlike a vessel at anchor amidst the sylvan surges. It is perhaps, however, in autumn, that the forest glory of Wharncliffe may be said most conspicuously to unfold itself, in those rich, deep, and mingling tints that precede the falling of the leaves. A person who has never watched the progressive changes of this tinting, from its earliest indications, to the full contrast of dark greens, deep yellows, rich browns — to the last uniform tone of full russet, can form but little idea of the mellowness of effect produced between a solemn sunset and such a forest: the individual who has never seen Wharncliffe Wood in any guise, may justly be suspected of having little taste for the beautiful in natural scenery. At the present moment, it might perhaps be deemed by most persons totally uninteresting, because leafless; but, as Du Hamel has justly remarked,

> "there is a beauty in forest vegetation all the year round: when autumn tinctures every fading leaf with dyes, from the refulgent gold to the full-bodied tint of russet brown; say, can the pencil's warmest touch convey the varying richness of the glowing scene? for even in winter, when the leaves have dropped, the ramification of the branches and spray is beautiful and interesting."

The buildings comprising "the Lodge", as seen from the road adjacent to the river, have rather a mean appearance on the whole. The situation, however, is most commanding, and would, one is tempted to think, be just the spot, not only for a castle, but even for a tower, a column, or any kind of conspicuous obelisk.

But why should I aim at a description of Wharncliffe, while the following glowing sketch — the pen-and-ink painting of a lady too! — lies before me?

> "Immediately on leaving Wortley, we descended a long and steep hill, and turning to the left, entered upon the vale. The road continued by the side of the Don, that emerged from its source in the moors above; but I am quite unequal to describe

the sublime and beautiful variety which the succeeding seven miles presented. On the left, the wooded amphitheatre; on the right, hanging copses, tufts of wood, interspersed with sloping pastures, and nestling cottages beetled over the road. These we drove too closely beneath, to see in their best effect; but all on the Wharncliffe side was in fine distance and perspective. I never saw the actual pomp of woods before, sweeping down the steep aclivity, from its lofty summit to the river's brink, advancing and receding as we passed the windings of the vale, and presenting their varied beauty in processional array. The road was laid high above the river's bed. The carriage passed close to its steep and rocky banks, and Lady Mary Wortley could not have been in more danger, when she awoke Mr. Wortley on their journey in Saxony, than we were in the domains of her descendant. Though the postillions were not nodding on their horses, or the Elbe rolling below, yet the banks were frequently as high, and the road as narrow, and the waters of the Don quite deep enough to have terminated our terrestrial career — if a horse had fallen or a wheel come off on its slaty verge. We looked up to the circular rampart that crowned the summit for several miles; and when we were opposite the lodge, that like an eagle's nest, appeared perched in the sky, we scarcely could believe that we had soared so high, or the foot of man could have reached there. Too elevated and too aerial to distinguish its architectural pretensions; its numerous chimneys that rose like small turrets, accorded well with the rocky line, of which it appeared to form a part; every object was in perfect keeping but one: a newly built coach-house, contiguous to the lodge, and there not unappropriate or otherwise, when seen from the vale below, interrupted the feathery line of wood, with its heavy square barn-like appearance." — *Life of a Boy.* *{1821}*

The "Life of a Boy" — what boy? and who is the lady who writes in that style? As to the first question, I can only reply "read the book" — to the second, Sheffield responds, MARY STERNDALE. I am glad of this opportunity of naming with respect a lady whose presence always reminded me of the old school of female geniuses — if I may use such a phrase. It so happened, that when a boy, I, like most other boys, read the narratives of the voyages of Captain Cook; and afterwards — unlike other boys it may be — I met with the monody on the death of the great circumnavigator, by the poetess of Lichfield; the style was brilliant and fascinating to my young imagination. *

* "The Elegy on Captain Cook", says Sir Walter Scott, in his Memoirs of Miss Seward, "was dictated by those feelings of admiration and gratitude, which, in common with Europe at large, Miss Seward felt for the firm and benevolent character of the dauntless Navigator, and for his tragical destiny. It would be too much to claim for these productions", continues the biographer, "the warm interest which they excited while the melancholy events to which they refer were fresh in the public mind. But even when the advantage which they derived from their being suited to 'the form and pressure of the times', has passed away, they convey a high impression of the original powers of their author". In the Elegy alluded to, "benevolence" is the attribute most elaborately lauded as characterising the designs of the intrepid Navigator in his voyages to the South Sea Islands. How much more transcendently, and in its sublimest acceptation, might that term be applied to the objects, the labours, and the success of those Christian Missionaries, who have given to many of those islands an aspect of moral beauty, surpassing even the charms of their natural loveliness.

To be sure, I presently outgrew my admiration of the Darwinian glitter in ode or elegy — but not before Mrs. Sterndale was pointed out to me as the friend of Anna Seward; and when I first spoke to the Sheffield authoress, I recollect congratulating myself on having talked with the lady who had talked with the lady, who had talked with Doctor Johnson — and if we do *not* believe Boswell, had the best of the conversation too! This was venerating by proxy with a witness. But whither am I rambling? *from* the banks of the Don certainly: well, then, I will conclude this chapter with good wishes for the welfare of the author of "The History of a Boy", in the retreat she has chosen in one of the prettiest of the spots designated by her graphic pen as "Derbyshire Vignettes".

No. XVI. — WHARNCLIFFE LODGE.

April 16th, 1836.

"O for a lodge in some vast wilderness,
Some boundless contiguity of shade,
Where rumours of oppression and deceit,
Of unsuccessful and successful war
Might never reach me more! My ear is pained,
My soul is sick with every day's report,
Of wrong and outrage with which earth is filled."

{From 'Slavery'} COWPER.

If the secluded dwelling-house {SK305956}, designated by the title
of the present chapter, cannot be said literally to realize the above
description of the amiable poet, it comes sufficiently near it, to
suggest the appropriate use of the lines as a motto in this place. The
"contiguity of shade", if not actually "boundless", is ample enough to
have served as a "wilderness" to one who had chosen to shroud
himself therein from the world — if not to the fullest extent from the
world's rumours. It is most of all a happy circumstance, that any
benevolent individual, with "The Task" in his hand, may sit himself
down in *this* "lodge", or dive into the shady recesses of *this*
"wilderness", and feel, while reading the above quotation and the
lines that follow in the original, how in his case are largely realized
the blessings so intensely sighed for by the devout bard of Olney.
"Rumours of oppression and deceit" are, it is true, rife — as they
probably ever will be in this fallen world of ours, whatever be the
general condition of society: but the harrowing details "of
unsuccessful or successful war", are, as regards this country, happily
no more heard: and best of all, that soul-sickening curse — Negro
Slavery, which with the still more horrible Slave Trade, filled the
dark places of the earth with "wrong and outrage", in Cowper's day,
have been abolished — but waving these cogitations, let us
endeavour to reach the Lodge.

There are three ways on this side of Wharncliffe, by which the rock-
crested summit of this wooded ascent may be gained: in the first
place, there is a good but steep road from Deepcar by Wortley, which
is that alluded to in the previous quotation from Mrs. Sterndale;
then, there is a gently rising turnpike which crosses the river at

Oughtibridge, about three miles nearer to Sheffield, and which is the way often preferred by parties from that town, who do not go by Greno-wood, on the other side of the hill: the third way, and one which in summer is pleasant enough to pedestrians, who do not object to its steepness, is to pass directly from the road *in medio res* {into the middle of things} — at once getting into the wood.

Nearly opposite the Methodist Chapel at Brightholmlee {SK298949} — and which stands close to the Manchester-road side, the pedestrian will see a green lane that leads down to the adjacent margin of the Don, in the direction of a cottage — called Wharncliffe Holm {Holmes Farm SK299954, 'The Holms' in OS First Series 1 inch}. In this part, the river will be found passable, (except at the period of high floods,) by means of the ordinary rustic contrivance — a line of *leapings* — and such, on account of their position and distances from each other, this row of huge boulders may well be called, in contradistinction to similar crossings which are formed of such small, square, commodious *stepping* stones, so placed that females feel little difficulty in using them — which could hardly be affirmed concerning this sequestered traject. This track of footstones is broken midway, by a little tree-covered islet which here divides the stream for a short distance {? SK298953 near Holmes Farm} — it seems an early and favourite habitation of that ever-welcome spring flower, the lesser celandine *(Ranunculus nemorosa {R. ficaria}),* which has been so particularly honoured by the muse of Wordsworth: and of its delicate companion, the wood anemone *(Anemone nemorosa),* both flowers at this moment starring the little copse as well as the adjacent banks, with their pleasingly contrasted colours.

The ascent up the wood is steep, but by no means unpleasantly so — particularly to those who take pleasure — and who in health does not? in climbing by such a verdant, flower-fringed, and oak-embowered path. The timber trees are thriving, but not large, owing to the periodical progress of the axe. There is a fall of wood in Wharncliffe every year, and the whole affair is so arranged with reference to the growth and condition of the trees, that twenty-two falls take place in twenty-one years. The section at present in preparation for the current season's felling, extends upwards from the Lodge by which the wood is entered from the Oughtibridge road. On account of the frequent repetition of this profitable process, the trees, as previously intimated, appear, when approached in detail by this inner path, to lose much of that impressiveness of effect which arises from viewing them in the mass, under the favourable circumstances presented by the road below or the eminence above. A considerable portion of the underwood, consists of flourishing hazles; and formerly, Wharncliffe was the grand resort of *nutters,* from different parts of the neighbourhood, including Sheffield. Owing, however, to the mischief and depredations so frequently committed by wanton or dishonest persons, the ancient charter of free warren in salvage fruits, has long been revoked by the noble owner of these domains, and the gatherers of nuts, now pursue their object at the risque of being startled or overtaken by the keeper of the chase. I am yet, in feeling, boy enough to love the recreation of nutting — not for the sake of eating the fruit — but for the pleasure of finding and plucking the clusters: for holiday nutters, like amateur fishers, derive much more pleasure from the pursuit than from the possession of the prize — aye, and occasionally there is a delight in hearing that "crash "among the green boughs which is sometimes inevitable — though I would not wilfully injure a spray; — therefore, I do not like, in the language of Wordsworth, to confess or rather to boast, that after enjoying the "virgin scene", where, thick and beautiful, the "milk white clusters hung", I ever,

> "———————— then rose up,
> And dragged to earth both branch and bough with crash
> And merciless ravage."

On reaching the brow of the wood, and approaching the Lodge, the appearance of the building as thus come upon, is even less interesting than as seen from below: on entering, however, the immediate enclosure, the scene changes: for while the structure reminds one of a plain, comfortable old-fashioned grange, there is a trimness and effect in the accessories that tell us the hand of taste, and the means of its indulgence, have had to do with the place. This house was in fact, during one period, the temporary residence of the Wortley family — here dwelt the celebrated Lady Mary Wortley Montagu; and this scene of the paternal domains seems to have remained as a verdant spot in the memory of this singular woman during her romantic peregrinations, for when writing from Avignon, in 1743; after describing the situation of that place at the junction of the rivers Rhone and Durance, she says: "Last summer, in the hot evenings, I walked often thither, where I always found a fresh breeze, and the *most beautiful* land prospect I ever saw, *except* Warncliffe, being a view of the windings of two great rivers, and overlooking the whole country, with part of Languedoc and Provence". The Lodge was, at a later period, the residence of the relict of John, Earl of Erne, and mother of Lady Wharncliffe.

Before describing the spot more particularly, let us turn and look back over Wharncliffe wood — but here I resign the office of *cicerone {guide}* to the autheress before quoted: —

> "Over the House the distant country united its purple tint with the horizon; and had we proceeded no further, we should have supposed the heathy outline was all the view it commanded — a House, humble as is its external appearance, exceeding in grandeur of situation, the palaces of kings — placed on the very verge of a line of perpendicular rocks, that sweep in circular pomp on either hand, and overhang a valley that lies many hundred fathoms below — the sides of its grand amphitheatre clothed with the richest mass of native woods that the kingdom presents; — their unbroken surface glowing with all the varieties of autumnal colouring. Below, rolled the dark waters of the Don, inclosed by its rocky banks, too far beneath, and too much shadowed by the overhanging woods, to be seen from the heights above. Compared even with those of the yeomanry of the present day, the House might be pronounced mean; but it must be remembered, it was built in the fifteenth century, when low ceilings and contracted windows were thought to promote the warmth and comfort within; and though the residence of a man of rank, it was only a Lodge or appendage to his extensive domains. That its situation was selected with a strong feeling of the grand scenes and sweet sounds of nature, is proved by the inscription within the House, and which the present owner, no doubt, highly values for its ancestorial testimony; the very stones proclaim his hereditary descent."

> "Turning the west-end of the building, that stood a few yards behind the line of its front, the grandeur of Wharncliffe bursts upon our view. Wood and rocks, and sky, deep valleys, and distant moors, in all the gorgeous display of a fine October day! Here was another little square enclosure, secured by an

almost invisible wire fence, extending from the corner of the retreating angle to the very verge of the precipice. Its fairy gate admitted us to that delight of a country residence — a half glass door, that at the end of the house entered into a handsome room, where two sash windows overlooked the deeply descending valley, to which the massy pointed grey-stones, rose in close approximation, just as though the house had been built within their natural buttresses, for its certain support and security. With all due respect for the absent lady, (the Countess Erne, then residing at Wharncliffe Lodge), we availed ourselves of the glass door, to *survey* the inside of the room from its outside — 'the guiltless eye enjoys but wastes not,' and there it luxuriated upon its home delights. A nice spinning wheel, the primitive employ of ladies, coeval with the house, was there; a cheerful fire, a reading table, with chairs around it, and cases containing books, combined with the view it commanded, to render this the sweetest spot I ever saw. From the little platform, ten or twelve steps of wood, painted dark green, were bedded in the steep declivity, to aid the descent to a small terrace lying below. Upon this sweet perch, we rested; the turf green as emerald, and soft as velvet, not exceeding five yards in breadth and length; from whence we surveyed all the brilliant scenery of the vale. The topmost boughs of the tall ash, and the sturdy oak, waved at our feet, sinking in abrupt and almost perpendicular descent. Upon narrow borders around the accessible walls of the house, the privet was planted. To soften and embellish the home-scene of a situation so wild is certainly desirable: but the town-growing privet seemed out of place there, amidst the oaks of ages, and the antique evergreens, that the same desire in its earlier inhabitants had planted. The perennial verdure, and the bright scarlet berries of the pyracanthus would have accorded well with the sylvan natives of the place, tinting the walls, and glowing in the winter scene of this aerial habitation, when 'clouds and darkness rests upon it'. "

The writer of the foregoing glowing description saw Wharncliffe in autumn, at which season, as previously intimated, the wood is in its glory: at present, the spring season is too little advanced to give much of beauty to the nobler trees: the birches, however, begin to toss their tufty masses of bursting green over the dark ramifications of the oak and the ash.

Until within the last two or three months the Lodge remained pretty much in the condition above described, except that a few years of desertion had given to the principal rooms an air of decadency. Since the death of Lady Erne {*}, to whose taste the decorations of the spot are attributable, the Lodge has remained the dwelling of a park keeper, the furniture of the late occupant having been left in a great measure undisturbed in the rooms. This romantic and far-famed house, perched like an eagle's nest on the craggs, was built by Sir Thomas Wortley, in 1510, since which time it has undergone so many alterations, and received such modern additions, as to leave it doubtful which was the original portion. This Sir Thomas, whose name will again occur in a still more interesting connection, and whose fondness for the bold magnificence of nature will not at all events, be doubted, seems to have had hard measure, if not positive injustice, in the celebration of his memory, as well from modern ballad rhyme as from local tradition; and this not only in the absence of all documentary evidence or allusion, but in spite of strong contemporary testimony in favour of the simplicity and worthiness of his character.

{* records seem to show that Lady Erne (Lady Mary Caroline Hervey) died in 1842 having, in her later years, lived in an apartment in Hampton Court.}

No. XVII. — WHARNCLIFFE CRAGS.

April 23rd, 1836.

"————— Again I hear
These waters, rolling from their mountain-springs
With a sweet inland murmur: once again
Do I behold these steep and lofty cliffs,
Which on a wild secluded scene impress
Thoughts of more deep seclusion; and connect
The landscape with the quiet of the sky."

{From 'Lines written a few miles above Tintern Abbey'}
WORDSWORTH.

IN describing the general aspect of Wharncliffe, I have already
mentioned the fine gritstone rocks which crest the lofty summit of
the Wood as viewed from the Manchester road, and add so materially
to the effect of the scene. In addition, however, to their pictorial
character, these rugged masses are identified with other matters of
peculiar interest. In 1639, Taylor, the "Water Poet", as he is usually
termed — *not,* as will presently appear, because he preferred *aqua
pura* to nappy ale {strong ale}, but for other reasons — visited
Wharncliffe. Of this visit he has left some account in a rare tract,
quaintly entitled, "Part of this Summer's Travels, or News from Hell,
Hull, and Halifax, &c., with many pleasant passages worthy your
observation and reading" {Halifax and Hull had a reputation for
strict law enforcement, as noted by Camden (in 'Britannia' (1607) in
his description of Yorkshire). John Taylor (1578-1653), also wrote
the Beggar's Litany (?1622) - "From Hell, Hull, and Halifax, Good
Lord, deliver us!". There have been suggestions that 'Hell' refered
to 'Hallam'!}. Proceeding with his narrative, our garrulous tourist
says, —

> "From Leeds I went to Wakefield, where, if the valiant Pinder
> had been living, I would have play'd Don Quixot's part and
> challenged him; but being it was so happy that he was dead, I
> passed the town in peace to Barnsley, and so to Wortley, to
> Sir Francis Worteleye's ancient house. The entertainment
> which himself, his good lady, and his most faire and hopefull
> daughter gave mee there, being such as I never did or can
> deserve, so I never shall be able to requite. To talke of meate,

drink, money, and free welcome for horse and man, it were but a mere fooling for me to begin, because then I should hardly finde the way. Therefore, to his Worship my humble thanks remembered, and everlasting happiness wished both to him and all that is his; yet I cannot forbear to write a little of the farther favour of this Noble Knight. Upon the 14th of September afternoon, he took horse with mee, and his lady and daughter in their coach, with some other servants on horseback: three miles we rode over rocks and cloud-kissing mountains, one of them so high that in a clere day a man may from the top thereof see both the minsters or cathedral churches, York and Lincoln, neere 60 miles off us; and as it is to be supposed that when the Devil did look over Lincoln, as the proverb is, that he stood upon that mountain or neer it; Sir Francis brought me to a lodge, the place is called Wharncliffe, where the keeper dwells who is his man, and keeps all this woody, rocky, stony, vast wilderness under him; for there are many deer there, and the keeper were an ass if he would want venison, having so good a master. Close to the said lodge is a stone, in burthen at least a hundred cart loads; the top of it is four square by nature, and about 12 yards compasse. It hath three seats in the fourme of chairs, made by art as it were in the front of the rocke, wherein three persons may easily sit, and have a view and goodly prospect over large woods, towns, cornfields, fruitful and pleasant pastures, valleyes, rivers, deers, neat {cattle}, sheep, and all things needful for the life of man; contayned in thousands of acres, and all for the better part, belonging to that Noble Knight's ancestors and himself. Behinde the stone is a large inscription engraven, where in an old character is described the ancient memory of the Wortleys, (the progenitors of the Sir Francis now living) for some hundreds of years, who were lords and owners of the said lands and demaynes, which he now holds as their right heire. About a bowshot from thence (by the descent of as many rings of a ladder) his Worship brought me to a cave or vault in a rock, wherein was a table with seats and turfe cushions round, and in a hole in the same rock was three barrels of nappy liquor. Thither the keeper brought a good red deere pye, cold roast mutton, and an excellent shooing-horn of hanged Martinmas biefe: which cheer no man living would think such a place could afford: so after some merry passages and repast, we returned home."

Independently of the far-stretching diversity of landscape, the gorgeous sweep of investing wood, and the romantic character of the crags themselves, the most striking object of curiosity to visitors is, in many instances, the inscribed stone mentioned by Taylor in the foregoing extract. It is, indeed, a rarity, unique in its kind — its great antiquity, simplicity of design, singular state of preservation, and perfect keeping with the surrounding scenery, at once contributing to its interest. The following is, perhaps as nearly as can be obtained, an accurate transcript of the record: —

> Pray for the Saule of
> Thomas Wryttelay Knyght
> for the Kyngys bode to Edward
> the forthe Richard therd Hare the vii. & Hare viii.
> hows Saules God perdon wyche
> Thomas cawsed a loge to be made
> hon this crag in mydys of
> Wanclife for his plesor to her the
> hartes bel in the yere of our
> Lord a thousand ccccc x.

{"Pray for the Saule of Thomas Wryttelay Knight for the Kyngys bode to Edward the forthe Richard therd Hare the vii & Hare viii hows Saules God perdon wyche Thomas cawsed a loge to be made hon this crag in mydys of Wanclife for his plesor to her the hartes bel in the yere of our Lord a thousand ccccc x"

"Pray for the Soul of Thomas Wortley Knight of the King's commands to Edward IV, Richard III, Henry VII and Henry VIII whose Souls God pardon. Which Thomas caused a lodge to be made on this crag in the middle of Wharncliffe for his pleasure to hear the hart's call in the year of our Lord 1510."}

It is always assumed that the individual here commemorated, *himself* caused this inscription to be cut in his own lifetime. Such a notion is certainly highly poetical; but, in the absence of direct evidence, does it not seem more reasonable to suppose from the phraseology, that it was a *post mortem* record of the generous Knight, executed by some one holding his memory in respect?

By whomsoever designed, this venerable specimen of engraving on the live rock was, it may fairly be presumed, exposed for more than two centuries to the elements; consequently, it has suffered much from the weather. At present, it is enclosed within the Lodge, forming, as it were, a sort of natural floor to a small outshot room, into which, by means of the door, window, and a low open arch, just sufficient light is admitted to enable persons to inspect the stone. The received opinion is, that this erection was made for the purpose of protecting the monument from farther injury: the appearance and connection of the room, I think, discountenance this idea, leaving it very probable that the convenience of the inmates was chiefly consulted in the construction of a buttery on so tempting a site. The stone — at least so much of it as is visible — is about twelve feet long by six feet wide, and slightly convex: the inscription, which consists of ten lines, running lengthwise, has been cut in a large, bold, square character — and probably of considerable depth: the lapse, however, of between three and four hundred years, has rendered the whole nearly illegible, without the aid of a transcript made when the writing was more perfect. Notwithstanding, however, that the

> "Old English letters, and those half pick'd out,
> Leave us unskilful readers much in doubt,"

as to the greater portion of the matter, some material words are still easily decypherable by the aid of the transcript above given. This famous lithograph will, it is probable, henceforth remain, perhaps for centuries to come, without farther sensible deterioration; as, with due regard to the value of so precious a memorial of the olden times and primitive manners, it is, in addition to the roof, covered with a moveable board, which is conveniently raised for the gratification of visitors.

The cave in which Taylor was regaled, evidently so much to his heart's content, and which he has, therefore, associated with such savoury recollections, has subsequently obtained a widely different celebrity as "the dragon's den" {SK305959}: it is a sort of quadrangular cavity, about four yards long by two yards wide, mainly formed by the accidentally favourable position in which a vast rock happens to lie upon certain subincumbent masses of stone: the floor is level with the lower greensward path alongside the craggs. The tradition of which this cave contributes to perpetuate the remembrance, will form the subject of a separate Chapter.

The rocks — or enormous masses of gritstone — are, for the most part, perfectly angular, in many instances lying confusedly upon each other, and appearing as if but recently disrupted: they not only present a rugged magnificence in keeping with the rest of the scenery, but afford numerous standing places, at different points of observation. To play the gypsy, to exercise their scansorial powers, explore these ferny recesses, gaze upon the distant landscape, or indulge in other like recreations, is usually the object of those who come hither "to enjoy liberty for a day". It is impossible, however, even amidst these immediate enjoyments, to resist the insinuation of a silent question — how came this rockery into its present dislocated state? Did some sudden rush of waters over this eminence, denude and dissever these ponderous blocks? — or, has it been the slow work of centuries to undermine the once uppiled masses by means of rain and storm, allowing them to tumble from their original state of superposition into their present romantic disorder? It would not be easy to give a satisfactory answer to the question suggested.

At whatever period, or under whatever circumstances, Wharncliffe Crags may have assumed their present arrangement, no small portion of their extrinsic beauty arises from their being so splendidly tinged with what are rather poetically than botanically called "timestains", consisting of an immense variety of lichens.

> "The living stains which Nature's hand alone,
> Profuse of life, pours forth upon the stone;
> For ever growing, where the common eye
> Can but the bare and rocky bed descry;
> There Science loves to trace her tribes minute,
> The juiceless foliage and the tasteless fruit;
> There she perceives them round the surface creep,
> And while they meet their due distinction keep;
> Mix'd but not blended; each its name retains,
> And these are Nature's ever-during stains."

CRABBE.
{from 'The Borough – Letter II' by George Crabbe}

In the month of February, I spent a pleasant day of botanizing on these crags and in the adjoining chase, with a friend, to whose well instructed eye every minute diversity of the various vegetable incrustations adverted to was familiar. To give some idea of the richness of this spot, as a study for the young adventurer in cryptogamic botany, it may be mentioned, that within a space of twelve inches across, on the surface of the rock immediately over the "dragon's den", we counted not fewer than a dozen species of lichens. It is stated by botanical writers, that the attachment and growth of this extensive tribe of vegetables, are among the means provided by Nature for effecting the slow destruction of the rocks upon which they nourish and decay; thus forming a pulverulent nidus {~ powdery nest} for other minute cryptogamia, as mosses, ferns, &c.; these, in their turn, affording by decomposition a vegetable mould adapted to the nourishment of plants of the higher orders.

But is the assertion first above alluded to quite correct, in the sense ordinarily conveyed by the terms? It may seem presumptuous even to attempt to contravene the authority of great names; but would it be less in accordance with facts, if, instead of attributing to the rock-growing lichens so directly *destructive* a tendency, we were rather to regard them as *protecting* the masses which they so closely invest, from the action of the weather? The late G. T. Burnett, Professor of Botany, in King's College, London — speaking, in his "Outlines of Botany", of Lichens, to which he applies the good, old expresive English name of *Time-stains,* says, in reference to the question at issue,

> "The first conquests of life over death, the first inroads of fertility on barrenness, are made by the smaller lichens, which, as Humboldt has well observed, labour to decompose the scorified matter of volcanoes and the smooth and naked surfaces of sea-deserted rocks, and thus to 'extend the dominion of vitality'. These little plants will often obtain a footing when nothing else could be attached. So small are many, that they are invisible to the naked eye, and the decay of these, when they have flourished and passed through their transient epochs of existence, is destined to form the first exuvial layer of vegetable mould; succeeding generations give successive increments to the soil, thus forming that from which men are to reap their harvests, and cattle to derive their food; from which hereafter forests are destined to spring, and from which future navies are to be supplied."

The foregoing passage is highly poetical surely — and if it be deemed to touch the confines of physical credibility, the answer to the question which follows, may perhaps be thought to pass that limit, "But", enquires our amiable and enthusiastic author,

> "how is the frail dust to maintain its station on the smooth and polished rock, when vitality has ceased to exert its influence, and the structure that fixed it has decayed? This is a point which has been too generally overlooked, and yet which is the most wonderful provision of all: the plant, when dying, digs for itself a grave — sculptures in the solid rock a sepulchre in which its dust may rest. For chemistry informs us that, not only do these lichens consist in part of gummy matter, which causes their particles to stick together, but that they likewise form, when living, a considerable quantity of oxalic acid; which acid, when by their decay set free, acts upon the rock, and thus is a hollow formed in which the dead matter of the lichen is deposited."

That in deriving their support more or less from the stone upon which they grow, some disintegration must take place, cannot be denied; but is that any thing more than a very inconsiderable tribute paid by the solid mass of rock, for the very efficient protection afforded by the living investiture in question? To say nothing of the manner in which some of the limestone rocks in the High Peak of Derbyshire are absolutely *encased* by various species of *Lecidea,* let us look at the crags before us. If there be any situation where one would expect to meet with traces of rapid atmospherial desquamation of the rocks, it would surely be at Wharncliffe: but instead of this being the case, the greater part of the immense sandstone blocks lying about, are strikingly angular; and this peculiarity is by no means least apparent with reference to those which are most abundantly licheniferous. To say that the decrement effected by the vegetables had been so uniform, as that no change in the shape of the block need be supposed to have resulted from its destruction, would be idle: let any person examine the effect of *weathering* on *naked* stones, and the conclusion will, I think, inevitably be in favour of the conservative tendency assumed.

How long these rocks may have lain in their present position, it would, as already intimated, be impossible to say; but let us suppose only a thousand years, and it will be difficult to imagine they would have been more entire in form and bulk, had they not been made the supporters of so dense, and in some places so compact, a coating of parasitic vegetation, — nay, we must believe they would have been less so. It may easily be possible to carry this view too far; but are those of our venerable church towers in the country, or even those old walls, which are covered with lichens, actually yielding most rapidly to the processes of decay?

From Wharncliffe Lodge to within a few fields of the village of Wortley, there is a good road through the wood, which was opened in 1827. This "new drive", as it is locally called, is for the most part carried along the crest of the hill, and, from various points, commands noble and diversified prospects of the country on the opposite side of the river, which, except in winter, when the trees are leafless, runs quite unseen, and as commonly unheard, below: indeed, almost the only feature wanting to complete the beauty of the panorama, as seen from Wharncliffe, is water. This romantic region is, as might be expected, the resort of numerous parties of pleasure during the summer season; nor does there seem to be the slightest barrier in the way of the most minute explorer of the beauties of the place, notwithstanding the presence of the following notification, which appears painted upon a board hoisted over one of the cliffs: — "Take notice, no person is permitted to scramble down these rocks into the private walks belonging to Wharncliffe Lodge". Although summer is the chief season when visitors, especially ladies, may be expected to ramble — if not, indeed, actually to "scramble" — among these rocks with pleasure, there is no part of the year, mid-winter scarcely excepted, in which Wharncliffe does not present appropriate and striking beauties to the observation of those who, having health and strength for the task, will be at the trouble of climbing up the hill to look at them.

No. XVIII. — THE DRAGON OF WANTLEY.

April 30th, 1836.

"The fabling seers anticipate
Philosophy of modern date,
Whose giant appetite devours
Thrones, principalities, and powers;
Establishment delights in munching;
Takes a cathedral for its luncheon.
And kindly condescends to sate
Its hunger on communion plate,
Chalice, or consecrated flagon,
Like Wantley's sacrilegious Dragon."

{From 'Bubble and Squeak' 1799} HUDDESFORD.

THE romantic spot where we have been so pleasantly detained, owes some considerable portion of its modern celebrity to its identification with an old ballad, once current in the neighbourhood, and the title of which, (commonly, however, misquoted,) and perhaps the fragments of a stanza or two, are still occasionally in the mouths of hundreds of persons who never gave themselves the trouble to read this notable composition. That Wharncliffe is in reality one of the places recognised in the story, appears to be admitted on all hands; yet are there some very important discrepancies in the evidence which goes to confer this somewhat equivocal honour.

In the first place, as to the title. It is quite common to hear persons speak of the "Dragon of Wharncliffe", as if that were the title of the ballad, which could leave no doubt of the locality intended by the poet; whereas the title — at least the material word of it — has always been printed as at the head of this chapter. But let this pass: "Wantley" may have been a clerical error for "Wharncliffe"; or, in the original manuscript, the principal word of the title (and it does not occur in the poem) might be "Wortley", or more likely, "Wancliffe", which, by an easy mistake, owing to illegible writing, might be transferred to type as above.

In the second place, as to the indications of locality furnished by the text. The poet says, in the fifth stanza, —

"In Yorkshire, near fair Rotherham,

> The place I know it well;
> Some two or three miles, or thereabouts,
> I vow I cannot tell;
> But there is a hedge, just on the hill edge,
> And Matthew's house hard by it;
> O there and then was this dragon's den,
> You could not chuse but spy it."

Here is certainly nothing very likely, apart from other information, to fix the reader's attention on Wharncliffe, which instead of being "some two or three", is rather some six or eight miles from Rotherham. How the rhymster could pretend to *know well* "the place", while he confesses he *could not tell* its distance from the last-named town more nearly, is difficult to say. Of the "den", we will speak presently. The only other two places named in the ballad, are More Hall and Sheffield: the former was, it seems, the residence of the redoubtable dracocide, who, as the hero of the ballad, is thus introduced in the first stanza: —

> "Old stories tell how Hercules
> A dragon slew at Lerna,
> With seven heads, and fourteen eyes,
> To see and well discern-a:
> But he had a club, this dragon to drub,
> Or he had ne'er done it, I warrant ye:
> But More of More-Hall, with nothing at all,
> He slew the dragon of Wantley."

This personage is thrice afterwards mentioned: his name in each case occurring with the same suffix of his place of residence. At the solicitation of "men, women, girls, and boys", who came to him "sighing and sobbing, and making a hideous noise", he determined, in the style of an ancient knight of romance, to encounter the dragon;

> "But first he went, new armour to
> Bespeak at Sheffield town;
> With spikes all about, not within but without,
> Of steel so sharp and strong;
> Both behind and before, arms, legs, and all o'er,
> Some five or six inches long."

More-Hall {SK292958} is situate in a low valley a short distance from the foot of Wharncliffe, on the opposite side of the Don; it is

— 118 —

very conspicuous from the Lodge on the hill. It was formerly the residence of a family named More; and this fact seems to be almost the only solid link which connects the metrical fiction under notice with the assigned locality. But here we encounter a startling anachronism; for the mention of More of More-Hall, as the hero, if taken literally, would fix the date of the action, if not the writing of the poem, to a period not only antecedent to the Reformation, as some have supposed — but much earlier, the family above-named becoming extinct in the time of Edward VI.; a species of evidence which the comparatively modern character of the ballad by no means sustains. Having said so much of the hero and the scene of his exploits, it remains that we note, in the third place, the person and accomplishments of the dragon :

> "This dragon had two furious wings,
> Each one upon each shoulder;
> With a sting in his tayl, as long as a flayl,
> Which made him bolder and bolder:
> He had long claws, and in his jaws
> Four and forty teeth of iron;
> With a hide as tough as any buff,
> Which did him round environ.
> Devoured he poor children three,
> That could not with him grapple;
> And at one sup he ate them up,
> As one would eat an apple.
> All sorts of cattle this dragon did eat;
> Some say he ate up trees;
> And that the forests sure he would
> Devour up by degrees.
> For houses and churches were to him geese and turkeys;
> He ate all and left none behind;
> But some stones, dear Jack, that he could not crack,
> Which on the hill you will find."

Such are the passages that contain any thing like allusions to persons and places: as to the period when the ballad was written, or to what time or transactions it may refer, there is no other internal evidence. It may be added, that the foregoing will not only serve as a specimen of the style, and a clue to the story, but is nearly all that could with propriety be quoted, — several of the nineteen stanzas containing such coarse expressions as would not now be tolerated, even as expletives in the rudest style of ballad-mongering.

At what period this ballad first made its appearance in print, I am unable to state. Dr. Percy, who has published it in his "Reliques of Ancient English Poetry" {1765}, by which means it has become somewhat familiar with the public, follows the text of a printed copy in the Pepysian collection, collated with two or three others. As the Rev. collector above-named had met with none but modern copies, he supposed the ballad to have been written toward the latter end of the seventeenth century.

Not having been able to obtain any specific facts which could be supposed to be at the foundation of the ballad, the Doctor was

> "obliged to acquiesce in the common account; namely, that this ballad alludes to a contest at law between an overgrown Yorkshire attorney and a neighbouring gentleman. The former, it seems, had stript three orphans of their inheritance, and by his encroachments and rapaciousness was become a nuisance to the whole country; when the, latter generously espoused the cause of the oppressed, and gained a complete victory over his antagonist, who with mere spite and vexation broke his heart."

All this seems the pure, gratuitous, and certainly not unreasonable hypothesis of some one excogitating the ballad, without the advantage of a particle of local knowledge or historical information.

In a subsequent edition of the "Reliques", the editor subfixed the following "curious particulars", in the words of the relator, as communicated to Dr. Percy in 1767: —

> "In Yorkshire, six miles from Rotherham, is a village, called Wortley, the seat of the late Wortley Montagu, Esq.; about a mile from this village is a lodge, named Warncliffe Lodge, but vulgarly called *Wantley:* here lies the scene of the song. I was there above forty years ago: and it being a woody, rocky place, my friend made me clamber over rocks and stones, not telling me to what end, till I came to a sort of cave; then asked my opinion of the place, and pointing to one end says, 'Here lay the dragon killed by Moor of Moor-Hall: here lay his head; here lay his tail; and the stones we came over on

the hill, are those he could not crack; and yon white house you see half a mile off, is Moor-Hall.' I had dined at the lodge, and know the man's name was Matthew, who was a keeper to Mr. Wortley, and, as he endeavoured to persuade me, was the same Matthew mentioned in the song. In the house is the picture of the dragon and Moor of Moor-Hall, and near it a well, which, says he, is the well described in the ballad."

Who the communicator of this information may have been, does not appear, as the editor has chosen to suppress his name — if, indeed, he was in possession of it himself; the relator does the same of his friend. The whole story has certainly very much the air of a pleasant joke, played off by some gentleman of the neighbourhood upon his friend. That Mr. Wortley may have had a keeper of the name of Matthew, is likely enough: indeed, that the name of Matthew Northall belonged to a succession of keepers in the Wortley family "for many generations", we have the express testimony of Mr. Bosville. That Wharncliffe was ever vulgarly called *Wantley,* except in relation to the ballad, is an assertion made on no sufficient evidence, as will be admitted by all persons acquainted with the place; and that there ever was in the house any picture of the character mentioned, seems as repugnant to probability as it is opposed to testimony, while it is equally unsupported by any thing like contemporary evidence. Be this as it may, the spot suits so well to the descriptive touches of the ballad, that the identification of "Wantley" with Wharncliffe, and of a cavity under one of the rocks, with the dragon's den, has ever since been taken for granted.

It was to be expected, that so puzzling and curious a question as the subject of this ballad, would attract the attention, and exercise the critical and antiquarian acumen, of the learned historian of this district: such has been the fact. In the opening of his first elaborate work, namely, "Hallamshire", Mr. Hunter expressed his opinion, that the true key to the subject of the far-famed ballad was to be found in the following tradition of the neighbourhood respecting Sir Thomas Wortley, which was committed to writing a hundred and fifty years ago by the Rev. Oliver Heywood {1630-1702}, of Coley, near Halifax: —

"Sir Francis Wortley's great grandfather being a man of a great estate, was owner of a town near unto him, only there were some freeholders in it, with whom he wrangled and sued until he had beggared them and cast them out of their inheritance, and so the town was wholly his, which he pulled quite downe and laid the buildings and town-fields even as a common; wherein his main design was to keep deer: and made a lodge to which he came at the time of the year and lay there, taking great delight to hear the deer bell. But it came to pass that before he died he belled like a deer, and was distracted. Some rubbish there may be seen of the town: it is upon a great moor between Penistone and Sheffield."

In his later work, "the Deanery of Doncaster", our candid author, after reconsidering the matter, with the aid of better evidence, abandons the popular opinion relative to the bearing of the ballad.

"That it was composed in reference to Sir Thomas Wortley's inclosure of Wharncliffe, I *now* think cannot be sustained; neither that it was composed while still the family of More resided at More-Hall."

Mr. Hunter then gives at length his reasons for assigning 1591 as the date of certain vexatious transactions between a person of the name of Blount, then of More-Hall, and Sir Richard Wortley; and out of which he conceives the song to have arisen. It should be with great diffidence, that a mere tyro in such questions ventures to demur, when so profound and cautious an authority as Mr. Hunter pronounces judgment; but after all, considering the nature of the evidence adduced, it seems to me scarcely to sustain the case: the facts set forth relative to the misunderstanding between Blount and Sir Richard are numerous and specific, and yet it is remarkable that not one of them coincides in character with the allusions in the ballad. To say that the latter was written by some one ignorant of, or willing to disguise, the precise facts, were to beg the question. The most probable opinion is, that the ballad — if, indeed, it ever had any very specific meaning — referred to some local squabble about tythes: this was attempted to be shewn in detail by some remarks of the late Godfrey Bosville, Esq., of Malton, published several years ago. We have already seen that Taylor, the water-poet, visited Wharncliffe Lodge in 1639, and that he is very explicit in his notice of the cave, now known as the "dragon's den": now had the spot possessed at that time any of the notoriety which it has subsequently acquired, it is difficult to suppose the knowledge of it could have escaped that garrulous writer: yet the period assumed by Mr. Hunter as fixing the date of the subject, was between thirty and forty years previous to Taylor's visit, during which it is difficult to suppose that either the notoriety of the dispute between Blount and Wortley, or the ballad, supposing their identity, would have slumbered in abeyance. It is barely possible that Taylor, being under the surveillance of his generous host Sir Francis Wortley or his servants during his stay at Wharncliffe, might not hear of that which was familiar to every one beside; or might, at all events, have sufficient reason for preferring to mention the hole in the rock as the depository of the "three barrels of nappy liquor", to adverting to its more equivocal denomination and legend. The reader whose curiosity is still unsatisfied, will find the particulars alluded to, in vol. ii. p. 332 of the work above mentioned.

{See also — Sorby Natural History Society (www.sorby.org.uk) — Sorby Record, No 31(1995), pp 53-8 ('The Legend of the Dragon of Wantley — A Suspected Methane Outburst' by R. F. Grayson).}

No. XIX. — YEWDEN BROOK.

May 7th, 1836.

"A limpid stream that issues from the hills,
Descending downward to a river swells;
Through meads, through woods, through pastures urges on,
Winds through the vale, and glitters to the sun,
In glassy substance to reflect the shades,
Or falls precipitate in hoarse cascades:
Its course to Wharncliff's endless wood it bends,
Closed in with that the varied landscape ends."

BOSVILLE.

LONG and pleasantly as we have been detained at Wharncliffe, there yet remain a few interesting notices to be collected and presented, before we bid farewell to that picturesque spot. It will, however, be pleasant, by way of diversifying these sketches, if we descend from the wood-clothed eminence, and, for the subject of this interchapter, bend our steps towards the lovely vale which forms so conspicuous a feature in the scenery descried from the Lodge.

Mr. Hunter has remarked, that "England presents few more beautiful scenes than are to be found at several points in the early progress of the Don." Perhaps to no point does the observation more strikingly apply than to that which indicates the junction of the stream named at the head of this article with the main river, at the foot of Wharncliffe. On all the old maps, the brook in question will be found distinguished as the Ewden — a term, of the significance of which, the old shepherds, who have long been wont to field their procreant *ewes* in this warm and sheltered *dene,* might possibly have had something to say. The learned topographer above-named has, however, preferred a derivation from the former prevalence of the tree, the name of which forms the prefix to the old English word for a valley. At present, the yew abounds too sparingly on either side of the stream to illustrate, much less to suggest, this etymology; but there are a few fine trees of this species — and these may be the survivors of a more numerous race. Persons living on the sides of the valley, rarely call the glittering stream which they perceive meandering below, by either the one or the other of the foregoing appellations — they call it *Sunny Bank Dyke* {Sunny Bank Farm,

SK283963}, — the prenomen being by them applied to the southern side of the hill extending from Bithoms {Bitholmes Wood ~SK294961} to Bolsterstone {SK270967}.

A summer's day may be pleasantly spent in exploring the sylvan recesses of this beautiful brook, which enters the Don from the west, about one hundred yards on this side the sixth mile stone from Sheffield. Let the pedestrian, who wishes to walk along the margin of the stream — and a more delightful walk need not be desired — enter the dingle by the wicket just where the water runs under the Deepcar Road, and he will presently find himself in a warm, secluded dell — warm at almost all seasons, so fully sheltered is it from the winds: here, with a book, the birds and the river for companions — even if he have not in its sweetest form the society of his own species, the spot will only be found just such a solitude as a holiday rambler would desire.

Two or three weeks ago I visited this valley, on one of those mild warm days which have with more than wonted rarity interpolated the chilling diary of the fickle month during the present season:

> "It was an April morning: fresh and clear
> The rivulet, delighting in its strength,
> Ran with a young man's speed; and yet the voice
> Of waters which the winter had supplied,
> Was softened down into a vernal tone.
> The spirit of enjoyment and desire,
> And hopes and wishes, from all living things
> Went circling like a multitude of sounds."

Feeling perhaps some emotions kindred with those experienced by the bard of Rydal Mount {William Wordsworth} when he composed the foregoing lines, I fancied how pleasant it would be to hail the cuckoo, or list her greeting betimes on May-day in the vale of Yewden. A moment's calculation shewed me that May-day would fall on the Sabbath: it would, therefore, involve duties and yield delights higher and holier than rural rambling. One might almost deem that May-day had so fallen at the time Chaucer wrote the following: —

> "And as for me, though that I can but lite, [little]
> On bookes for to read I me delight,
> And to them give I faith and full credence,

— 125 —

> And in mine heart have them in reverence,
> So heartily, that there is gamé none
> That from my bookés maketh me to gone,
> But it be seldom, on the holy day,
> Save certainly when in the month of May
> Is comen, and I hear the fowlés sing,
> And that the flow'rés 'ginnen for to spring, —
> Farewell my book and my devotión.
> — Now have I then eke this conditión,
> That above all the flow'rés in the mead,
> Then love I most these flow'rés white and red,
> Such that men callen Daisies in our town:
> To them I have so great affectión,
> As I said erst, when comen is the May,
> That in my bed there dawneth me no day
> That I n' am up and walking in the mead,
> To see this flower against the sonné spread."

This passage is so poetical, so true to nature, so indicative of the noble simplicity of the Father of English Song in his rural tastes, that I should think a visit to the vale of Yewden well repaid, by the pleasure of enjoying such a quotation in such a spot. And then the Daisy — see, how delicately it dimples that green bank there! What British poet but has celebrated this unobtrusive flower? Chaucer, Wordsworth, Montgomery, Burns, have respectively honoured it in delightful verse; so true is the sentiment of our Sheffield bard, that amidst the votaries of song as of the vicissitudes of the floral year,

"The Daisy never dies".

The more convenient route, however, for commanding a view of the vale, is to proceed along the opposite side of the water, to that just adverted to. Immediately beyond the bridge rises a bold projecting knoll, called Bithom's Hill {?SK294959}, along the "sunny side" of which runs the old road to Bolsterstone, and from which the stream of the Yewden is seen winding gracefully along the bottom of the valley.

After a very short walk, we pass Moor Hall {SK292958}, the spot noted in the ballad of the "Dragon of Wantley", which formed the subject of the preceding chapter. Here, as we have seen, a family of the name of Moor was seated some centuries ago. As the ballad alluded to makes the "cunning champion creep down into a well" previous to his attack upon the dragon, one commentator, adverting to the situation of Moor Hall, says, it "lies so low, that it might be said to be a well". Others have found the well in question within the yard of Wharncliffe Lodge. The fact seems rather to be, that this part of the story is taken from the old rhyming legend of "Sir Bevis", in which the hero attacks a dragon from a well, in a manner not very remote from that of the ballad. It is, however, from the green slope on the opposite side of the river, that the house is seen to the best advantage — presenting the front of a comfortable dwelling, with ample outbuildings, such as a man of moderate ambition, with moderate means, might have no objection to occupy — apart from the celebrity of the spot, or the rendering, as ancient customary tenure, a rose yearly at the court of the Lord of the Manor at Oxspring, which I suppose the owner still pays. The house has been, for the most part, modernised: it is to be regretted, however, for the sake of curious visitors, that neither the big ale-pot, the hedgehog armour, the quarterstaff, nor any other vestige of the equipment of the redoubtable ballad hero, have been preserved! An angler, to be sure, will find his disappointment on that score abundantly compensated, if he can but obtain leave to fish for trout in the Yewden below the house, where, if he knows how to throw a fly, he may soon increase the weight of his basket with fine fish.

The course of the stream above Moor Hall is very sinuous and picturesque. The upland slopes on either side are prettily scattered with trees: these, though mostly of but moderate size, give, especially during the summer, a pleasing character to the landscape: the hedges and walls, too, having rarely been indebted to the line or square in their original setting out, seem to maintain a sort of quaint independence of modern tastes, which is far from displeasing in this wild region.

If the pedestrian have kept the road along the hill-side to Bolsterstone, he may now turn down the lane from the chapel toward the river, which is here seen to great advantage. Passing "Yew-trees House" {SK269964} — so called from a couple of ancient yews there standing, — we presently gain the stone bridge, under which flows the sprightly Yewden.

Just on the brow of the hill above the bridge, stands Broomhead Hall {SK244961, the hall was demolished in 1980}, the seat of James

Rimington, Esq. {1786-1839}, one of his Majesty's Justices of the Peace for the West-Riding. The house, which appears of good size, is built of excellent dressed stone: the design is mostly derived from what may be called the better domestic style of the time of Elizabeth — half octagon projections, bay windows, gabled roofs, clustered chimneys, and embattled parapet. The interior of the mansion is finished in a style of great richness and beauty: the greater portion of the ground story of the eastern or principal front, is fitted up as a library, and contains a splendid collection of modern books. The situation is delightful — in summer, — overlooking the fine slopes right and left of the Yewden, including the winding channel and glittering curves of the river itself; the whole scene shut in at the bottom of the valley by the vast triangular curtain of Wharncliffe wood. Indeed, it may be remarked, that as this valley lies pretty much in the direction of east and west, it is often, during the summer, filled with a glorious effulgence of that rich mellow light which is poured forth at sunset and sunrise.

The only apparent drawback on the local beauty of Broomhead, as to the front view, is the comparative nakedness of the home grounds: there are, however, some thriving plantations of fir, and considerable numbers of promising trees have recently been planted in the park; but one misses those forest giants — oaks of centuries, whose fantastic arms and gnarled spray harmonise so well with this picturesque style of architecture. Immediately behind the house lies Broomhead Moor {~SK234955}, a bleak, open, uncultivated tract, upon which are many low mounds, that are considered to have been tumuli, or burying places, of distinguished individuals in very remote ages; for having in many instances been opened, they were found to contain comminuted bones, or other sepulchral vestigia.

Broomhead is classical ground to the Hallamshire antiquary, the present mansion having been built on the site of the old house, formerly occupied by John Wilson, Esq. {1719-1783}, to whose indefatigable exertions in collecting, through a long life, whatever deeds, records, or other evidence he could obtain, illustrative of the history, topography, genealogy, &c. of the neighbourhood, we are greatly indebted for so accurate a knowledge of those matters. Mr. Hunter, to whose use the entire collection was ultimately destined, has not only rendered abundant justice to the memory of Mr. Wilson, by the acknowledgment of his labours, in the "Hallamshire", but has given in that work a portrait which can hardly fail to inspire respect for the amiable and ingenuous character of the Broomhead Antiquary.

The "Owdin", as the rustics hereabouts term the river, flows, about a field's breadth to the north of the Hall, down a sweetly-wooded dell, which is crossed by a rustic stone bridge, whence the road runs over the hill towards Midhope. The vista which opens up this umbrageous valley to the Moors, where lie the sources of the river, forms a pleasing view to a person standing on the moss-grown bridge, particularly when the glory of a summer's sunset is streaming down in all its effulgence.

But we must return to the spot where the Yewden joins the Don, and there take our leave of this cheerful brook, with the quotation of a much-admired passage, descriptive of the Hallamshire tributaries: —

> "Five rivers, like the fingers of a hand,
> Flung from black mountains, mingle and are one
> Where sweetest valleys quit the wild and grand,
> And eldest forests, o'er the sylvan Don,
> Bid their immortal brother journey on,
> A stately pilgrim, watched by all the hills.
> Say, shall we wander, where, through warriors' graves,
> The infant Yewden, mountain cradled, trills
> Her doric notes? Or, where the Locksley raves
> Of broil and battle, and the rocks and caves
> Dream yet of ancient days? Or, where the sky
> Darkens o'er Rivelin, the clear and cold,
> That throws his blue length like a snake, from high ?
> Or where deep azure brightens into gold
> O'er Sheaf that mourns in Eden? Or, where, roll'd
> On tawny sands, through regions passion-wild,
> And groves of love in jealous beauty dark,
> Complains the Porter, Nature's thwarted child,
> Born in the waste, like headlong Wyming? Hark!
> The pois'd hawk calls thee, Village Patriarch!
> He calls thee to his mountains! Up, away,
> Up, up to Stanedge! higher still ascend,
> Till kindred rivers, from the summit gray,
> To distant seas their course in beauty bend,
> And, like the lives of human millions, blend

Disparted waves in one immensity."

ELLIOT
{'An Excursion to the Mountains' from
'The Village Patriarch' by Ebenezer Elliott}

No. XX. — THE POACHER

May 14ᵗʰ, 1836.

"That nailor there, or much his neighbours wrong him,
Knows more of woodland paths and holes in walls,
Of how the hares run and the pheasant roosts,
Than needs to boot well handling of his hammer:
Some say he hath a taste for contemplation,
And hence affects the starlight and the gloom;
Some call him idler — and all wonder much
How he doth keep the bailiffs from the door."

FREQUENTLY on passing the roadside alehouse, you see in certain districts, a man leaning on the wall or gate adjoining, or if you step inside, he may be lolling on the langsettle or dozing in a chair: perhaps, near him may be lying — and exhibiting much the same nothing-to-do sort of indolence as that displayed by his master, a dog, — the very obvious cross of his breed, to say nothing of his temper, suggesting clearly enough that he belongs not to the race of honest hounds.

The lounger in question, has probably somewhat of the terrier in his look: of wiry muscle, and limbs little encumbered with flesh. Nor is the singularity of his dress often to be mistaken: if only an under-graduate in the class of nocturnal depredators, he wears a large fustian or duck jacket with enormous pockets: if he have taken the higher degrees of his profession: namely, been before the magistrate — had his gun taken from him — paid the penalty for hunting and shooting without license — or been in prison, then, his status being no longer to be mistaken, he affects the garb of a gamekeeper — the profound sacculated sub-coat aforesaid — a plush waistcoat — laced half-boots, and leather leggings: such is the Poacher. When there has been a slight snowfall, you will sometimes perceive this curious personage spelling out the not-to-be mistaken footprints of "poor puss" — or he may occasionally be noticed doing the same on the soft ground. The gamekeeper and our slyboots will at times meet on the road, when they exchange salutations, something in the leer of each seeming to say: — "I could a tale unfold". Sometimes of a night you may perceive in certain smeuses {a hole in a hedge or wall} of yonder wood — if you chose to risk your safety or your reputation in looking for them — loops of wire cunningly suspended — hark! heard you not a footstep — saw you not a shadow? Sure, 'twas not a ghost! A movement, a slight motion of the bracken there —

"And the snared hare, screams, quivers, and is dead!"

The character in question has commonly a range of acquaintance beyond nodding to the gamekeeper, and idling with the alehouse keeper; — the coachman knows him, and exchanges with him significant nods — and, at certain seasons, ejaculates sentences not quite unintelligible to "those on the top": indeed a pretty bit of business is sometimes pushed between the parties: dead hares and black cocks tell no tales as to how they came by their deaths; and if coachee does but once get them fairly hung beside his seat, he well knows they are safe — they need no certificates now to ensure their delivery — neither judge, jury, nor informer can touch them.

Now let us look into the Poacher's dwelling: filth, squalidity and raggedness may characterise its inmates — but this is by no means always, nor commonly the case, at least in this neighbourhood — the house is poor but clean, the wife is industrious, the children's habiliments are commendably patched; there is a monthly rose tree in the window, and a goldfinch in the cage — but there is an expensive gun on the balk, and a something in the looks of the poor woman, and of the bigger children too, which tells you that mystery and apprehension are no strangers to their bosoms.

On one occasion, between twenty and thirty years ago, a gamekeeper was pursuing his nightly rounds in a covert not very far from the banks of the Don; he fell in with several poachers, one of whom, after no small difficulty, was captured and carried before the lord of the domain. Having been taken *flagranti delicto,* gun in hand, wire in pocket, and as added to the report of his gun on his spot, he enjoyed the report of the neighbouring hamlet, as a first-rate operator in his line, — one who, if he could not see a hare past quite so well in the pitch-dark as by the young moonlight, knew, even without the aid of his dark lantern, every smeuse in Wharncliffe or Tankersley parks, as well as he knew the door of his own house.

With the advantages of this first rate reputation, Fielding was brought up to render some account wherefore he, being unlicensed, did assume and persist in the exercise of the privilege of sporting in woods, chases, and grounds over which he held no charter of free warren? Fielding was a man whose figure, ingenuity, and boldness had been worthy of a better calling; but, alas! misled by temptation, he preferred to enact, in his humble way, the character of a freebooter, in times when the memory of his illustrious precursor in that line had ceased to be odorous, save in ballad or romance. Nevison, who was born at Wortley, and became the most notorious highwayman of his time, might perhaps have been a hero of laudable fame, had his genius been developed on the field of Waterloo instead of on the turnpikes of Yorkshire — so our hero, whose birth-place was not far from that of the gallows-tassel just named, would, no doubt, had his lot been cast in the days of Robin Hood, have been a sort of Will Scarlet, even had he not rivalled Little John himself — but this is hypothesis — the fact is, he was taken in the inglorious predicament above described.

To have caught one poacher, — and one of such notoriety too, — was something; but as repression of the offence, rather than punishment of the offender, was the prime object of the owner of the pillaged domain, his first anxiety was, to obtain, through the confession of the culprit before him, the names of his companions in crime. This design Fielding resolutely, but not rudely, withstood — threats, caresses, promises, all were tried, and equally in vain: he would not "peach". There was evidently bottom in the man — and seemingly something better, which, had it been cultivated under other auspices, might perhaps have turned to account; in short, it was apparent, not only that he was sensible of the unlawfulness of his career, but that the fidelity which he maintained toward his accomplices in guilt might, if set in a right direction, admirably qualify him for a situation of trust. He was liberated. Before he had time to return to his old habits, or almost receive the caresses of his old companions, an authorised person put to him this question: — "Fielding, will you renounce your unlawful practices, and become a keeper: you would know well how to act in such a situation?" The man considered the proposition — reflected on the desperation and danger of his former course of life, thought upon his family, and consented to take the perilous appointment. He went to live at one of the lodges in the wood, and thenceforth took his rounds by day and by night, as a faithful conservator, in the recesses of those grounds where he had so lately played a very different part. This unexpected arrangement produced as might be supposed, no small degree of consternation among the poachers of the neighbourhood — one being quite sure that Fielding *would* never touch him; another, that he never *should* touch him; and a third fancied he would now criminate them altogether.

One thing, at least, is certain, that the gamekeeper's integrity was never suspected by his employer: his courage and fidelity were well understood by his quondam companions, who, whatever might be their comments upon his conduct in having "taken office", considered it prudent, at least, for some time, not to encounter him on enchanted ground. Well would it have been, had they one and all continued to keep close by such discretion!

It was a fine Sunday morning in October; the foliage of Wharncliffe, glorious in its deepest autumnal tints, lay shrouded in obscurity, save in so far as the gloom yielded to the feeble light afforded by a waning moon at this very early hour. Fielding and his colleagues were pursuing their usual rounds in the outskirts of a neighbouring preserve, when they espied four men proceeding toward them on the high road, and whose persons, accoutrements, and manners left the keepers no room to doubt but that the object of the party was unlawful sport. What was to be done? The tenters would have concealed themselves, but there was no chance for doing so, as they knew they were seen: so they walked onward, until they confronted the poachers. "Well, Joe, thou hast got thy gun with thee this morning — and plenty of snickles too, I doubt not", said Fielding familiarly to the fellow, whom he knew, stroking him at the same time with his hand over the jacket, whose bulging pockets suggested the operation. Little more occurred — the man raised his piece — the wood echoed with the report — the shot passed through the body of poor Fielding, who instantly fell upon the ground. The party then attacked the other keeper, whom they presently floored with the butt end of the gun, at a short distance from his murdered companion, belabouring him with their bludgeons. Fielding heard the words "Stick him, stick him", uttered over his fallen companion. Unable to rise, or render him any personal assistance, he managed to reach his gun, fired it at the party, one of whom fell, and the rest, not considering whence the shot came, immediately made off. Both the keepers managed to crawl home: the latter recovered of his bruises — but poor Fielding lay in his chamber a corpse the day following.

Swiftly the news of this fatal rencontre spread through the

neighbourhood: many went to look at the scene of the affray, steeped, as the ground was, with blood, and battered with agonistic trampling. Anxious and self-accusing hearts were beating in the hamlet of Grenoside, which stretches along the eastern crest of yonder hill. The gang were severally apprehended, and tried at the ensuing York Assizes. The evidence was clear — the details were aggravated — the culprits were found guilty of the capital offence, and received sentence of death. At the earnest solicitation of the worthy prosecutor, punishment was remitted in each case, except that of the actual murderer, who suffered the extreme penalty of the law. This tragical occurrence produced a deep sensation, not only in the neighbourhood where it occurred, but throughout the country; and, perhaps, even tended, in some degree, to bring about that alteration in the Game Laws {?1831}, for which the Lord of Wharncliffe long unsuccessfully contended — the legalizing of the sale of game in our markets, in the same manner as any other like commodity.

Whether the change adverted to has diminished the temptation to poaching, or reduced the number of its votaries, is not very clear: that it has reduced the quantity of game, is admitted on all hands. And certainly, to us, who recollect the legal impediments which formerly existed, to counteract the sale of game, and also the stories about secret but well-conducted depots, where it might at all times be bought and sold, few sights were, for a time, more striking than that of hares, partridges, pheasants, and grouse, hanging side by side with ducks, rabbits, and barn-door fowls, at almost every poulterer's stall in the town.

No. XXI. — WHARNCLIFFE VIGNETTES.

May 21st, 1836.

"Wharncliffe, 'tis sweet, amid thy hoary crags
To spend the sultry day — to lie at ease
Beneath thy moss-grown oaks, yews evergreen
And pensile birches — while the mountain ash
Shews its red berries, and the holly shines
With glossy leaf. Romantic Wharncliffe! hail!"

T. A. WARD.

Such is the salutation of a September visitor to the delightful spot from which, after so long and pleasant detention we must now prepare to descend. Before, however, we rejoin the river at the foot of the wood, let us string together a few miscellaneous sketches, so as to form a valedictory chapter in our description of Wharncliffe — and first of the trees.

PEELING OF THE OAK.

Hear you that cranching noise? 'tis not like the riving of timber, or the collision of dry tree tops in a storm; — no, 'tis produced by the rending of the rugged bark from the mighty oak! It is a sound I like to hear — apart from the association that wherever it is heard, there, the regality of the forest is about to be laid low — it leads us to an acquaintance with one of the most interesting operations of woodcraft: and how little has it been noticed, if noticed at all, by the illustrators of rustic life, either in picture or song. The "Woodman" of the winter scene, is in graphic representation quite familiar with tens of thousands of individuals who never saw any thing like the original: the resonance of the Fellers' axe echoes through various poems descriptive of the country — but the Peeler and his "life in the woods", appear to have been thought unworthy of attention. This is the more remarkable, inasmuch as spring is the season when the enlivening operation of divesting the oak of its bark is performed: when the light hut is built, the rude ladder constructed, the bough-loppings bundled up, the bark rucks set out — in short, when numerous sylvan operations pleasingly impress a looker-on with the idea that there are yet arts that can never be transferred from the forest to the town. I have mentioned in a previous chapter that the section of Wharncliffe Wood, destined to the axe this year, is above the Entrance Lodge, near Oughtibridge — you may even now see the naked trees standing at a distance from each other amidst the verdant array; and perhaps hear some stalwart bough-strider singing, to a simple tune,

THE PEELER'S SONG.

Oh! Spring's brave prime is a joyous time,
And worth a workman's prizing;
Where'er he sees the fall-marked trees,
Just when the sap is rising.

Then — then with joy, to his stout employ,
The glad sun sees him hasting,
While, o'er the lawn, the cheerful dawn,
Mist, twilight, dews are wasting.

The woodman's stroke must fell the oak, —
The forest monarch hoary,
But to strip him, through both bole and bough,
Is first the *peeler's* glory.

Or ere the axe one tree attacks,
The *boddle* must precede it,
Ere wide or tall its beauty fall,
Whoever hath decreed it.

And who can tell how his muscles swell,
With strength his task while driving!
And hark, O hark! how sounds the bark,
When merrily it is riving.

'Midst flood and fire, earth, air, or wood,
To rigid limbs or limber,
There's no delight, from morn to night,
Like peeling noble timber!

THE OAK-BORNE BIRCH.

Within the enclosure in front of the Lodge, stands an old oak, of considerable girth, greatly decayed in its arms, and so hollow in the bole, as to suggest the idea of a hermitage; but most remarkable on account of its bearing aloft, as it were upon its aged shoulders, a large and flourishing Birch tree. At first sight, the stout stock of the parasite seems to be actually incorporated with the substance of the bulky bough which sustains it — the junction of the two masses appearing as perfect as that of a scion with the stem upon which it is engrafted. A more common, though scarcely less incorrect notion, run away with by many is, that a seed of the birch having fallen upon a mass of the decayed substance of the oak, there germinated, and having shot its roots into the rotten wood, thence derives its nourishment. It is obvious, however, on a nearer inspection, that whether the birch may have sprung up by chance, as just intimated, or have been designedly planted when young within the oak, that although indebted to the ruin of the latter for support, it does, in reality, derive its nourishment immediately from the ground, by means of a stout healthy tap root or sucker which descends inside the hollow tree: the whole is a curious illustration of what writers on vegetable phenomena have said of the manner in which plants sometimes *adapt* themselves to peculiar situations.

ANOTHER NOTABLE TREE.

Just without the enclosed verdant plot, in which stands the last mentioned tree, may be seen another ancient oak, quite hollow, and apparently in the last stage of sylvan decrepitude.

> "———— we have admired that antique oak
> Of size immense; not six, with outstretched arms,
> Can span its mighty round, and more than six
> Might stand within its huge and hollow trunk."

The circumference of this venerable elder of the chase, is certainly not less than seven yards: it is a favourite with visitors — young persons especially, being fond, of squeezing themselves into its time-hollowed trunk. There is something interesting in the contemplation of a venerable tree thus standing as it were in the last stage of vegetable decrepitude. This fine patriarch of the forest, the survivor, no doubt, of a goodly race of oaks, might probably stand here a century ago in all the glory of mature treehood — its branching head having in summer the greenness and amplitude of a grove "una nemus", as Ovid says of a similar oak: but what a change has taken place: —

"———— The vigour of his root now gone.
He stands dependent on his weight alone;
All bare his naked branches are displayed,
And with his leafless trunk he forms a shade:
Yet though the winds his ruin daily threat,
As every blast would heave him from his seat;
Though thousand fairer trees the field supplies
That rich in youthful verdure round him rise;
Fix'd in his ancient state he yields to none,
And wears the honours of the grove alone."

Pharsalia, i. 37. {by Lucan (Marcus Annaeus Lucanus)}

THE EAGLES.

About a hundred yards from the Lodge, there is a small building,
having a railed but roomy enclosure in front, where a pair of fine
brown eagles are kept. The birds, which were brought, I believe,
from Ireland, and placed there while young, six or eight years ago,
appear to be in fine plumage, and perfectly at ease in their prison.
Possibly they might be taken from the nest, and, therefore, as to the
loss of freedom, we may say of them as Cowper did of another bird,
"That privilege they never knew, and, therefore, never miss'd", At all
events, their lot is far preferable to that of the poor eagle chained to a
stone to give effect to a bit of mimic rockery pertaining to the
Coliseum, and whose fate is so touchingly deplored by a poet in
Fraser's Magazine this month; or it may be, to that of the fine
individual of the tribe who was tethered to the pole from which at a
late National celebration in Boston, the flag of the United States
unfolded its glittering stripes — the eagle being fastened there, to use
the words of a describer — "as *the emblem of Liberty!*"

What the species of these birds may be, I am not ornithologist
enough to determine: neither could I learn any thing of their habits:
a considerable portion of their food consists of rabbits, which are
plentiful about the Lodge. Satisfied as these two fine full fed, and as
fully feathered prisoners appeared to be with their ready furnished
meals, comfortable perches, and secure enclosure, it was impossible
not to believe but that they would gladly have exchanged their cage
comforts, for the freedom of their natural state — to see such a pair
of aquilines fairly afloat on their broad wings over Wharncliffe wood

were a picturesque spectacle. That such sights were once witnessed here, might be inferred from the couplet of Mr. Bosville, in which he says —

> "The imperial eagle rises on the rocks;
> The Don below conceals the wily fox."

The fox is still frequently found, as well as the marten: formerly the badger was common in the crags — the constable's books at Wortley containing numerous items of sums paid for "bowson's heads".

LADY MARY WORTLEY MONTAGUE.

It would scarcely be pardonable to quit Wharncliffe Lodge, without interweaving even with these slight memorials of the place, the names of the celebrated Lady Mary Wortley Montague, and of her talented but eccentric son, the Honourable Edward Wortley Montague. Of the voluminous collection of letters written by this lady from Constantinople to Pope, Addison, and others, several editions have been published: and at this moment a new and much improved edition of the letters, poems, &c. is announced under the editorial auspices of the Right Honourable Lord Wharncliffe, her ladyship's great grandson. The celebrity, however, of Lady Mary as a captivating letter writer, forms a less splendid halo about her name, than the distinction of having been the first to introduce the practise of inoculation into this country. Addison invited Mr. Wortley's assistance to the *Spectator:* in one of his letters he says, "If you have any hints or subjects, pray send me a paper full. I long to talk an evening with you." It does not appear that Addison ever visited Wharncliffe, although importuned to do so by his friend Mr. Wortley. In a letter dated Wortley, July 28, 1711, "We may eat", says he, "in the woods every day, if you like it, and nobody here will expect any kind of ceremony." — Yet that spot — or, at all events, the Hall adjacent, stands connected with the *Spectator,* by means of the celebrated love letter from James to Betty, printed and illustrated in No. 71 of that work. The real name of the love-smitten swain who calls upon his absent fair one to "remember her lover who lay bleeding from the wounds Cupid made with the arrows he borrowed at the eyes of Venus, which is your sweet person", was James Hirst. He was a servant to the Honourable Edward Wortley at this place, and in delivering a parcel of letters to his master, gave him by mistake, the epistle he had prepared for his sweetheart, under date of May 14, 1711, and which was transmitted to London. It appears that James ultimately married the sister of Betty, (the latter dying before the nuptial contract could be ratified); and died in the neighbourhood of Penistone many years ago. It may be mentioned that Lady Emmeline Stuart Wortley, the daughter-in-law of Lord Wharncliffe, is favourably known to the muses — her Ladyship's work entitled "The Village Church Yard, and other Poems", published last year, containing passages of power and feeling that require not the adventitious circumstance of noble authorship to recommend them.

LORD WHARNCLIFFE.

The picturesque and celebrated spot from which we are now about to descend, gives title to a statesman of the most distinguished character. James Archibald Stuart Wortley, descended of a line of ancestors who derived their local surname from the adjacent village of Wortley, where the family mansion stands, was ennobled in 1826, by his late Majesty George the Fourth, by the style of Baron Wharncliffe of Wharncliffe. The circumstances under which this well merited and gracefully-worn dignity was conferred, reflected at once honour on the sovereign and the peer. It was alledged by parties politically opposed to his Lordship, that the peerage was bestowed at the instance of Mr. Canning, and was a sort of subterfuge to avoid, on Mr. Wortley's part, a contested election for Yorkshire, which at that time he represented in Parliament. At a public dinner given to his Lordship in Sheffield, on the 14th September, in the same year, he indignantly repudiated both parts of the allegation: "I have", said his Lordship,

> "a high respect for Mr. Canning; I look up to him as a man of powerful abilities and the kindest heart, and I am proud to think that I am in habits of friendship with him. But I am too proud to receive such a favour at the hands of Mr. Canning. It has often been said to me, not by persons of my own family, or particularly interested in me, 'You are in a situation to ask a peerage; why do you not do it ?' My answer has always been — I feel myself a greater man as a representative of the county of York than I should as a peer; and, besides, I will never ask a favour of any Minister, — I never did ask it. The King, in the kindest manner, in a manner which will never be

forgot either by me or my family to the last hour of our lives, offered it to me. He told me that he did not offer it to me at the instance of his Ministers, that there were many parts of my conduct in Parliament which he did not approve, that there were subjects on which he differed from me; but, he added, that my character and station in life were such that he thought me a proper individual to receive a peerage. A title so offered could not be refused — a peerage is a thing not to be slighted; — and I do not see why I should be debarred from that station more than any other man. I would never do a base action to obtain it; but it having been given to me, I will prize it as I ought. But, forsooth", added his Lordship, "I took it in order to avoid a contested election! I know, indeed, what a contested election is, though I have never been engaged in one as principal: I know the horrors of it, and to what it leads; and if the seat for the County of York could only have been kept by me at the enormous expense at which it would appear it is to be kept — an expense which would ruin any man of moderate fortune, then, I say, I would not have retained the seat for the county. But those persons are very much mistaken who think I have feared a contested election. I should have been present in the Castle-yard at York, I should have defrayed the legal expenses of the election, and have left the freeholders to say whom they would choose."

THE DEER PARK.

Immediately east from the Lodge lies an enclosed piece of ground called the Deer Park, and containing two or three hundred head of those graceful quadrupeds. On the north side, this portion of the ancient chase is overspread by an immense quantity of gritstone rocks, lying as in the case of the crags before described, in confused heaps. Here are many very ancient oaks — coevals, it may be, with the "Sir Thomas", who in 1510, built the adjacent lodge "for his pleasure to hear the hart's bell". Having long passed the period when they might have been profitable for timber, they stand in no immediate danger of the axe that pursues its annual progress through the ranks of their juniors in the neighbouring wood. Here again, the minute botanist may lay open his vasculum and commence operations on the rugged bark, which is not less abundantly licheniferous than the rocks before described: indeed almost every old weather-beaten tree, like that so graphically described by Wordsworth, appears

> "——— a mass of knotted joints,
> A wretched thing forlorn :
> Each stands erect and like a stone
> With lichens it is overgrown.
> Like rock or stone, is overgrown,
> With lichens to the very top,
> And hung with heavy tufts of moss,
> A melancholy crop."

Here, indeed, the student may not only collect several species of those beautiful foliaceous lichens which no person can fail to notice on every tree, and even extract from crevices in the bark those minute caliciums, which it requires a sort of microscopical eye to distinguish — he will find the branches literally and profusely hung with what the poet calls "heavy tufts of moss" — namely, the *Evernia prunastri* {'Oak Moss'}, and the still more abundant *Usnea plicata* {'Old Man's Beard' or 'Tree Moss'}.

DON-SIDE FLOWERS.

The spring weather, so tardy in its approaches this season, has at length come in all its beauty and congeniality ; the oaks, which a fortnight ago exhibited hardly a trace of foliage, now give promise of being somewhat out in leaf by the "Twenty-ninth of May" {Restoration of the Monarchy in 1660, 'Oak Apple Day', public holiday abolished in 1859}. The rambler will notice too, on that sloping bank of the river the delicate and fugacious blossoms of the Bird Cherry *(Prunus padus);* there also may just now be seen in flower, the Sweet Cicely *(Myrrhis odorata)*; and along the wood bottom by the water side — indeed, wherever the trees overshadow a damp spot, the elegant cymes of the *Luciola sylvatica* {*Luzula sylvatica* Great Wood Rush, *Luciola* is a genus of Japanese Firefly!} are most profusely present. I specify the habitat of these plants, as I have done those of some others, not on account of their rarity, but from the conviction that many persons will find the gratification to be derived from these rambles increased, by knowing the names of the less common vegetables which may present themselves. On this account, it will not be uninteresting to mention, that the large stones lying scattered over the bed of the river, hereabout, owe their dull green — almost black appearance, mainly to the presence of two kinds of moss, — the *Cinclidotus fontinahides* {? Smaller Lattice Moss}, and the *Jungermannia asplenoides* {syn. *Plagiochila asplenoides,* a spleenwort}. If a person will take the trouble to gather a specimen of the latter, he will find the plant elegantly formed, and the leaves remarkably large and distinct for a moss.

WHARNCLIFFE IN SPRING.

I gazed on Wharncliffe when the year was young, —
When vernal airs were mildly breathing round;
When the first timid flowers peeped from the ground,
Under the warm hedge sides, ere Spring had flung
Abroad the treasures of her open hand;
Then, through yon rich immensity of wood,
The strong, quick spirit, stirring in each bud,
Made the whole blush with green: the breezes bland
Wooed forth the infant leaves, till soon the trees,
Erewhile so naked, smiled in bright array :
So seemed the sylvan scene, that hour, to pay
A silent homage to His power, who sees,
Pervades, upholds, destroys, and renovates,
What, in Creation's round, his high behest awaits.

WHARNCLIFFE IN SUMMER.

I gazed on Wharncliffe when, in summer pride,
The tall trees spread their leafage to the sun:
Then was the scene magnificent! Not one
Of all those forest nobles, but supplied
Some sylvan feature that improved the whole.
'Twas noon; and o'er them Stillness, as a soul
In contemplation lay. Ah! who could gaze,
As then I gazed, nor choose but gladly feel
A kindred influence through his bosom steal ?
Cold is the heart that never thus obeys
Even the weak hints of Nature, to adore:
I would not walk beside the man whose eye

Could light on this fair earth, yon beauteous sky,
Or ocean's wondrous swell — nor feel his heart run o'er.

WHARNCLIFFE IN AUTUMN.

I gazed on Wharncliffe, when autumnal change
Had passed upon its trees — and such a scene!
Who could have deemed that leaves of living green
Involved of mingling hues so rich a range!
'Twas not the colouring of noon's seven-fold bow,
Nor that whose fainter tints the moonlight sheds;
Nor iridescent light, like that which spreads
O'er the calm sea: 'twas of a graver show —
'Twas the time — coloured scarf which Nature dyes,
And, graceful, flings o'er the expiring year:
To mortals still adorning to endear
The woodland scene, e'en as its beauty flies:
Till, with each deepening hue familiar grown,
We mark the foliage fall, one mass of deepest brown.

WHARNCLIFFE IN WINTER.

I gazed on Wharncliffe, when the Winter's breath
Was keen but still: the snowfall, through the night,
Had clothed the trees in delicatest white;
There was a beauty in the scene of death,
Brief as it was, that scarcely when endight
With summer foliage, lovelier looked the trees:
But with the sun upsprung a thawing breeze,
And soon the woodland lay in plashy plight:
So cold, fair, fugitive, how oft one sees
Some charm of earth, that tempts to love awhile,
On which deluded Hope doth fondly smile:
But of ten thousand glistening things that please,
How many, while we view them, melt away,
Like snow-wreaths from the trees at touch of solar ray!

No. XXII. — BEELEY WOOD BOTTOM.

May 28th, 1836.

"When in the sweet and pleasant month of May,
We see both leaves and blossoms on the tree,
And view the meadows in their best array
We hopeful are a joyful spring to see;
Yet, oft, before the following night he past,
It chanceth that a vapour or a frost.
Doth all those forward bloomings wholly waste;
And then their sweetness and their beauty's lost."

WITHERS. {'Seed Time and Harvest' by George Withers}

IMMEDIATELY on leaving Wharncliffe, the Don passes Oughtibridge {SK307933}, a hamlet so called from a stone structure of two arches, under which the river flows, and over which, as previously stated, one of the nearer roads to Wharncliffe passes. A very short interval of farm cultivation occurs to separate that far-famed and magnificent sylvan tract which previously engaged our attention, from another fine tree covered slope called Beeley Wood {SK320922}, — a sort of Wharncliffe "in little", as to its adornment of the hill side; but wanting at once the cresting rocks and crowning lodge of the more celebrated scene to complete the comparison. Upon this "rich mountain robe of living green", the eye reposes with delight, particularly at this season, when the trees are fast assuming their compliment of summer foliage: the vernal season, to be sure, is somewhat backward — but although we have had, during the week, a prevalence of bleak northeasterly winds, their effect has not realized the mischiefs noticed in the motto above; and which, having been written in 1634, may serve to remind us that occasional destructive frosts occurred in the month of May two hundred years ago — popular notions to the contrary notwithstanding.

At the bottom of Beeley Wood, as at the foot of Wharncliffe, the road and the river run for the most part alongside each other; the intervening slip being, in many places, very steep — in some, so precipitous as to become almost perpendicular; tall trees or low bushes skirting the steep from the footpath down to the water's edge. The bed of the river is, in many places, scattered with large blocks of stone, that appear to have tumbled one knows not from what neighbouring rock, — or to have been laid bare by the long continued effect of the running water on the matters in which these stones were formerly embedded. These sturdy impediments, by breaking the equable flow of the current, add not a little to its beauty: and in winter, when the moorland tributaries swell the river with their torrents, the noise with which it frets, and foams, and tumbles over these rugged obstacles, presents a striking contrast to the quiet musical murmurs with which the water eddies its way amongst them in ordinary summer tranquillity. To timid persons carried rapidly along this valley on the coach, the glimpses which are caught of the river, through openings in the trees, are often very pleasing, — to be sure, the thought as to what might happen, should a wheel fly off, or an axle snap just here, is very likely for a moment to present itself — and but for a moment — the mind presently resuming its interest in the beauties of the vale. The general steepness of the intervening acclivity has been mentioned — it may be added that in one spot, where a hollow has been filled up to level the road, the side next the river, consists of a vast and rugged wall, over the superior edge of which it is not easy to look down upon the rushing flood below without something like giddiness. Such are some of the aspects presented by the river to the road: it is possible, however, to get along by the water's edge on the opposite side; for although the sylvan beauty of Beeley Wood, in common with that of Wharncliffe, extends down

> "To where the hard rocks dip their rugged feet
> In Don's dark wave."

the stones are neither so rough, nor the bushes so tangled as to forbid all progress.

At Oughtibridge {SK308936}, Middlewood {Middlewood Rolling Mills SK313926, Middlewood Forge and Tilt SK308931}, and Beeley Wood {SK317912} respectively, we pass some of those rattling water-power establishments for the working of iron and steel, which occur at intervals all the way from Wortley to Kilnhurst. Uninviting as these places commonly appear — and astounding as persons of delicate nerves must find the noise and vibrations of the machinery, it will be worth the while of the pedestrian who has never witnessed these or similar Cyclopian forges, to step in and take a peep at the operations — even ladies may do this with perfect safety and comfort in most instances. There are two descriptions of hammers used in each place — the one for forging the other for tilting: the former, which is the largest, and is lifted and dropped by means of knobs projecting from an immense roller, revolving very slowly, is commonly used for working scrap iron into bars: the latter, which is smaller, and worked by the successive impinging of a series of cogs upon the end of the shaft, so as to kick the hammer up, is employed in reducing stout bars of steel into long slender rods fit for the farther and multifarious operations of the hand-hammer men at Sheffield. The forge hammer makes from one hundred to two hundred strokes in a minute; the tilt, however, as many as three hundred: hence, as may well be conceived, the sounds produced by the two are not less distinct than the modes of manipulating the metals on the anvil. The iron scraps are piled in conical heaps upon round slates about the size of a trencher: these are introduced into a wind furnace, the intense heat welding them as it were together: the glowing mass is then withdrawn, and placed under the heavy hammer, which is at first worked very slowly, the rapidity of the strokes being increased as the iron cools: much less skill seems to be displayed in the management of these lumps under the hammer, than appears to be exercised in the tilting of steel bars, where, owing to the rapidity of impact, a degree of dexterity is shown by the workman, the effect of which is very pleasing to a looker on.

As the three establishments before named are all below the road, and immediately between that and the river, the ruddy flare or the lurid light produced by the flame from their furnace chimneys, has often a most singular effect when the night is dark or the vapours dense. Loth to venture at the description of what has exercised the graphic pen of the lady with whose sketches I have enriched one or two preceding chapters, I transfer another "bit of picture" from her pages.

> "The river now became more expansive, and its surface smoother; [than along Wharncliffe bottom,] the banks less rugged, yet still high; the woods drawing closer together, and their outline gradually declining to their termination, darkening all the vale, over which the mists of evening began to spread, that just before we quitted, presented a new and striking object — a low and extensive building, apparently placed in the water, called in the provincial language of the country, 'the works.' From its very high cupola chimney, bright flashes of fire threw their lurid light upon the woods,

which was again momentarily darkened by its emitting a
heavy volume of coal-black smoke, the precursor of another
illumination: —

> Dark red the heaven above it glowed;
> Dark red beneath the waters flowed.

Whilst from the unglazed windows, descending to the water's
brim, the reflection of the fiery furnace was spread in 'blood
red light' over its whole surface. The dark figures at work
within could only be distinguished in contour; and as they
passed and repassed, bearing red-hot iron bars with them, I
thought of the abode of the Cyclops, preparing their
firebrands of destruction, and with thundering hammers
frightning silence from her sylvan haunts."

The foregoing extract concludes with a very natural sentiment: it
will, nevertheless, be at once admitted that however dissonant the
rattling of these hammers to the rural Muses, the sounds would not
only be still more unwelcome, but — it ought to be added —
absolutely intolerable, amidst a town population. But combination
wonderfully modifies the harshness of sound — and I have
sometimes listened to the distant and rapid strokes of the tilt-
hammer, as they mingled with the softened tones of life in this valley
on a still, sweet summer evening, with real delight.

The manner in which the stream is made available for giving motion
to the various works on the Don, as well as on the other rivers in the
neighbourhood, is not by placing the water wheel, whether overshot
or underfloat, directly in the main current, but by diverting a
sufficient volume of water for the purpose required, by means of an
artificial cut branching from one side. With this view, advantage is
taken of any convenient fall of the river, sufficiently considerable to
allow of the water-level being carried by a pen-trough to an overshot
wheel; or, where the descent will cause a stream velocity at least
sufficient to give motion to a float-board wheel. The lateral canal,
alluded to, is, after passing the water wheel, carried by the nearest or
most convenient course to the river, into which the water, after
having been diverted for a while, again falls; In most cases there is,
a considerable dam or head of water, laid up at a little distance from
the river, the running out of the contents of which is found preferable
to depending directly upon a supply from the river which is

sometimes overfull, and at others not sufficiently replenished for the work. In all cases, however, the whole of the main stream, when inconsiderable, or if swollen, go much of it as may be necessary, is diverted into the side canal by means of a weir, or artificial barrier thrown obliquely across the bed of the river; this impediment is built with large stones so as to descend sloping on both sides, somewhat like the roof of a house, having a stout beam or piece of timber along the edge. Owing to the intervention of these dams or weirs, the levels of which are matters of careful arrangement in the adjudication of stream privileges, so much of the water as may be wanted is, as already stated, turned aside, while the remainder is suffered to flow over the weir — often forming very pleasing cascades. The supply is regulated by means of flood-gates, or, as they are called hereabouts, *shuttles;* where the small canal that carries the water to and from the wheel, is the *goight;* and the overplus stream that passes away, the *by-dyke.* It is not uncommon, in the summer season, to find the by-dyke — on that portion of the river, between the upper and lower ends of the goight, completely dry, the water pursuing its circuitous course by the last named channel. It frequently happens, during the summer, that the tilter or grinder can only work a few hours at a time — that is, so long as the dam or head of water takes to flow off. As the river may be too low to yield a constant supply to the water-wheel, so it may be too high to allow of its motion; that is, when the volume of water is so considerable at the lower opening of the goight, that instead of flowing out, it suffers a sort of reflux or stagnation: this is called "back water" — and is rarely an inconvenience of more than temporary duration. 1 am not prepared to state with certainty, what may be the elevation of the Don at its sources, above the German Ocean: it may, however, be mentioned here, that the fall of the river from Grayson's tilt at Oughtibridge, to the paper mill at Brightside was, in 1794, stated to be 69 yds. 0ft. 8in., there being at that time twenty eight different works on the stream, and a like number on the Loxley, the fall of which, between Bradfield corn mill and Nether Slack tilt, being 84yds. 1ft. 6in. At the same time, there appear to have been seated on the Rivelin twenty establishments, mostly grinding wheels, worked by a fall of water of 98yds., between the uppermost wheel, (then Greaves's) {SK287869} and the Grogerham wheel {Grogham Wheel SK325892} below Mousehole forge. At the period referred to, there were in Sheffield only five steam-engine mills.

No. XXIII. — PREACHING IN THE HAMLETS.

June 4th, 1836.

"Observe the cottage in yon hazel copse,
Round which the cornfields wave their yellow crops;
Green tufts of velvet moss adorn the thatch,
From many a crevice grows the verdant patch;
A spot it seems, where poverty might rest,
Unknown, unhonoured, and by man unblest:
Hark! hear ye not the Christian hymn arise ?
Loud swells the chorus — the sweet cadence dies.
Now, gently on the heart, as snow-flakes melt
Into the unruffled lake, that evening tune is felt."

IT would hardly be possible for the most indifferent observer to walk along the line indicated by these papers, — in short, to follow the course of the Don and its upper tributaries, without noticing the repeated occurrence of little stone chapels, — sometimes built close by the road side; occasionally lifting their plain roofs above the surrounding cottages; and, rarely objects of picturesque combination with the circumjacent scenery. That the appearance of these frequent, unadorned, and almost portable "preaching houses", would excite different emotions in different individuals may well be supposed: the mere Methodist may be expected to regard with, perhaps, something like exclusive complacency, those chapels in which the preacher and the services are altogether Wesleyan: the mere Independent, on the other hand, accords a like decided preference for those, in which the ministry is identical with that of his own peculiar denomination: while the mere Churchman, must regard them alike as unauthorised intruders upon the clerical jurisdiction of the incumbent in whose pariah they happen to be situated. The man, however, whose Christianity is not bound within the walls of his sect — and many such there are among the parties just adverted to especially in this neighbourhood — regards every one of these little chapels as a house of God, in which the blessings of the sanctuary are dispensed every Sabbath day, to many — very many, who otherwise would attend no place of worship at all — except, perhaps their distant parish church on certain high occasions, such as weddings, christenings, and burials.

In common with certain of our charming rural village churches, which are placed as snugly as bird nests in the bushes, some of the little rustic preaching houses, even in this neighbourhood, are so situated, that it is almost impossible for a person inside to turn his eye toward the window without getting a glympse of distant woods, green fields, or perchance the orchard plot close at hand — and, when the casements are open — which is not seldom — not only does there blow in the most exhilarating airs, but at intervals such puffs of fragrance from the apple blossoms, that the God of Nature and of Grace seems to remind his worshipper by the affluence at the same moment of both his gifts, bow great the amount of his obligations — and that the altar which is sanctified by the sublime mysteries of Christianity, is that on which also may be presented the sincere thank-offering of him who feels the outflowings of intense gratitude to the power who gives to man "*all things* richly to enjoy".

Many of these out-of-the-way chapels are supplied on the Sabbath, with what are called in the economy of Methodism, "Local Preachers", an extraordinary class of men, which the energetic genius of that religious system has a direct tendency to develope. These are men who have not only given among their brethren and before the world the requisite proof that they are living "as becometh the gospel" — but who have also shewn that they possess certain "gifts", which qualify them to minister for the edification of others. Gentle reader, see you that plain pedestrian, with open countenance, humble garb, and steady pace? He is a poor industrious smithyman, who, having toiled at his anvil during the week, undistinguished from his fellows, with black face, horny hands, and in leathern apron, is now going to preach the gospel in the chapel of yonder hamlet — see, he draws from his pocket a paper — is it his sermon? No — it is "the plan" — a printed arrangement indicating for every Sabbath during a quarter of a year the times and places where he and his brethren are to preach: he peruses it, and finds that he must announce that a "Love Feast", will be held in the chapel, to which he is going, on the ensuing Sunday afternoon. Let us follow him into the house — 'tis a Methodist Chapel, gentle reader, but don't be alarmed. — See, the preacher is already in the pulpit, and, strange as it may seem, appears quite at home there. He gives out the hymn — i.e. reads two lines at a time: how lustily — how sweetly they sing — young, old, both sexes swelling the song of praise with a joyousness of look and tone, which assures us that most of those who so cheerfully raise the tune with their voices, are at the same time making melody to God in their hearts. In almost all places the rustics have naturally, as it were, a taste for music and singing; and what a sweet world of latent talent, emulation, and delight has not these village choirs elicited? Indeed the extent and variety of the attainments sometimes displayed in executing complex tunes, by persons in these humble situations, would probably be noted as astonishing, were the instances less common.

The singing over — the closing cadence of the last lines of the hymn appearing to linger in dying sweetness on the lips of the congregation — all bow their heads, and now the minister lifts up his voice in prayer: it is in this holy exercise that he often appears peculiarly free, animated, and eloquent: a power, a fervency, a fluency, to possess which a bishop, were he influenced by the spirit of Simon Magus, might in vain offer his mitre as the price, not seldom characterises the extemporaneous devotional aspirations of the man who "all unnoticed and unknown", occupies his useful and providential place at the anvil during six days of the week. The fact — and the secret of the thing is, he constantly lives in this holy atmosphere — while on the Sabbath-day, he may not only be said to breathe it more freely, but to breathe it audibly — and sure, many of his auditors are in the same element — how frequent, how fervent, how pithy their responses! Truly, this may be regarded as one illustration of what is meant by "the communion of saints": —

> "At once they sing, at once they pray;
> They hear of heaven, and learn the way."

And then comes the sermon; in the case of the preacher before us, it is less remarkable for its originality than for its applicability; for its expository than for its experimental character. The preacher is evidently less careful — as indeed he may well be supposed less able — to exhibit new and striking deductions from his text, than to make it the vehicle for conveying and enforcing clearly recognised, and, it may be, old-fashioned truths. His auditors are not merely called upon to *assent* but to *act.* In Methodism all is motion; and the good man before us could as easily "square the circle "to the satisfaction of mathematicians, as adapt his own views, or balance his phraseology, to the idea of "a stand-still believer".

There are mysterious movements in tens of thousands of human hearts, of which the owners have, perhaps, never done anything to distinguish themselves, in the eyes of the world, from those other tens of thousands which appear to make up what Shakspeare calls "the ranks of common men". In very many instances, these mysterious spiritual or mental movements are never revealed to any human being; in many others, they are rarely, cautiously, and confidentially disclosed. In almost all cases, experience has taught, that worldly curiosity is stronger than worldly sympathy; moreover, that the power of the worldling to "minister to a mind diseased" relief or consolation is often even more feeble than the will to do so. Religion, while it finds the heart thus close shut, as it may be, upon "secret workings" to which none but the eye of Omniscience can penetrate, not seldom tends, by its powerful operation, to develope at once the cause, the conflict, and the cure.

Could you hear the members of the religious society, who sit mingled with the general congregation as worshippers in that little rustic chapel — could you hear them individually relate by what processes they have been, as the cases may be, transformed from neglecters of the sabbath to its stated observers; from men of profanity to men of prayer; from bad husbands to lovers of their wives and children; from drunkards to sober persons; from individuals who scarcely knew the alphabet, to those who can read the word of God in short, from bad men to good men, by whatsoever criterion tried, — could you hear the villagers, in their simple way, thus tell their *experience,* you, gentle reader, would surely rejoice in the blessed effects which have resulted from the preaching of the Gospel in the hamlets on the banks of the Don.

Nor speak I of the Methodists alone, in reference to these rural preachings — I have mentioned them in particular as most illustriously exemplifying the practice: but the Independents have their hamlet chapels; and even from the Established Church are there found young men full of zeal and piety, going out to those places which are remote from Church, and there speaking unto the people "words by which they may be saved". And why should it not be so? Why should not our venerable Establishment at once recognise and encourage these extra-clerical agencies, so as to promote their efficiency a thousand fold? — yea, and render them ten thousand times more effective than they are.

Not a few of these useful places of public worship are indebted for their origin to the introduction of Sunday Schools: and to a mind imbued with Christian philanthropy, the circumstances out of which they have sprung (and upon which in turn they have so powerfully reacted) afford a delightful picture for contemplation. In the autumn of 1818, George Benett, Esq., a gentleman, who afterwards circumnavigated the globe, on a missionary voyage, chiefly with reference to an enquiry concerning the progress of the Gospel in the islands of the Southern Pacific, and Mr. Montgomery, the celebrated poet, visited the Sunday Schools in this district. These gentlemen, in a report of what had been seen and done by them during the progress of their interesting mission, thus write; —

"In these Sabbath walks, while we enlarged our knowledge of the adjacent district, its mountains and vallies, its tracts of waste and cultivation, its woods, its waters, and its inhabited places, till every hamlet was endeared to our remembrance by some particular and delightful association, we were more and more deeply impressed with the utility and necessity of Sunday Schools." "We remarked", they afterwards add, "with peculiar pleasure, in several country schools, especially those which were recently established, that the teachers were masters and mistresses of families, elderly persons, who, after having been engaged in husbandry or handicraft business during the week, rested on the seventh day, not in indolence, but hallowing it by works of faith and labours of love. It was a patriarchal and affecting spectacle to contemplate an old man, with the crown of glory on his head — 'gray hairs found in the way of righteousness', and soon to be exchanged for that crown of glory which fadeth not away; — it was truly a patriarchal and affecting spectacle to contemplate such a man of years, teaching an infant of days the name of Jesus and his love. But this, indeed, was beginning the good work at the right end; the example, authority, and sanction of age in these cases being frequently necessary to lead younger people from their vanities and pleasures to the self-denying duties of giving or receiving religious instruction, where nothing of the kind had been done or required before. We observed also", proceed the visitors, "that in every neighbourhood where the Gospel was preached in a house built for that purpose, there was a Sunday School attached to the same, either within its walls, or in an adjacent erection. On the other hand, where a school had been begun, even for a few weeks only, where no other place of worship was found, and perhaps where none had ever existed from the foundation of the world, — there the school room was occasionally converted into a temple, and the Gospel preached to those who previously had been almost as ignorant of it as Jews, Mahometans, or Pagans. Thus, where a school was established first, a chapel soon arose within its enclosure, or at its side; and where the chapel first appeared, the Sunday School followed as its necessary accompaniment. One means of grace faithfully improved, is never long alone. The prayer meeting in a private room leads to preaching there to a few neighbours; in due course, a congregation is formed, and a congregation, in these days of hope and promise, of enterprise and achievement, will not always be passive hearers of the word; they must be doers also; and they presently find employment for young and old in Sunday Schools, in Bible, Missionary, and Tract Societies, and other benevolent institutions, in which the Christian shews his love to God, by love to his neighbour".

It is delightful, amidst descriptions of natural and artificial objects, to turn aside to contemplate the foregoing moral picture, sketched on the banks of the Don by such parties as those above named — and this delight is enhanced by the consideration, that time, so far from having obliterated any thing of the verisimilitude of the picture, has, in many respects, only added depth and harmony to the colouring.

No. XXIV. — THE LOXLEY AND THE RIVELIN.

June 11th, 1836.

"Dear to my childhood were the banks of Don!
As year to year succeeding passes on;
And Memory still is adding to her store
Of honied sweets, she never charms me more
Than when she leads me, or by day or dream,
Through the wild beauties of my native stream.
From Wharncliffe wood, where, yet unknown to fame,
The moorland torrent falls without a name,
To where the Loxley, down his shelving bed,
Rolls to the Don his waters tinged with red.
No whispering reeds, no meads like velvet neat,
Tempt to his banks the summer wanderer's feet;
But broken ground and scattered stones are there,
And roots, long washed by wintry torrents bare.
Tall woods descending meet the water's edge:
Swift sluices, gushing down the rocky ledge,
Far o'er the windings of the footpath way,
In misty showers, throw the hoary spray."

HOMFRAY {'Thoughts on Happiness' by Francis Homfray}

ALMOST immediately before it reaches Sheffield, the Don receives
a considerable increase from the two picturesque tributaries named at
the head of this chapter, which, after gathering on the skirts of the
moors to the west, descend by separate valleys to a point of junction
a little above Owlerton {Malin Bridge SK325893}, whence their
confluent waters run in a common channel, until they enter the main
river near Wadsley Bridge {SK341894}.

The Loxley chiefly originates in two streams, — one running down
Bradfield Dale {? above Agden Reservoir SK243939}; the other
descending on the south side of Bradfield Moor {? via Strines and
Dale Dyke SK234906}. In the earlier part of its progress, this rivulet
is not remarkably different from many others whose earliest course
lies in the moors. About three miles, however, above the point of its
confluence with the Don, the valley through which it flows opens out
in a style of great interest and beauty: steep, rugged cliffs, strongly

broken or gently undulating ground, precipitous banks, on the one hand — or, on the other, sloping fields; the whole space on the south and rocky side being, more or less, clothed with the native birch, or other wood. Such, in brief, were the natural features of the Loxley valley, before the hand of man had interfered with them, otherwise than by damming up the water at intervals, and erecting thereupon his tilts, grinding-wheels, and flour-mills. About thirty years ago, however, an attempt was made, not only to improve (by the addition of some artificial embellishments and alterations) the local beauty of this sequestered glen, but likewise to attract visitors to the spot, by spreading the fame of its picturesque attractions, and at the same time establishing a house for the convenience of rest and refreshment {Robin Hood Inn SK311892}. A substantial house of entertainment was accordingly built; the rugged hill-side was cut into terraces, and perforated with grottoes; walks were made, and seats erected, where either seemed desirable; larches were planted in effective situations; while the merry mountain-brook, which art could neither spoil nor adorn, pursued its trickling course amidst these alterations, giving life and beauty to the whole. For a while, "Little Matlock", as the place was called, attracted numerous pleasure-parties from Sheffield; and few are probably the adult individuals, having any taste for rural scenes, who do not recollect to have spent the afternoon of a summer's day delightfully with their friends at this place.

Little Matlock {SK309892} appears to have lost, in a great measure, its attractiveness for fashionable visitors; the grounds are neglected; the house looks anything but picturesque, its situation notwithstanding: and the following inscription, cut on a stone over the door, (and which, I recollect, I thought wonderfully in character some twenty years ago), appeared, when I last saw it, to have little congruity with the vulgar signboard on another side of the building :—

——————————— Nec vos dulcissima mundi
Nomina, vos montes, cataractae, pascua, sylvae,
Rupes atque cavernae, anima remanente relinquam.

T. HALLADAY.

{A misquote from Abraham Cowley (1618-1667) substituting mountains, etc. for muses, etc. A rough translation (based on

Cowley's own translation in his essay 'On Myself') might be —

> Nor by me e'er shall you,
> you of all names the sweetest, and the best,
> you mountains, flood gates, and pastures,
> forests, cliffs and caverns, forsaken be,
> as long as life itself forsakes not me. }

At the foot of the craggy steep on which stands the public house just described, there is a cluster of dwellings, upon one of which is the following inscription, comprising, in common with that above given, the name of the individual whose taste, aided by classical associations, sought to render permanently sacred to health, friendship, contemplation, and love, a spot so richly endowed with natural amenities: —

> Anno Christi M.DCC.XC.IX.
> Thomas et Martha Halladay
> sine liberis, aetate provecti, necnon jam nunc morituri,
> has construxer{u}nt cedes.
> Sic vos non vobis mellificatis apes.

> {1799
> Thomas and Martha Halladay
> without children, advanced in age, and about to die,
> these houses have built.
> 'Thus you bees make honey, but not only for yourselves'
> (Virgil). }

{Hunter (1819) includes these two quotes (on p3) but appears to have their locations reversed – 'Nec vos dulcissima …' 'above the door of a substantial mansion', and 'Anno Christi …' on 'a house of refreshment'.}

{Thomas Halladay was the Unitarian Minister for Norton – he also built Loxley House SK316903 (rebuilt 1826).}

A little to the north of the spot where this river unites with the Rivelin, lies an extensive plain called Loxley Chase, and traditionally pointed out as the birth-place either of Robin Hood, who was sometimes called Locksley, from the place of his birth — or at least of one of his followers, whose name in sound if not in spelling is identical with that of the place referred to; though what grounds of identity are traceable between our Hallamshire locality and the "Sweet Locksley town in merry Nottinghamshire", where, according to the ballad, "bold Robin was born and bred", it would be difficult to say. The question has its interest with ballad-antiquaries: but evidence that proves too much will be received with suspicion — the story, therefore, that some fragments of a building formerly pointed out were the remains of the early dwelling of the Sherwood royster, or the fact that his well is still pointed out in Cliff Rocher {Robin Hood's Well ?SK 310892}, are circumstances rather amusing than elucidatory. The dreary scalp of this tract known as Loxley Edge, acquired in later years a still less enviable celebrity as the site of a far conspicuous gibbet, happily now removed.

The Rivelin rises not far from Stanedge, between Ughill Moor {~SK239887} and Lord's Seat {SK249851, a building of this name disappears between the 1948 and 1955 OS 1:10k maps, the area is now plantation}, about eight miles west of Sheffield. In the volume of its stream and the character of its banks, it may be said generally to resemble the Loxley: being, however, somewhat nearer to the town, its picturesque beauty has been more frequently no less than deservedly celebrated: the tourist from a distance concurs with the local explorer in awarding this praise. The interest attaching to the banks of the Rivelin does not indeed arise from the presence of the grand or the romantic: these terms imply the existence of pictorial features on a larger scale than any which can be claimed for our river — its charm consists rather in that sort of quiet, snug, attractiveness which is more easily conceived than defined. Nor can it boast of that sylvan distinction which, according to Evelyn, constituted its boast for two hundred years. In the seventeenth century, there stood "at the upper end of Rivelin", an immense tree called the "Lord's Oak", having a bole twelve yards in girth, and a proportionate amplitude of branches: this forest giant — "the pride of Rivelin's dale", was cut down in 1690.

To a person visiting the Rivelin from Sheffield with the design of merely glancing at the scenery, the shortest cut will be to pass the Dams {Crookes Valley Dams SK337873 or Pisgah Dam (later Hadfield Dam, now underground (since ?1946)) SK331873. Mount Pisgah, at ~SK331871, is also the name of the mountain from which Moses first saw the Promised Land, perhaps this location was so named because of the views over Sheffield} and get over the hill by

Crooks {?via Lydgate Lane SK326871}: or else to go by the Mount {Broomhill SK334867}, leaving the main road on the right beyond the toll bar {Fulwood Toll Bar SK331867}, and after passing Lydgate, a smooth verdant lane presently brings the pedestrian in a strikingly sudden manner upon the brow of the hill overlooking the scene in question. A party, however, intending a summer afternoon's ramble, would, in general, find it most pleasant and convenient to hire a coach to drive them on the Glossop Road, as far as the Paper-mill on the Rivelin {also known as Third Coppice Wheel, SK296873} — a distance of about three and a half miles from Sheffield: for although there are, even above that place, several pleasing points of view, the country soon falls or more properly opens out into the ordinary moorland character, and may well be resigned to afford time for the more leisurely and luxurious enjoyment of rambling along the banks, or leaping from stone to stone along the bed of the river lower down.

The interest of the scenery on the Rivelin, is, as already intimated, less directly attributable to the size, form, or even the quality of the materials, independently considered, than to what may be called the *composite* character of the whole — meaning by this term the congruity which one part bears to another, and with which all the parts coalesce in the production of a picture. Indeed, rich as the neighbourhood of Sheffield is acknowledged to be in subjects for the pencil — particularly on the line of its romantic rivers — there is probably no stream, the banks of which have yielded such ample contributions to the artist's portfolio as this is known to have done. The bold sweep and sometimes broken surface of the hills, as they rise on the one hand toward Stannington, and on the other to Walkley — scattered as it may be with timber trees, or brushwood, or, at least, covered with furze, ferns, or herbage — the inequalities, obstructions, and diversions of the watercourse at the bottom — the low-roofed grinding wheels, perched, or rather, buried in all sorts of quaint situations, each accompanied by its rudely-outlined dam, and often no less rudely constructed by-dyke — bushes here, and bushes there, softening the whole to harmony, and not least so in the season when the copsewood is overrun with wild roses, and festooned with honeysuckles, the former oftentimes of a deep blush colour, and the latter in racemes of great sweetness — at least so they have always appeared to me — these are some of the items that would be found in the memory or the minute book of the person who should explore the course of the Rivelin from the point above mentioned.

Having adverted to the colour and the fragrance of the wild flowers, it may not be out of place to add that here the youthful botanist will find considerable amusement in collecting various plants which, if not rare, are pleasing: as geraniums, speedwells, epilobiums {willowherbs} — the gaudy lychnis {Campion}, the pretty blue and the delicate white varieties of polygala {Milkwort} — gentians are seen peeping through the rushes on the grassy border of the dams, and equisetums {Horsetails} may be pulled from the water at the risk of a foot-splash if not a ducking. If I am not mistaken, I noticed, when down the Rivelin last summer, that a person might sit upon the rough bankside, and almost without moving from his position, gather four species of the elegant genus *Hypericum*, "by poets praised", namely, the *perforatum* {St John's Wort}, which is common with its pinhole leaves; its less frequent companion, the *quadrangulum* {?*H. tetrapterum*}, so called from its square stem; the delicate *humifusum* {Trailing St John's Wort}, oft coyly hidden under the grassy fringe of the gutter; and the *pulchrum* {Slender St John's Wort}, whose compact and graceful habit, no less than the striking red colour of its flower buds, renders it a favourite of the race: it would not, perhaps, be easy to find within so narrow a space four species of any other genus of British plants — the Veronicas {Speedwells} hardly excepted.

Memory hath its delicate vignettes, as well as its ampler and more deeply lined pictures — memorials of golden moments never to be recalled, but which have left forms and colours in the mind not easily effaced. It so happened that emerging once, on the evening of a fine summer's day, from the verdant lane above mentioned, I found the subjacent bank scattered over with a group of juvenile flower-gatherers, whose lovely forms, pleasant voices, and lightsome motions gave a most expressive effect to the scene. The temptation to moralise was irresistible: —

> Thought I, how sweet a wreath — leaves, buds, and flowers,
>   Of frail humanity, adorns yon slope!
>   Some, in which girlish innocence to hope
> Hath scarcely turn'd; and some, whose opening powers
> Give promise of fair minds enriched with thought:
>   Life at this period, liveliest, loveliest seems,
>   While in no waking hour, and scarce in dreams,

Hath man's ingratitude sad knowledge taught.
Sweet wreath! said I, deep sighing in my breast —
   May no rude wretch e'er, feigning virtue's smile,
   Pluck off one flower, admire its charms awhile,
Then cast it down, neglected and distressed:
No: Heaven on each the happier lot bestow,
Ne'er of life's bitters more than at this hour to know.

It must be acknowledged that the water-side path along the Rivelin is neither altogether sleek greensward or smooth causeway; nor have the grinders in all cases been mindful of lady-like convenience, in the matter of nice crossing-stones or covered gullies; but with parties bent on the enjoyment of an afternoon's ramble, the trifling obstacles to be overcome tend rather to increase than to diminish the ultimate gratification.

The grinding-wheels so repeatedly alluded to, and of which there are about a score on the Rivelin, afford opportunities for inspecting the machinery used for giving edge and polish to cutting instruments, upon what may be deemed nearly the primitive model. The interior of Wolf wheel {SK302875}, for example, being as spacious, will repay a peep, even to the least curious loiterer down the charming glen in which it is situated. The rapid whirling motion of the stones, buffs, &c., is derived (through intermediate cog-wheels and drums) from bucket-wheels, the bulk and slow revolution of which are generally pleasing to the eye; while the low, intermitted splash of the water upon the bucket-boards, as heard in the stillness of the evening, produces a no less pleasing effect on the ear, especially when harmonised by the consideration, that those sounds of liquid impact are the pulses of a powerful natural agent, unweariedly beating in aid of the labours of man. It were impossible to witness the prodigious velocity with which one of these grindstones revolves, and not to be struck with the jeopardy in which the workman's life must be placed should one of them break while thus in motion. The fact is, that loss of life from this cause does sometimes occur, the splitting stone not only tearing up the grinder's seat, strongly as it is chained down, but the fragments, in some instances, actually passing through the roof! The tremendous hazard of instant death, however, from this appalling cause to which all the grinders using large stones are liable, is a trifling matter, when compared with a more subtle but almost universal source of fatality, to which one class of them is constantly exposed, — namely, those who use dry stones in grinding certain articles, especially forks. Any person looking at one of these grinders at work will perceive a constant stream of sparks issuing from the metal at the place of its contact with the stone: these sparks consist of particles of iron or steel, many of which in a state of impalpable minuteness are, along with pulverulent matter from the grindstone, constantly inhaled by the workman; the result is a distressing and generally fatal disease, too well known as "the grinder's asthma". It is only of late years that this incurable complaint has become so frequent among grinders. Dr. Knight, in an Essay on the subject, published in 1822, has justly remarked, that

> "until the beginning of the last century, grinding was not a distinct branch of business, but was performed by men who were also engaged in various departments of the cutlery trade, and who were consequently exposed but seldom, and then only for a short time, to the injurious effects of the grinding wheels. Up to that time, also, the grinder's asthma was not known as a disease peculiar to the grinder; then, however, an important change took place in the divisions of labour, and grinding became the sole employment of the grinder. A few years afterwards, about the middle of the last century, several grinders were observed to die of complaints nearly similar; the attention of their companions was aroused, and they found the complaint was peculiar to themselves."

The Doctor then proceeds to state that the ravages of the disease have been fearfully extended, by the substitution of unremitted steam power, and small pent-up rooms, for those open airy establishments which were seated on the streams. Such had been the increase of the disease and such its effects, that when the above statement was published, it was asserted

> "that out of twenty-five hundred grinders, there were not thirty-five who had arrived at the age of fifty years, and perhaps not double that number, who had even reached the age of forty-five: of above eighty fork grinders, exclusive of boys, it was said there was not a single individual amongst them thirty-six years old."

When this subject began to excite attention, various remedial schemes were suggested; the two most striking of these were a mouth-guard of magnets to collect the ascending dust; this contrivance, suggested by Mr. Abraham, although ingenious, was not found of practical utility; and it was left for the late Mr. John Elliott to devise and complete an effectual and simple preventative of the evil, by the application of a sort of wooden funnel or chimney, the near end partly enclosing the stone, and the other end passing through the wall; as it was found on experiment that such a current of air was excited by the mere revolution of the stone, as to carry the dust evolved from it through the tube to the outside of the building. This contrivance is now generally — not to say universally — adopted by the dry grinders.

The appearance of these rustic wheels, and their adaptation as subjects for the pencil, has been mentioned; it remains to be added, that the grinders themselves are often the most striking accessories of the scene, in a pictorial point of view. "They are", to adopt the words of a highly graphic describer,

> "nearly the only inhabitants of the valley, and they do not reside in it. There is scarcely a dwelling-house throughout the whole length of it. They are a rough, half-civilized class. Removed thus from the restrictions of society, and the observation of all authority, they associate only with each other. In summer, when the mountain streams which feed their infant river are almost dried up, they have not a supply of water to employ them half their time. As, however, it is uncertain when the uppermost dam will be sufficiently filled to enable the wheel to work, and to dismiss the fluid element to the expecting wheels below, they are under the necessity of being upon or near the place, to take advantage of the supply when it does arrive. At those times, groups of human beings may be seen near every wheel, which, taken with the surrounding scenery, form such subjects as are well fitted for the pencil of a Salvator {perhaps referring to Salvator Rosa (1615–1673), an Italian Baroque painter, poet and printmaker}. Athletic figures, with brown paper turbans, the sleeves of their shirts rolled high up, exposing their brawny arms bare almost to the shoulders, their short jackets unbuttoned, and their shirt-collars open, displaying their broad, dark, hairy chests; their short leathern aprons, their breeches knees unbuttoned, and their stockings slipped down

about their ancles, the whole tinged with ochre-coloured dust, so as to leave the different colours and materials faintly discoverable — form a figure, when taken singly, sufficiently picturesque; when grouped, as they generally are, they become strikingly so. You there see them, some seated on the stone raised, turf-covered bench at the door, with their copious jug and their small pots, handing round the never-cloying English beer; others reared up against the large round grinding stones supported by the walls of the building; others, again, seated on the same kind of stones, lying upon and against each other on the ground, whilst some are stretched at their length, dozing or contemplating, in the verdant sloping banks of the mill-dam; some are amusing themselves with athletic exercises, and others are devising, or slyly engaged in executing, some rude practical jokes. At times you may perceive, as an exception to the general habits, a solitary wandering ruminator with a book, but much oftener with a pipe."

But we must leave the grinders, and hasten down the valley towards Owlerton.

The two streams unite at Malin Bridge {SK325893}, in the glen called Wadsley Bottom, and, flowing thence under the name of the Loxley, reach the Don just beyond High-house {SK339894 on 1854 OS}, near Owlerton. The bridge here has been already named. I may add that Elliott, in what may be safely asserted to be his most beautiful poem, "The Village Patriarch", thus adverts to one of the "mason-works" of his age-blind, hoary-headed hero: —

> "Come, let us wander where the flocks delight
> At noon to sun them, when the sun is warm;
> And visit, then, beyond thy uncle's farm,
> The one-arched bridge — thy glory and thy pride;
> Thy Parthenon; the triumph of thy skill;
> Which still bestrides, and long it shall bestride,
> The discontented stream, from hill to hill,
> Laughing to scorn the moorland torrent still.
> How many years hath he slept in the tomb,
> Who swore thy bridge would yield to one year's rain!
> E'en London folks, to see and praise it, come:
> And envious masons pray, with shame and pain,

For skill like Enoch Wray's, but pray in vain."

A pencil note, inscribed by a friendly hand in the margin of my copy of the poem, propounds the following inquiry:

> "Was this Hill Bridge? — since removed, and a stone *cartway* built across the river, with the architect's name (no Enoch Wray) chiselled upon it. I could", adds the writer, "have knocked my head against it for vexation, the first time I saw the upstart — only it was my own head; had the builder's been on my shoulders, then I would have done it with all possible good will."

Whether the structure referred to by the poet as the master-piece of the village architect, may or may not have been the bridge at the foot of the hill below Walkley, that bridge was certainly a most graceful and pictorial object, as any one may yet convince himself by a reference to the faithful representation of it in one of a series of six engravings of local scenery, by David Martin {? 1791}.

No. XXV. — THE OLD PARK — JONATHAN SALT.

June 18th, 1836.

"Stranger! whose steps have reached this solitude,
Know that this lonely spot was dear to one
Devoted with no unrequited zeal
To Nature: Here, delighted be has heard
The rustling of these woods, that now perchance
Melodious to the gale of summer move;
And underneath their shade on yon smooth rock,
With grey and yellow lichens overgrown,
Often reclined; watching the silent flow
Of this perspicuous rivulet, that steals
Along its verdant course: Stranger! perchance,
Therefore the stream more lovely to thine eye
Will glide along, and to the summer gale
The woods move more melodious."

SOUTHEY. {'In a Forest', Robert Southey}

THE third and last of those fine masses of wood, which so luxuriantly mantle the hills, and sweep down to the — very margin of the Don in its progress from Wortley to Sheffield, is the Old Park {comprising most of the hillside from Parkwood Springs (~SK347891) to Shirecliffe and Herries Road (~SK344908)}, comprehending, as the appellation may be allowed to do for the present purpose, the scarcely separated Cook Wood {above Neepsend, ~Rutland Road, ~SK352890}. In general aspect, this sylvan ornament of the neighbourhood of Sheffield, resembles Beeley Wood; the ground, however, which it covers is of a more undulating character, and at one point it rises to an elevation conspicuous to a great distance. The prospect of the circumjacent country, as commanded from the highest point of the wood — a point easily attainable by pursuing the path from the Lodge {SK343892} near the Rolling Mill {SK342894} — is one of the finest which it is almost possible to conceive. Shame on the indifference of the hundreds of intelligent and, it may be, prospect-loving individuals who have never given themselves the trouble to walk from Sheffield to the top of Old Park Wood, to look upon such a scene! The approach to the wood from Sheffield, is by Hill-foot Bridge {SK342888}, and for a short distance along the water side — or rather along the pleasant margin of a side cut, upon which at no great distance from each other, stand two buildings, both in appearance the reverse of elegant certainly, but respectively interesting to a person who is apt to make visible objects, not always in themselves striking, the nuclei of thoughts and feelings depending in a peculiar manner on the association of ideas. I allude to the Club Flour Mill {SK342897} and the Old Rolling Mill {SK342894}.

The former building was erected in the year 1795, on a sort of "joint stock" principle, by the members of the various Friendly Societies, or, as they were then more familiarly designated, "Sick Clubs", of Sheffield. The object of the speculators, who had as little knowledge as experience in such matters, and still less of suspicion as to the difficulties and trickeries likely to be encountered — was to produce good flour on better than the regular retail terms, at a time when this "staff of life" was at a high price. There was nothing wild or unwarrantable in this project of a subscription Flour Mill, simply considered; and hence, nothing absurd in the demonstrations of joy which accompanied the laying of the foundation; the scene was thus described by a spectator: —

> "I remember, from an elevated station in a field, seeing the procession moving along the high road and crossing the bridge at Hill-foot, to lay the foundation stone of the intended edifice. Forty-three clubs, and their thousands of members, with banners flying, music playing, and drums beating, marched to the fatal spot" — fatal to the prosperity of many of the clubs "It was", proceeds the describer, "a triumph before the opening of the campaign: that campaign proved a most disastrous, a most destructive one. Not content with attempting to insure bread at a reasonable rate, the patriotic clubs established a cheap shoe warehouse, and projected a plan for supplying themselves with milk, at such a price as the dealers would not accept. All these schemes failed in the course of a very few years. The loss of the clubs can hardly be estimated at less than six thousand pounds."

The building was actually raised on a leasehold site held only for the term of twenty-one years! Thus was there exhibited at the outset a most egregious want of foresight in regard to the legal position of the property; and, as it presently appeared, so full a measure of difficulty and dishonesty in the administration, that it was scarcely a wonder that the scheme should have proved abortive — the participants constantly losing more at the hopper than they saved in the bag; — the mill itself being ultimately clutched by a party who found all the considerations of a charitable object too feeble to withstand the temptation to accept as welcome the falling in of a lease with such a property upon it. It seems impossible to quit this instance of speculative or rather practical infatuation, without recollecting how lately we have seen great numbers of working men inveigled into the much more absurd and delusive scheme of what are called "Co-operative Societies" — arrangements by which individual consumers are associated in trading companies: in other words, arrangements by which the combined selfishness of five hundred individuals was, by the mere magic of words to be transformed into the purest personal disinterestedness! It may consist with the notions of people of a certain sentiment, to seek to institute this exclusive dealing, while talking about free trade — but Providence or human infirmity seems to have interposed a bar to its success.

The other building {the Rolling Mill} above referred to, is interesting as the first mill established in the neighbourhood for laminating by means of steel rollers, and with water power, the copper plated with silver, which has now, for nearly a century, been used in such immense quantities in one of the most elegant and successful staple manufactures of Sheffield. Mr. Hancock, who built the mill, and of whose family an interesting notice will be found in Rhodes's "Peak Scenery" {Ebenezer Rhodes, 1824}, had been one of the earliest adventurers in the matter of perfecting and extending the application of the beautiful metallic fabric in question.

> {Rhodes states that "About the year 1750 a Mr. Joseph Hancock, [a descendent of a Family buried at Riley Graves, Eyam] discovered, or rather recovered, the art of covering ingots of copper with plate silver, which were afterwards flatted under rollers, and manufactured into a variety of articles in imitation of wrought silver plate." Sheffield Plate was originally developed in ~1743 by Thomas Boulsover, but it was initially only used to make small items such as buttons. Hancock was responsible for introducing industrial scale

manufacture in 1751.}

But wherefore dilate I thus on the history of yonder mills, fortunate or unfortunate as their founders might be! When I sat down on this gentle green slope, and wrote at the head of my paper the names of this charming wood, and of a man who formerly wandered in its recesses with an eye exquisitely alive to their vegetable beauty, my purpose was merely to link by a single paragraph the present reference to these shades with a transcript of the splendid testimony borne to the unambitious pursuits of Mr. {Jonathan} Salt {1759-1815}, by a highly gifted fellow-townsman.

There are three prime sources of enjoyment which are, generally speaking, open to all without respect of circumstances, though not precisely in an equal degree: Religion, Literature, and Nature. As to the first, no person can be precluded, except by his own act, from a participation in all the pleasures of religion: moreover, the amount of happiness derivable from this source, is in no way necessarily measured or stinted by worldly condition. Literature, although in a certain sense, restricted in its indulgence by the means of the individual, is, nevertheless, in a practical sense, within the reach of all; for, however hundreds, and it may be thousands, of persons may have found themselves too poor to purchase such books as they might wish, there is probably not a man living who can truly say, that with an intellectual taste, and after every effort, he is debarred the means of its appropriate gratification. The largest, the loveliest, and at the same time the least mutable sphere of sensible delight, is the study of Natural History — using these terms in a large sense. In every individual, through every period of life, wherever placed, and during every season of the year, responding harmonies, touched from no chord of that artificial harp whose strings are wealth, power, ambition, pride — will occasionally break forth; and sometimes persons the most deeply immersed in the concerns of sophisticated society — yea, even those who are chained to the rugged oar of daily toil, are found devoting what leisure they can command, to studying the works of Nature. Of such studies, Botany is by no means the least fascinating and recreative; for while its scientific nomenclature, and physiological phenomena exercise the intellect, its wide range of illustrative exemplification calls upon the student for no small amount of active exertion.

"But where", enquires the man of business, "is the profit of acquiring a knowledge of flowers?" — This might be answered by proposing another question, did it not appear almost irreverent to do so: "Where was the necessity for the creation of flowers at all?" And are there, then, individuals so wholly dead to the charms — the non-pecuniary charms of Nature, as to care nothing for the floral beauty of the earth? Utilitarians, who see nothing in the richness of the apple blossoms, but a prelude to the market bushel and the cyder press — nothing in the appearance of the sweet green grass, but the measure of sordid profit on butter and milk, or the still less poetical association — the value of a haystack! O what a world we should have could these men only extirpate from the soil what they term "useless weeds", — how would the butter-cup, the daisy, and the dandelion disappear from our pastures! The furze {gorse}, and the foxglove, and the bracken from our heaths! And then, could they give a railroad celerity to the growth — a steam-engine rapidity to the ripening — and a utilitarian perfection to the nature of the productions of the earth — how would the corn be carried up from the germination to the ripening, without the present unprofitable interval of lingering green: how would the filbert, the walnut, and the acorn, instead of interesting the botanist and beautifying the wood by their slow process through incipient stages, be expected to start at once into full ripe existence, if not from the bough to the wallet of the collector! Yea, the oak and the ash of the forest, instead of vibrating as they are wont, their delicate stems, and shaking and shedding their curious leaves, during a long period as feeble saplings, liable to be trodden down by the heifer in her path, and even for years after that stage lingering through a nonage {immaturity} in which they are scarcely fit for hop-poles, would, no doubt, could wishes promote their growth, rise suddenly from the ground into fine trees, not to be admired for their bulk or their beauty, but to be sawn into timber, and exchanged for gold.

Happily the earth but little — forest trees as to their growth, hardly more — and the seasons not at all, yield to the impatient haste of mercenary man — happily, too, there have been many, and still there are a few who cultivate a taste for the investigation of the productions of the earth, not professionally or scientifically merely, but fondly and implicitly, as yielding to those instincts of admiration which He who adorned this earth with such a profusion of loveliness, and at the same time made man especially capable of enjoying it, seems to have intended should have play.

It is impossible for an inhabitant of Sheffield, especially one possessing any interest in the history of the intelligence of the town during the last half century, to pass the Old Park Wood, much less to enter its precincts, without being reminded of one, whose noiseless pursuits, occasionally participated by his friends, but much oftener pushed in solitude under the shadow of its trees, as well as carried over every open field, into every secret dell, and across all the moorlands of the neighbourhood, in quest of botanical rarities, were strikingly illustrative of the foregoing sentiments. "Botany", said Mr. Montgomery, in his beautiful speech at the establishment of the Sheffield Literary and Philosophical Society, in 1822, —

"Botany might be presumed to be the last walk of science in which a Sheffield manufacturer would be found; yet, within my remembrance, there lived in the heart of this town ONE who was attracted into that path by a peculiarly delicate sense of whatever is beautiful and curious in the loveliest productions of nature. The late Jonathan Salt {1759-1815} — for he is now no more — engaged in this interesting pursuit with such patient ardour and uncloyed delight, that he not only acquired a correct and comprehensive knowledge of plants, but was regarded by the first professors of his day as an ornament and a benefactor to the science, having, by his elaborate researches and discoveries, even in this neighbourhood, added something to the stock of general information. A late friend of mine, highly gifted with genius, and accomplished in every branch of natural philosophy, was so charmed with the genuine intelligence of Mr. Salt, on subjects with which few have more than a showy acquaintance, that he considered an hour in his company, when they could freely interchange thoughts, (giving and receiving fresh hints on their favourite topic), as an hour of privileged enjoyment. With a pleasure which none but botanists can know, (for such congenial spirits do not encounter every day), they were wont to welcome each other when my friend came to Sheffield. On such occasions, while I have watched their countenances, and hearkened to their discourse, though, from my ignorance, I could enjoy but little of the latter, the expression of the former was perfectly intelligible, and highly exhilarating to a spectator who had anything of human sympathy about him. I have known Mr.

Salt mention a certain rare plant as growing in this neighbourhood, when my friend, for joy scarcely believing that there was no mistake, desired to be conducted immediately to the spot; and away they went to the depths of the OLD PARK WOOD, where the one had the triumph of showing his discovery, and the other the joy of seeing, for the first time (I believe) on British ground, the coy recluse, which was then in full flower."

Thus far the allusion of the elegant minded poet to the wood; but the remainder of the sketch of this amiable and indefatigable local botanist must not be discarded: —

"There must have been", proceeds Mr. Montgomery, "a native elegance in the mind of him who could thus attach himself to a solitary study, and in a range beyond his ordinary occupation; and there must have been an unconquerable love of it in that man who, in such circumstances, could make himself master of its terminology, (the engraftment of all manner of barbarian words on a classic stock), and its technical phrases, borrowed from a language in which he was unskilled, except in its adaptation to botany. I cannot choose but envy the pure transports of an enthusiast, who could quietly steal away from the bustle, the care, the dirt and meanness, (if I may hazard such a term here), of the warehouse and the workshops, and visit, according to the season of the year, one locality or another, within his pedestrian circuit, where he knew that he should meet with peculiar plants that flourished there, and nowhere else. Conisbrough, the Woodlands, the High Moors, the Peak of Derbyshire, were so many rounds of amusing excursion to him. On every hill and in every valley, he was welcomed and accompanied by *the Flora* of the scene, who showed him her loveliest children, crowding in her path, or beautifully scattered throughout her little domain. He is gone, and the places that knew him know him no more. Who among our youth will tread in his footsteps, and be the heirs of his innocent pleasures, in the fields both of nature and of science? His humble name and praise deserve an apter eulogist than I am. Such as they are, however, these few flowers of speech are gratefully scattered upon his grave by one who, at least, knew how to respect his modesty and worth."

As a pendant to the foregoing eulogium, the subjoined verses, written a few years since in the album of Miss Salt, as a tribute to the memory of her father, and containing an allusion to Mr. Montgomery's remarks, may not be improperly introduced in this place: —

Unknown to wealth and noisy fame.
    To circles where ambition climbs,
Was he, whose unpretending name,
    Inspires these tributary lines:
It was his highest joy to meet
With Science in some lone retreat.

With Science, leading Flora's band,
    A gaily-coloured, fragrant train;
Trees, shrubs, and flowers; — whate'er the land
    Brought forth throughout each season's reign:
These — every figure, size, and dye,
Became familiar to his eye.

He knew their names; in each could read
    Its various history with delight;
And oft some coarse or humble weed,
    Would strangest ecstacies excite:
Some weed, which, all uncommon, hath
Appeared beside his devious path.

Nor deem ye loftier minded race,
    That mean his quest who gathers flowers;
Who loves the coyest steps to trace
    Of Nature, in her secret bowers :
Who finds some vegetable gem,
In every blossom, leaf, or stem.

Nor scorn, ye proud, his curious lore,
    Who courts the sweet Botanic muse;
Who loves minutely to explore,
    What pride with cold indifference views, —
The woodland depths, — the mountain's brow, —
Wide plains; or vales where streamlets flow.

Such were the haunts of him, who made

LINNÆUS his companion dear;
Who gathered, classified, displayed,
    Through every season of the year,
Those products of his native soil,
Which now attest his pleasant toil.

Those curious specimens which fill
    His ample *Hortus Siccus,* stand,
Like autographs of wondrous skill,
    Traced by the great Creator's hand:
They show how warm, and how sincere
A friend of science placed them here.

Long may they be preserved with care;
    And with the tribute of the bard,
Claim for the Botanist his share
    Of merited, — of kind regard:
While students, moved by kindred zeal,
Shall to these treasures oft appeal.

J. HOLLAND.

Of the industry and ingenuity of Mr. Salt, as a botanical collector, the
hortus siccus {herbarium, literally 'dry garden'}, which he left behind
him, and which, coming into the possession of the late Mr.
Staniforth, surgeon, was by him presented, in 1826, to the Sheffield
Literary and Philosophical Society, is the best memorial. {The
herbarium is now held by Museums Sheffield.} The collection
consists of several hundred specimens — indigenous and exotic —
all neatly glued upon sheets of paper, containing the name, class,
order, habitat, &c. of each, and disposed in fasciculi {bundles}
according to the arrangement of Withering — the most popular
adaptator of the Linnæan system to the Flora of Britain, then known.
At the time Mr. Salt began to form his herbarium — neither Smith
nor Hooker had given to the public those laborious works which have
so wonderfully elucidated botanical science — between thirty and
forty years ago, it was not expected that Sheffield would, in 1835,
expend upwards of £14,000 in the formation of Botanical Gardens,
or that students in Mr. Salt's pursuit would, at that time, purchase a
dozen originally drawn and faithfully coloured portraits of British
plants for a shilling! What the identical plant alluded to in the above
speech was, does not appear. It is, indeed, more than probable, that

Mr. Montgomery's memory may have served him less exactly as to the habitat of the "coy recluse", than as to the fact of its discovery. I have had an opportunity of examining the specimens in the collection, at the Music Hall, and of sixteen plants described as "gathered in the Old Park Wood", not one can be said to be rare; — in fact, they are mostly of common occurrence — at least in this neighbourhood. There are, indeed, two plants, of which the places of growth are specified with a much greater degree of exactness than the rest, namely, the broad-leaved heleborine *(Epipactis latifolia),* and the sweet cicely *(Myrrhis odorata),* already noticed as growing on the banks of the Don. It was probably the latter of these (the habitat or identity of which may have been doubted by Mr. Salt's friend, the late Rev. Henry Steinhauer) that led the botanists off to the Old Park Wood: this is the more likely, as the excursion took place at midsummer, at which time the myrrhis would be in flower. There is, however, a plant, *Carex elongata,* which was gathered by Mr. Salt, in 1801, in a marsh, a little below Aldwark Mill, and to which the name of our late townsman is generally attached in British Floras: the specimen in the Sheffield Herbarium is distinguished by the note

"Now first discovered to be a native of Britain."

{The *Carex elongata* specimen is now missing.}

The neighbourhood of Sheffield — using the term in its limited sense — cannot perhaps be said to be generally interesting to the botanist; but it is otherwise, if we extend the lines of exploration to a distance of from twelve to twenty miles, or a long day's walk, in every direction around. In this circuit will be comprised not only great variety as to soil, but also of elevation; and, as might be expected under such circumstances, almost every mile traversed, presents something to enrich the vasculum of the student.

No. XXVI. — NEEPSEND — ORNITHOLOGY

June 25th, 1836

" — Birds, the free tenants of land, air, and ocean,
Their form all symmetry, their motions grace;
In plumage delicate and beautiful,
Thick without burthen, close as fishes' scales,
Or loose as full-blown poppies to the breeze;
With wings that might have had a soul within them,
They bore their owners by such sweet enchantment,
 — Birds small and great, of endless shapes and colours,
Here flew and perched, there swam and dived at pleasure;
Others, more gorgeously apparelled, dwelt
Among the woods, on Nature's dainties feeding,
Herbs, seeds, and roots; or ever on the wing,
Pursuing insects through the boundless air:
In hollow trees or thickets these concealed
Their exquisitely woven nests. "

PELICAN ISLAND {James Montgomery (1771–1854)}

AFTER quitting Owlerton, and skirting the Old Park, the Don, which has now become a fine, broad, placid river, passes under Hill-foot Bridge {SK342888}, a substantial structure of timber, thirty yards long; and, margined with one of those charming plots of little gardens formerly to be seen every where in the suburbs, may now be said to enter the town. At this spot we have the General Infirmary {SK344882}, a noble edifice, embosomed in a rising plantation, just on the right, and St. Philip's Church, immediately in front {SK347882 – the church is now demolished and is a 'shrubby' traffic island!}. The river, however, instead of running straight toward the last-named pile, goes off to the left, toward the point indicated by the title of this chapter; and, after passing Sand-bed tilt {N. of Hillfoot Bridge, ~SK342891}, it spreads out at a place called the Butts, opposite the celebrated Britannia metal works of Messrs. Dixon {SK353878, behind current Law Courts}, into a pool of considerable breadth. A number of small boats are moored hereabouts, for the accommodation of pleasure-taking parties, or the convenience of crossing from one side to the other; this is, indeed, the only spot in the immediate vicinity of the town where the pleasant and athletic exercise of rowing can be even in a slight degree indulged. This portion of the river, although by no means so much sheltered as decency would wish, is much resorted to by summer bathers, and accidents from drowning repeatedly occur. Mr. Wesley, in one of his journals, records a striking case. That celebrated individual used himself occasionally to bathe in the Don, during his visits to Sheffield: his bath, however, was not the pool at the Butts, but rather a well-known deep near the Walk Mill {SK362881}, just below where the river quits the town.

In former years, before the religious denomination of the Baptists had a water-tank made inside their Chapel, for the immersion of adult converts, it was customary for them to resort to the river, as John the Baptist went to "Enon, nigh unto Salem, because there was much water in that place", for the performance of the sacred rite; and assuredly, whatever might be thought of the ceremony, as one to which, in the opinion of this people, it behoves every Christian to conform, the whole transaction, conducted, as the services invariably were, with the utmost decorum, was one which few could observe with indifference, and which, to many, was undoubtedly an occasion of direct religious edification. Within the last two years, the still, capacious expanse of water at the Butts, has been more than once selected as the scene of adult baptism by a small party of this persuasion in the town. On these occasions, the boats, previously alluded to, have been filled with spectators, while others crowded the banks — the singing of hymns, preaching a sermon, and immersing the neophites in the water, in such a spot, forming, in connexion with the scenery about Neepsend, a spectacle of a striking character.

Hereabout, as already intimated, especially on the side of the river called "Harvest-lane" {SK351884}, are a considerable number of small gardens, mostly belonging to the workmen engaged in the various manufactories, and who spend such leisure time as they can command in the mornings and evenings, including sometimes the whole of "Saint Monday", in cultivating fruits, flowers, and vegetables. Sheffield, until the extension of the buildings pushed the cheap land comparatively beyond the reach of the poor — or, in other words, rendered the vicinal soil, in most cases, too valuable to be allocated — Sheffield, previously to this much-to-be-regretted circumstance, was remarkable for the beautiful zone of little gardens with which it was surrounded and adorned, "like the swart {swarthy}

Indian with his belt of beads". The healthful, harmless, and commonly even profitable recreation of gardening, was highly appreciated by the artizan: and many of these prized plots, containing perhaps hardly a greater number of superficial yards than there are squares in the multiplication table, produced gooseberries, polyanthuses, auriculas, (the splendid dahlia had not *then* found its way within these humble enclosures,) and other "poor man's favourites", in a very high degree of abundance and perfection.

From the Butts, above mentioned, the river flows along the bottom of what formerly were, as the site is yet called, Coulson's-crofts {shown on Fairbank's 1771 map as area from Kelham Island to Spring Croft (Spring Street). Coulson Street ~SK355877, is now site of Law Courts.}, and where, until toward the latter end of the last century, the water was crossed by means of stepping stones, placed in the bed of the stream, and standing about a yard high. In the year 1795, an iron bridge, calculated for foot-passengers, and cast by Messrs. Walker, at Masbrough, was erected over the Don at this place, and has proved of immense benefit, as a means of communication between the town and the populous suburb here called Bridgehouses: the necessity, however, of a more substantial structure, for the passage of heavy vehicles, has long been felt by the inhabitants about and beyond Neepsend. {The original Iron Bridge was damaged in the Sheffield Flood in 1864, but the replacement Iron Bridge can still be seen at SK354881, visible between the carriageways of the Ring Road. It apparently remains because it carries a water main.}

In former years, and before the buildings had so completely environed the river in this direction, various birds, of species now seldom seen, used to frequent the water — rarely, however the King's Fisher, the Grebe, and the Sand Piper, are still shot. How elegantly does Audubon, the celebrated ornithologist, describe, under the more common name of the bird, the habits of one species of Grebe, as witnessed in the lagoons of America. I have presumed, very slightly, to metaphrase the passage, in order to present, with the charm of verse to the eye, what, any one referring to the original will find, was previously poetry to the ear and the imagination.

> There go the little dobchicks, right among
> Tall rushes and aquatic grasses, bordering
> The marsh. But they have seen me; see, they sink
> Each gently backward into the deep water,

Like frightened frogs. Yet still, ye cunning things!
Ye "Water Witches", still I see your bills, —
All else withdrawn — you're sneaking slily off
Towards yon great bullrush bunch. Well speed you on,
May safety long attend you! To elude
Your numerous enemies, hath nature given
The various means; and glad I am to see,
That you have profited by her instructions.
I know, too, you can fly. How happy you,
Enabled thus to migrate through the air,
Instead of being obliged, month after month,
To labour with your curious scolloped feet,
As "Authors say", in seeking each far country.
Ah! you have reached a small secluded pool,
Where you in peace and safety mean to tread :
There you are gathering rushes and lank weeds,
To form an ample matted bed, whereon to lay
Your beauteous pearly eggs. Then labour on,
And mind not me, true friend — admirer of your race.
Among those plants, I see securely fixed
Your tenement, in which will shortly shine
Five eggs green tinged, but seeming purest white.
I wish I knew how many days of heat —
Heat constant from your bodies will suffice
To hatch these eggs — this time, perchance, may tell me.
Now, of yourselves, the miniatures, I see,
Each swimming, skipping, springing, gliding, dipping,
As gaily as yourselves. I see you catch
The crawling insect, yea and gorge yourselves
With leeches, fish, and herbage. Fast in size
Your younglings grow, apace, exchanging vesture —
The down for hairy-feathers — silken plumes.
On winglets now they cross the clear bright pool,
And on the farther shore enjoy the warmth
Of the bright sun. But lo! September comes —
And plump and strong here seven of you are:
Evening is calm and beautiful — sweet birds!
You spread your wings, and flying swiftly, reach
A proper height, then, swift as meteors, glide
Through upper air; till, greeting warmer waters,

There down you drop, and spend the gentle season.

Apropos of this celebrated ornithologist — the transcription of the foregoing lines suggests to me that the present will be as suitable an occasion as any that may occur, for inscribing my humble tribute of respect to the name and genius of one who, although not an Englishman, sought and has found, mainly in British munificence, the means of executing, in one department of natural history, a work of unequalled enterprise, fidelity, and skill — I allude to the "Birds of America".

Most persons at all conversant with our current literature during the last few years, must have heard of this splendid monument of individual genius; but it is utterly impossible for any one who has not actually seen and examined the drawings or the plates, embodying the spirited and faithful delineations of so many of Nature's most buoyant, graceful, and joyous children, to form more than a very inadequate conception of the force of character, the felicity of sketching, grouping, and illustrating, displayed in hundreds of birds, all represented of the size of life, in their appropriate attitudes and habitats, and perched upon, or associated with, those vegetable productions which are suitable to each.

There is another reason why I may be excused for selecting this place as that in which to indulge my ornithological rhapsody. In the second volume of the "Birds of America", our author describes, as somewhat of a rarity, a fine and genuine jerfalcon {Gyr Falcon, *Falco islandicus*} from Iceland, as in the possession of his friend Mr. Heppenstall, of Upperthorpe — the pleasant brick house on the near hill-side yonder. Aye, there may be seen one of the few sets in this part of the country, of the plates of the magnificent work in question. There, too, Audubon spent a few days on a visit, a month or two since; and moreover, Mr. Heppenstall is the fortunate possessor of a splendid picture, of a large size, representing a number of pheasants startled by dogs in a woodland recess, painted and exhibited by Audubon, some years ago, in London.

I once met with Audubon — and thankful I am for the gratification! To turn over the plates already referred to, is a treat of no ordinary kind: how much greater the pleasure of examining a large port-folio full of the original drawings, some exquisitely finished, others in various stages of progress — and then to talk over the history of each with the artist — such an artist! I shall not soon forget the evening I spent with John James Audubon, and Lucy his wife. He was one of the few men that a lover of natural history, or a lover of mere adventure either, would have gone a great way only to have seen. Truly, a fine figure he is, with the eye of an eagle, the limbs of an antelope, and the simplicity of a real child of the forest; yet was there a quiet dignity in his demeanour, and a placid energy in his conversation, which impressed me with the idea of being in the presence of a man whose spirit was with future times, in the assurance that the moderate award of his contemporaries would not be the full measure of his renown. Perhaps he may be at this moment in the wilderness depths of the western world, pushing, amidst toil, danger, and death, those inquiries, which are to complete his claims to future celebrity — if so, safety and success attend him!

We have often read — especially in the essays of modern poetical commentators, of the dignified complacency with which our glorious Milton, indifferent to the neglect and disparagement of his own times, relied on the award of posterity, as to the merit of his immortal work. The notion is certainly poetical — and when advanced by a poet, it is affecting: moreover, "Paradise Lost", which *was* neglected by its author's contemporaries, *has been* honoured by an after age, and *is* honoured by our own as one of the noblest productions of the human mind — still, it does seem to require a little conceding of probability to authority, to enable us fully to accredit even the poet himself with so prescient a magnanimity. Be this as it may, I never happened to meet with any other man, in whom so really as in Audubon appeared to exist a confidence — not avowed indeed, but reposed, in the award of posterity. And, surely as America is a great and growing country, the population of which is for the present too busily employed in providing the substantialities, to find time to pursue the elegancies of life — so surely will the descendants of these same active people in an after stage of society, discover, with rapturous interest, the merits of a countryman, who had devoted himself with such unparalleled enthusiasm and originality, to the illustration of a science that will not want studious admirers. Nor let these expressions be deemed extravagant, even by those who care as little about Ornithology as they do about Botany. A person who reprints a book containing numerous references to, or extracts from classical or obsolete authors, informs his readers with something like pride, that he has "verified all the quotations;" and this, by those who are acquainted with the difficulties of the task, is received as no small proof of skill and diligence. Another publishes a plan of a town, or a map of a district — it may be of a country, and laudably boasts that he has remeasured the distances, and revised the bearings; while a third, whose object is geological research, complacently states that he has not described any appearances which he has not personally noticed and examined. These, and fifty other instances which might be mentioned, are creditable to the parties, nay indispensable to reputation in each case, but what of extended enterprise or vigilant observation do they ordinarily evince, in comparison with his achievement who has undertaken to see, to delineate, and to describe the "Birds of America"? Here is an individual, tethered to the ground like the rest of us — admiring, pursuing, overtaking, exhibiting, as it were, a world on the wing! And yet, say you, the distance between the enthusiast and his object is measurable; and the "winged beauty" rendered as tangible as a dead bird can make it, by means of a super-excellent rifle and a super-excellent aim. This is easily said by one who perhaps has shot eighteen pigeons out of twenty, as the poor birds have been released from a trap; or who may have bagged forty pheasants in a day at one of those merciless *battus* in a preserve, which make the heart sicken in the very description; or still more, by one who has shot grouse on the wing, or ducks on the mere. But let any one of these "sportsmen" try some of those Kentuckian tests of a good shot described in one of our author's romantic interchapters, and then let him tell us how easy a thing it is, by means of a projected bullet, neatly to unbutton the glossy vests of the winged denizens of the swamps and forests of the western world. It were indeed, methinks, a delectable recreation to spend a week with our ornithologist in the woods — at least, it is delightful to indulge this notion while reading some of his pages — the effect of *others* is to reverse the impression.

No. XXVII. — THE DON AT SHEFFIELD.

July 2nd, 1836.

"The scene has changed, Sir: where those buildings stand
    They say the water once spread out: but now,
As firm and solid seems that slip of land,
    As the stone terrace on yon green hill's brow:
    Some say there's clayey moisture hid below,
And sand and pebbles like a river's bed:
    'Tis likely then, the flood had ampler flow,
What time this land with trees was overspread,
    And men a forest life in the deep thickets led."

ANON

WE have now arrived, with our pleasant companion the river, at the most celebrated — or rather, perhaps, we should say — the most important place on its banks: here we shall, of necessity, be detained awhile — a thousand attractions soliciting our delay. It were impossible, however, for a person who regards with any degree of interest the physical history of the Don, to quit the margin of the river for the streets, without first asking himself whether it be probable that the ample channel by which the volume of water at present finds its way from Neepsend to the Wicker, is or is not the same which sufficed for the stream in very early times? That we ought to adopt the negative conclusion seems next to demonstrable on two grounds — first, the general appearance of the locality, and second, the evidence of reliquiae frequently brought to light.

It would be difficult for a person, having this inquiry in view, to look upon the level space stretching along both sides of the river from the Butts {? The Wicker, SK358879} to the Lady's Bridge {SK357877}, without believing that the water must, at some time, have overflowed a much larger extent of ground than at present serves for its conveyance past the town. It is, indeed, very likely that, at a period antecedent it may be to historical evidence, the level tract in question was either a vast but shallow lake, through which the turbid current found its way, or a stagnant morass, deluged at intervals by the descent of more than usually copious floods from the moors: in either case, forming a scene widely different from that which we now witness. Of that lacustrine and — (must we not add?) — miasmatic era, nearly all that can be surmised — for nothing is really known — is set forth in the following bit of "Prose, by a Poet", — in which the ingenious writer {? 2 volumes of this name were published by James Montgomery in 1824}, giving a history of Hallamshire, from the Creation to the present period, says: —

"There *was* a time, when the mountains and valleys, the woods and streams, comprised in the district of Hallamshire, were a solitary waste; when neither men nor animals inhabited any part of it, except that, as fishes were not destroyed in the universal deluge, it may be concluded that the *Don,* and the *Sheaf,* the *Riveling,* the *Porter,* and the *Loxley* continued to be peopled as they had been from the beginning of the world. There *was* a time, when, though the whole of the region remained as thoroughly a wilderness of nature as ever it had been, yet four-footed beasts, flying fowls, and creeping things carried life and enjoyment wherever they moved on the earth, through the air, or through the mazes of the grass. There *was* a time, — no, we are not sure of that; but *they say* that there was a time, when Britain was possessed by a race of giants, (whencesoever they may have sprung), and that they were exterminated by a colony of Trojans, who under the conduct of a leader named *Brutus,* fled hither from the conflagration of their city. Whether giants or Trojans ever existed here, except in the dreams of tradition, we will neither take the trouble to doubt nor to inquire, but with *true* historical *veracity* at once roundly assert, that however puny and common-place in size and feature the living population may be, this neighbourhood was for ages the haunt of the former magnificent personages, prowling through forests and sleeping in dens of rocks which may be seen at this day; and that afterwards Hallamshire became the refuge of the immediate descendants of the Heroes of Homer, who were reminded every morning, when the sun rose upon its beautifully undulated landscape, of the loveliness and fertility of their own dear land on the borders of Asia, — while they missed nothing here but the towers of Ilium itself, which they carried every where in their hearts, and took down with them into their graves. There *was* a time, when Caesar, landing with his Roman legions upon the shores of this island, found it occupied by tribes of human beings, who could scarcely be descended from the classical Trojans, for the latter wore fine clothing, lived in superb palaces, and spoke most excellent Greek, as every page in the Iliad will testify; whereas the Britons, on Caesar's arrival among them, gabbled in a gutteral jargon more like Welsh than anything else; were poor, wandering savages living in huts or roosting in caverns; went naked and painted more frightfully than tattooed Indians, or were swaddled in the skins of wild beasts, with whom they held divided empire. Be this as it may, — such were the barbarians who hunted, and fished, and fought, and ate, and drank, and lived, and died, at that time, on the banks of the five rivers aforenamed."

It was probably somewhere within the period so ingeniously undefined by the foregoing quotation, that the waters of the Don expanded freely, and deposited their sediment slowly over the ample level at the foot of that fine eminence which, in the Norman era, was surmounted by that sacred edifice whose lofty spire has therefrom pointed heavenward during the intervening seven or eight centuries.

Whatever the circumstances which may have conduced to compel the waters of the Don to run in a more contracted channel, — whether the mere process of silting up the bed, as afterwards noticed, or the deposition of rubbish from the town, or both, aided by various artificial contrivances, it is likely that swampy meadows and damp osier grounds would succeed to feculent pools and lazy gutters. The memory of the former, indeed, seems to be indicated by the spot afterwards known as the Coulson Crofts, and the latter by the Wicker, an ancient salictum {thicket or grove of willows} of which Sheffield has no existing specimen.

We must now advert to the more decisive evidence of the existence of this fluviatile state of things. Four points on the progressive line of the river may be mentioned as having afforded, at a considerable depth below the present surface, the following results: —

1, Indications of the ancient river bed;
2, Deposits of blue clay, apparently derived from the moors;
3, Vegetable reliquiae; and
4, Traces of the operations of man.

The highest point at which I am aware of the three first mentioned deposits having occurred, is at Philadelphia; these appearances presenting themselves on digging for the foundation of the Globe Works {SK348882}. The next spot to be noted in connexion with their occurrence is the site of the Poorhouse (the old Cotton Mill) {SK352880}: when the foundations of that building were sunk, traces of fluvial action alternating with sedimentary beds were discovered. The third locality is lower down, and still farther from the present course of the river: it was discovered in excavating the ground for the purpose of making a tank for gasometers, on the north east side of Spring-street (SK354877}, about twelve months since {mid 1835}. On the occasion referred to, a large tree was laid bare, evidently lying as it had been cut, marks of the axe being visible at the kerf: the wood of this tree was interiorly a bluish black, looking as if recently dyed with ink: a considerable number of hazel nuts, thoroughly coloured in like manner, were found in a sludgy blue clay, lying above what appeared to have been the ancient river bed. The nuts might have been brought by some heavy flood down from Wharncliffe. Vegetable exuviae have likewise been found on the margin of the Sheaf, near its confluence with the Don, "Branches of hazel", says Mr. Hunter, "a tree with which the vale of Beauchief abounds, are sometimes found deeply embedded in the earth near the course of this river".

Similar indications of the wide license of the river, and the coincident operations of man, were discovered only a few weeks since in digging the foundations of the new Gas Works behind the canal basin {SK368880}. Exactly in the spot where the tall chimney of the retort-house stands, the workmen laid bare an immense piece of timber, to which remained attached by iron cramps, in a horizontal position, the trunk of a large tree which had evidently been channelled artificially, and laid as a conduit for water. These timbers, like the trees in Spring street, lay under a thick bed of moist blue clay, over which spread a stratum of rolled stones, indicative of this spot having been formerly comprised within the ample extent of the bed of the river. Precisely the same proofs of the ancient prevalence of fluviatile action over a much more considerable space than that now occupied by the river, presented themselves to the workmen employed in making the new cut behind the Ickles mill {~SK420920}, near Rotherham; and, indeed, they have generally been observed at the same depth below the covering of vegetable mould along the vale of the Don.

It were perhaps impossible, as already intimated, to form any rational conjecture as to the exact period when these depositions — especially the lower one — took place. The source of the blue clay was doubtless those argillaceous beds which existed either in a schistose, or less indurated state, about the upper part of the river, and which, having been laid bare and dissolved by the action of floods, would be held in mechanical suspension by the water, until the turbid stream, which flowed rapidly from the heights, would slowly deposit its load of sediment on reaching the lower ground, where its volume, no doubt, became diffused, shallow, and lazy. During the period first adverted to, whatever its duration, the tract over which it appears man had carried his conduits, must have been changed into an extended but shallow lake; for it is difficult to conceive that the vast accumulations of clay — little as it is removed in consistency from the state of mud — could have taken place in a very short space of time.

If this hypothesis of the former existence of a lacustrine era in what has since become the north western suburb of the town of Sheffield be admitted, two causes present themselves as unitedly sufficient to account for the subsequent contraction of the bed of the water. In the first place, however ample the Sheffield lake and stagnant its sides, as the water had undoubtedly vent in the direction of Rotherham — unless we choose to consider the submerged land as extending so far — and, indeed, whether that were the case or not, there would be a current somewhere: *where* the maximum force or set of such current might be, would depend partly upon the general dip of the space flooded, and also upon accidental causes; but most probably towards the middle of the lake. This current would, in the first place, cut through, and carry off the softer material of its bed; thus forming a channel, to which, of course, would be restricted the entire discharging volume of water, whenever any circumstance should occur to diminish the supply, so as to leave the silted margins uncovered. All this is on the supposition that the clayey stratum, resting on the most ancient river bed, was derived from the subsidence of the water during a long continued and tranquil occupation of the site, and not any sudden or violent flood, which came from the hills heavily charged with the debris of its mountain track — which seems, indeed, likely to have been the case.

The stratum of water-worn stones which lies between the clay and the surface soil, resembles the present bed of the river, and is probably of no great antiquity: it indicates, in common with the substratum, a wide expansion of the stream at the time of its deposit, but not necessarily any greater violence in the current than we now witness. The power of running water, even under small velocity, to tear up or transport solid matters is greater than many persons suppose – a velocity of three inches per second is ascertained to be sufficient to tear up fine clay; — six inches per second, fine sand; twelve inches per second, fine gravel; — and three feet per second, stones of the size of an egg. Many remarkable illustrations of the power of running water in moving heavy bodies are recorded in accounts of the great flood which occurred in Aberdeenshire, in 1829. "The river Don", observes Mr. Farquharson in his account of the inundations, "has upon my own premises forced a mass of four or five hundred tons of stones, many of them two or three hundred pounds weight, upon an inclined plane, rising six feet in eight or ten yards, and left them in a heap." But why cross the Tweed for examples from the Don and the Dee of Scotland, when we witness almost yearly in the higher part of our own river, sufficiently striking indications of the power of heavy floods to move large stones and other materials?

It has been already stated that in the first place, the natural effect of the middle current of the Don would be to work out a better defined and more limited channel — another cause would be the location of inhabitants and the increase of society along its banks. Slowly, but certainly, must this cause have operated in abridging the freedom and extent of the rivers' overflowings on the margin of the town of Sheffield: this is abundantly evident from the rubbishy appearance of the soil immediately overlying the sedimentary fragments in the sections laid open in the vicinity of Spring-street, and elsewhere. The rich alluvial soil, on each side of the Don much lower down the valley, has been largely accumulated by land floods, aided by annual overflows of the river.

The argillaceous beds associated with the lower coal, are wrought in some places with considerable advantage, for firebrick clay: and at Midhope there is a small pottery work; while at Storrs, near Stannington, a kind is obtained of sufficient purity to be mixed with the Stourbridge clunch in the manufacture of the crucibles used for melting metals. With the exception, perhaps, of the above-named partial use of this substance in the formation of furnace pots, it contains too small a portion of alumina — the pure potter's earth — and too much silex {silica}, by reason of the fusion of which vessels melt at an intense heat, to render it a substitute for the Staffordshire clay, which is used in considerable quantities in Sheffield. The yellow clays which abound so much in the neighbourhood of Sheffield, and which are so valuable in an economical point of view, owe their peculiar colour to the presence of oxide of iron in the form of ochre: this also gives the red appearance to the bricks when burnt: the readiness with which this clay yields to vitrification, may frequently be witnessed when the kilns have been accidentally overheated.

No. XXVIII. — SHEFFIELD — RETROSPECT OF LOCAL CHANGES.

July 9th, 1836.

"Where far around the dwellings stand
Of those who own his ruling hand,
Arise on high the rampart-walls
Of mighty Talbot's native halls, —
Proud as the chief for whom they swell,
And, as his arm, invincible."

ROYAL EXILE.
{(1822) by Mary Roberts (1788–1864),
daughter of Samuel Roberts (1763–1848),
cutler, author and pamphleteer }

START not, gentle reader, at any self-conceived notion that, having escaped from the mud, the clay, and the morass amidst which we beheld the waters of the Don making their way in the last chapter, the tourist is about to dive deeply or formally into the annals of Sheffield, either historically, topographically, or biographically — that were, indeed, an onerous, as well as an here-out-of-place undertaking. On the other hand, the banks of the Don at this place are too redolent of past times, too crowded with passing associations, not to compel an individual who has traced the great river of the district from its fountain source in the moors, to the most important town on its banks — and his own native spot — to linger awhile for congratulation, reflection, or review.

And, after all, say what the worst part of the world will on the subject, there is in human nature — at least as that nature as developed in this country, indeed, in persons of British descent generally, an instinctive hankering of curiosity after, and a respect for almost every thing that has either been long familiar to ourselves, or that remains as the memento of times antecedent to our own. Laugh at the Antiquary's pursuits as he may, almost every "true-born Englishman", who has not reduced himself to a mere money-getting machine, or been reduced almost as low as that by indigence, has a spice of the Antiquary in his nature. The man, says a pleasing author, who can miss with indifference even stocks and stones, with which he has been familiar for thirty or forty years, must have become a stock or stone himself. A determination to retain his rightful possessions, or the wish to plant or bring to maturity noble institutions, may nerve with valour the settler in a new country — but patriotism must have an historic connection with the soil: it looks forward to the happiness of future — but backward also to the glory of past generations — "Pro patriae" would be an absurd motto for the shield of a cosmopolitic warrior. He bears no English heart, to whom the history of his country is a dead letter. And surely, the individual who, living, amidst the changes of a great and growing town, feels no anxiety to learn something of its past history — no veneration for its time-honoured monuments, must be made of strange stuff indeed. This innate sentiment of respect for objects which the lapse of ages has in a manner hallowed by historic or other associations, is not remotely akin to some of the purest forms of patriotism: in some cases, indeed, its prevalence is remarkably exemplified in spite of strong political bias, or professions of indifference. What numbers of individuals, for example, are constantly coming over hither from the United States — not with commercial objects merely, nor to exchange courtesies with their friends, — but because the "Old Country" is rich in memorials of past times, transcendently rich in records of valour, learning, piety, and skill — in short, an intelligent American most commonly visits England pretty much for the same reason that a student goes to Oxford or Cambridge, namely, to "obtain a degree" which shall stand him in stead another day. Not a few of these transatlantic graduates extend their visits to the continent; and only a few days ago, I met with two most intelligent — I will not say, unsentimental, republican tourists, whose travelling trunks were each a sort of reliquary, so full were they of fragments of lava from Vesuvius, of pottery from Pompeii, of marble from Florence — all queer things, methought, to gratify Philadelphian tastes! But we are on the banks of the Don, and must cross the river by "The Lady's Bridge" {SK357877}. The very name of this structure transports the imagination into those mysterious times, of which it is, perhaps, impossible now to form a true estimate. The old bridge, at the foot of which stood a chapel of "Our Ladye", has long since been removed; it was built toward the latter end of the fifteenth century, at which period we find

> "Sir John Pleausance, vicar of Sheffield, and William Hill, of the same, maister mason", bargaining "for the making of a

brygge of stone over the watyr of Dune, nighe the castell of
Sheffield, well and sufficiently; the whych shall be made V
arches embowed, IIII jowels and II heedys, with sure
butments at eyther ende, and shall have for the making of it a
C. marks." {Hunter, Hallamshire, 1819, p193}

Where must we now look for foundation, or trace of the house of that
illustrious Saxon Thane, who, previous to the conquest, owned that
ample district of which Sheffield, in after ages, became the capital?
Its very locality is forgotton. "And yet", says Hunter, *"somewhere*
within the manor of Hallam, Earl Waltheof, had his aula." How
precious to the antiquary must have been a single brick of direct
evidence on this point, will be apparent to any one who examines the
long passage in the "Hallamshire", where the author endeavours to
fix the site of the *aula* mentioned under *Hallun,* in doomsday book.
The learned ingenuity, by which a few remote allusions are, in Mr.
Hunter's work above-named, made to bear in favour of fixing upon
the present Hallam as the site in question, is less admirable than the
frankness with which, in a later work, that gentleman seems to have
surrendered that elaborate hypothesis, in favour of the naked
probability that, after all, the mansion of Earl Waltheof — whatever
its character, may have stood where, ages afterwards, the massive
and more stable structure of the Furnivals reared its towers; in that
well-selected, if not absolutely

> "———— Safe retreat,
> Where the gay Sheafs clear waters meet
> The sober Don; — in after time,
> 'Twas there the castle rose sublime,
> And on the wild adjacent ground,
> The walls of Sheffield spread around."

ROYAL EXILE.

The latter pile, solid as were its materials, has been swept from the
face of the earth as effectually as the former: its site, however, is
well known; its foundation, embattlement, sieges, and demolition
are matters of history. To rebuild, even in imagination, Sheffield
Castle {~SK357876} — to recal to life, and exhibit in action, though
but on paper, the splendid line of Hallamshire Lords — to give body
and pressure and visibility to actors and actions of which the records
certainly do exist, would require a volume rather than a chapter —

would demand the genius of a giant in literature, rather than the timid approaches of a pen like mine — yea, would ask, what has happily been found, an historian with the taste and the talents of Mr. Hunter. But while it would be preposterous to aim at displaying any such breadth of canvas or depth of colouring as these remarks presuppose, it will not be difficult to sketch a few vignettes which may represent, in some measure, the progressive changes which the town has undergone. It would, to be sure, have been, in the estimation of many persons, a splendid enhancement of the local attractions of a town not remarkable for its antiquities, had the noble Castle, so richly associated with the Lovetots, the Furnivals, and the Talbots, been suffered to remain in its perfect state. Next to this, gratifying would it have been to thousands, had the "sleighting" of this strong building, been left beyond a certain point to the hand of Time: we might then, at least, have had a picturesque object in the ruins — and if the Castle-hill had been less usefully appropriated than at present, the mind would have dwelt upon the mouldering walls and moss-grown turrets which had witnessed so many remarkable transactions, with an interest widely different from that excited by the buildings which now occupy the site. So completely, however, has the Castle been demolished and supplanted, that, as already intimated, there remains not a vestige of ancient masonry to gratify the research of the curious explorer: and what is still more remarkable, I believe there is not known to be in existence any pictorial representation of Sheffield Castle, any more than of the entire Manor House in the Park, notwithstanding the interest that must three centuries ago have attached to both spots in connection with the Queen of Scots, and various other circumstances.

Let the reader imagine, if he can, the state of the town in the thirteenth and fourteenth centuries, when Sheffield began to be noted for its manufactures in iron, — especially falchion heads {falchion — a one-handed, single-edged sword}, arrow piles, and "an ordinary sort of knives called whittles". The Church would occupy its present position on the commanding eminence so wisely chosen for its site. To the munificence and piety of the Lovetots, who were Lords of Hallamshire in the reign of Henry II., we owe the erection of a parish church {now the Cathedral, SK353875}: nor is this the only good work for which the people of Sheffield have had cause to honour the name of that house. But as the rhyming monk of Worksop says of the Furnivals —

> "To report the good deedes, that they did to us
> Right long time and space they wold have; I write
> Bot in special: reward them our Lord Jesus
> Progenetours and successours, and in heaven them quyte."

Various crosses stood in different spots; about one of them, no doubt the market was anciently held. In the earliest periods of their history, one or other of these crosses may have witnessed processions, penances, preachings, proclamations, and what not: doubtless, during the interregnum, the market-cross of Sheffield, like that in other towns, would be the rostrum whence banns of marriage would be published, preparatory to the union of the individuals before a justice of the peace. Judging from the tone of certain parties, there are not wanting those who would be glad to see the practice of 1656 in the *non-solemn*-ization of matrimony again enforced! The name of "Townhead-cross" {~SK352874, no 18 on Gosling's map, 1736, removed ?1736}, is still occasionally heard, as applied to the site of an object no longer seen: there may be persons still living who recollect the successor of the old Market-cross {?the Market Place, ~SK356874} — though I do not: while the shaft of the "Irish Cross" — why an *Irish* cross in Sheffield? — having been removed from its original situation at the top of Snighill {SK356876, no 17 on Gosling's map, 1736, removed ?1792}, is still standing, though in miserable plight, in Paradise-square {SK353875}. Was this cross originally set up out of compliment to the sister island, by "Gilbert Earl of Shrewsbury, Washford, and Waterford, High Seneschal of Ireland", to quote the inscription on his coffin?

How mean, scattered, and insignificant would be, at that time, as we may reasonably presume, the dwellings and the workshops of the population.

> "A few straggling huts and smithies, forming an irregular street, extending from the castle and bridge to the Church-gate, (for the Church at that time existed {SK353874}), with a few houses lying toward the Town Mill {at Millsands SK355878, demolished 1939}; and perhaps a branch extending in a south-west direction, forming what is now called Fargate {SK354873}, in respect of its distance from the castle, seem to have formed the whole town of Sheffield."

That the articles manufactured at this early period were really of iron, the produce of local ores and smelting, seems hardly to admit of a doubt. Deeply buried collections of the slag or scoria produced by these operations, and supposed to indicate the situations of ancient bloomaries, occur in many places in the neighbourhood. In what style the manufactures were finished, and also whether the artisans had begun to avail themselves of the water-wheel for grinding them, are questions by no means so easy to decide. It is more than probable that the ingenuity of the Sheffield workmen, at an early period, greatly improved the quality and form of the articles, for the manufacture of which they had become famous; for it is remarked by historians of the battle of Bosworth Field, that unusually large arrows were used — that the pile-heads were bigger, well pointed with steel, and hardened — the backs were sharper, being ground in flutes, and much better polished than heretofore. Improvement in trade would bring increase of means; and while one portion of the men of Hallamshire would be sharing the fortunes of their superiors in wars at home or abroad, the rest were, no doubt, engaged in the local handicrafts.

At this time, the houses were probably constructed, for the most part, of timber; the lower spaces filled up, it may be, with stones and mortar, the upper parts connected by that description of wood-work called stoothing, the whole being finally plastered and thatched. Building-stone and slate, however, being obviously plentiful, the Sheffielders seem at an early period to have adopted these more durable materials in the erection and covering of their dwellings — long retaining, however, more or less of the massive frame-work, of which curious specimens remain to this day. The taste never appears largely to have prevailed for the construction of those more elaborate specimens of architectural carpentry which we meet with elsewhere, especially in and about Manchester — "calimanco houses" {variant of calamanco – a woolen fabric with striped or checkered designs}., as they have been called, and of which we have specimens at Norton Lees and at Carbrook — to which may be added, though less striking, the old castle laundry in the Ponds {now the Old Queen's Head pub, SK358872}.

Underlaid as the site of the town was by a rich bed of clay, which must have presented itself to the casual excavator thousands of times before the year 1696, yet the late Rev. Edward Goodwin preserved a tradition, that about that time was built, in Pepper-alley {now Surrey

Street SK354872}, the first brick house in Sheffield — a fabric which, although not large, was, it is said, viewed by the inhabitants with wonder and ridicule, they supposing it to be built of such perishable materials, that it must soon yield to destruction. The building in question is still standing.

That the house alluded to might be built in some new manner, as to the application of the materials, or even be the first in which bricks were used, to the entire exclusion of stone or timber in the walls, is possible: bricks, however, must have been known at a much earlier period, as of them the gate-towers of the Manor Lodge were mainly built, and in the foundations of which they are still conspicuous. Be that, however, as it may, from the latter end of the seventeenth century, the buildings began, and have continued, to be erected generally of a dark red brick. While this is the common building material in Sheffield as in Birmingham, the former town strikingly differs from the latter in this, that the houses have neither tiled roofs nor brick floors, an abundance of cheap slate and flag-stones interfering to prevent us from making our dwellings entirely of earthenware.

No. XXIX. — SHEFFIELD — JAMES MONTGOMERY.

July 16th, 1836.

— "Hither from my native clime
The hand that leads Orion forth,
And wheels Arcturus round the north,
Brought me in life's exulting prime:
— Blest be that hand! — Whether it shed
Mercies or Judgments on my head,
Extend the sceptre or exalt the rod —
Blest be that hand! — It is the hand of God."

DEPARTED DAYS. {by James Montgomery (1771-1854}

On the 12th of December, 1822, a public meeting was held at the Cutlers' Hall, for the purpose of establishing a Literary and Philosophical Society in Sheffield, on which occasion, the highly-gifted and excellent individual whose name I have presumed to write at the head of this chapter, delivered a speech which can never be forgotten by those who heard it. One of the most striking features of this elegant and appropriate address was its allusion to "four Hallamshire Worthies", as the parties have since been called. After mentioning the nations, the arts, and the literature of antiquity, and adverting to the contrast between the middle ages and our own, Mr. Montgomery said —

> "I have never pretended, nor could I be guilty of such sophistry and falsehood as to insinuate that Sheffield can boast of poets, historians, and philosophers to rival those of Greece and Rome; yet I am prepared to shew, that, within the present generation, this humble corner of the kingdom has given birth to four men, each of whom may be placed in the first rank of Britons in their respective professions, whether science, literature, or the fine arts, — the late Mr. Jonathan Salt, in botany; Mr. Chas. Sylvester, in experimental philosophy; the Rev. Joseph Hunter, in antiquities; and last and greatest of all, Mr. Francis Chantrey, in sculpture."

To these names would, doubtless, have been added that of Mr. Montgomery — had any other than the poet himself been the speaker on the occasion.

James Montgomery — *the* Montgomery, as contradistinguished from a person who latterly enjoyed a certain kind of celebrity as a versifier, originating mainly in a curious species of confusion, created, and for a time kept up, by the identity of surnames — Montgomery The Poet, although not a native, has so long been a resident in Sheffield, and during that long period has become so intimately identified with almost every local affair of importance, that his name stands — and ever ought to stand, first and foremost among those that have done honour to the town.

To tell the lover of his country — the hater of political strife and falsehood, that Montgomery for many years published a newspaper, in the management of which he constantly and conscientiously acted up to its conciliatory motto —

> "Ours are the plans of fair delightful Peace,
> Unwarped by party rage, to live like brothers",

were unnecessary: to enumerate the poetical productions of Montgomery would be a still more uncalled-for task — thanks to the beloved bard, that he has just now given to the public those productions in such an entire, compact, and available form! May I not add, — that, not to have read, and having read, not to admire these poems, would argue, in the case of the individual, who could make such an admission, an entire absence of taste and feeling — or at least, a most circumscribed acquaintance with the purest and most delicate examples of metrical achievement?

To deem it necessary to describe Montgomery's fervent, sincere, and effectual advocacy of some of the noblest institutions which have been set on foot of late years, for the propagation of Christian truth as established in the Gospel of Jesus Christ, would be to suppose that there could be many persons greatly interested in these matters, who had never listened with delight to the outpourings of the very soul of the "Christian Poet", at Bible Society or Missionary Meetings: to state that Montgomery's benevolent exertions are not confined to his pen or to his tongue — freely, and ably, and willingly as these are always accorded — might indeed be necessary toward those who may not have examined the various reports of charitable associations in Sheffield, and the private books of those that publish no reports — to most others, his liberality is as well known as his kindness; and often must this feature of his character have been either unfeelingly or thoughtlessly taxed: last and least of all, need it be averred to any one who ever saw, or heard the name of Montgomery, that for his piety, his talents, and his truly benevolent disposition, he is as much and sincerely beloved by those who know him personally, as he is universally admired by those who are only acquainted with him through his works.

Although by what my Lord Morpeth has called the "accident of birth", Sheffield, as already mentioned, is prevented from reckoning Montgomery among her natural children, his voluntary residence among her population for so long a period has constituted even a stronger relationship, happily and gratefully recognised on both sides; nor — to say nothing of local obligations on every-day grounds — is it small honour to Hallamshire to have been the soil from which has sprung such various, such beautiful, such fragrant flowers of poesy! Could I, a sensitive rambler on the banks of the Don, be expected to pass without notice, or recal with brief and hasty indifference, the fact, that *here* patriot sympathy was claimed for the "Wanderer of Switzerland", when driven by the scourge of Europe from his native mountains; — that *here* Britain's long-delayed, but finally glorious act of justice to the "West Indies", was worthily celebrated; — that *here* was indulged and declared that glorious vision of the "World before the Flood", the master effort of Montgomery's muse; — that *here* was revealed in the song of "Greenland", one of the most remarkable, and perhaps also one of the most successful, modern examples of Missionary devotion which Christendom has witnessed; — that *here* was shadowed forth in the history of a "Pelican Island", an exquisite parable of creation, providence, redemption, commencing with a description of one of the most marvellous exhibitions of formative Nature to be met with in the world; — yea, that *here* hath been most richly displayed in "Songs of Zion", those abilities, which "are the inspired gift of God, rarely bestowed; and are of power to inbreed and cherish in a great people the seeds of virtue and public civility; to allay the perturbations of the mind, and set the affections in right tune; to celebrate, in glorious and lofty hymns, the throne and equipage of God's almightiness, and what he works and what he suffers to be wrought with high providence in his church." I envy not the man who cares for none of these things.

It is a very natural, not to say laudible curiosity, which prompts the desire to obtain a sight of individuals in any way remarkably distinguished from mankind in general. And, perhaps, the gratification of this desire, is in no case more frequently indulged at the expense of its object, than when it fixes on the man of literature — may it not be added — the poet. In hundreds of instances has the question been put, by strangers visiting Sheffield, "Where does Montgomery live?" — "Oh, with the Misses Gales, in the Hartshead — it is a large bookseller's shop — you will readily find it", would often be the reply. Away started the querist: easily found the shop, entered, and after purchasing some trifling article of stationery, returned, as might be expected, *without* seeing Montgomery; sometimes, indeed, the interloper was more lucky — the bard was seen to flit from one door to the other, or perhaps have come down into the shop, to speak with a caller there, on some matter of business. The more desperate, or regularly introduced individuals of the class alluded to, of course, mostly found their way into "the presence", and were, probably, in nearly all cases, gratified in the proportion that they were entitled to purchase gratification at the expense of time so precious as that of the poet must always have been. Those who have been disappointed in getting a peep at the poet in *propria persona,* have generally been gratified by a sight of the fine full length portrait of him by Barber, now in the Museum of the Philosophical Society, at the Music Hall {a head and shoulders portrait by Barber is in the collection of Museums Sheffield.}. Why have we no *bust* of Montgomery by Sheffield's own sculptor, Chantrey? I say *Sheffield's* own sculptor, because, although the *man* was not born in that town, the *artist* was. The poet has done honour to the statuary in song — would that the latter had returned the compliment in marble! But, at all events, let Sheffield secure while it may this bust, lest to the regrets of posterity be *some time* added the self-upbraidings of Montgomery's local contemporaries.

The works which have gained for their author the reputation of a poet of the highest order, were all written in the Hartshead, which is nearly in the centre of the town of Sheffield; and almost one of the last spots which, judging from appearances round about, a poet might have been expected to select for his residence; but the truth was, he had, in the first place, properly speaking, no choice in the matter; and being once fixed, and long fixed, a sort of strong local attachment, added to some other causes, seemed sufficient to have tethered him for about forty years to a residence which may appear to others the reverse of interesting. The little upper room behind, in which it is understood his in-door cogitations were mostly indulged, and his writing done, must at all times have looked only upon filthy back yards, black brick walls, shelving roofs, and a grotesque array of red chimney-pots; whether, amidst such a cluster of substantial obstacles to the common day light, its richer display in the form of bright sunshine, ever penetrated the sanctum of the bard, does not appear; the *disagremens* in question, it is probable, however, were rarely, if at all noticed, by one, who looked much into the fields, more into his own soul, and not at all out of his study window for themes and inspiration.

But while thus located in the midst of a large town, mingling in its affairs municipal and benevolent, and not seldom taking a very prominent part in them too, Montgomery was an intense lover of the country: often has he sung its delights, and drawn his similies from its appearances: and never, save when breathed upon by the spirit of Religion, have the warblings of his lyre found more exquisite responses from the hearts of its admirers, than when it has been tuned to the simple music of nature — animate or inanimate.

Whether the elegant apostrophe to "Twilight", which occurs in the "World before the Flood", was composed by the poet while lingering at the close of some sweet summer's day through Endcliffe Wood, where Montgomery might sometimes have been met in past years, or whether studied in his little garden-house at Leavy Greave, or caught in that least likely of all spots, the Hartshead, — certain it is, that Javan's "Address to Twilight" is but a transcript of the author's own feelings. To take an example in prose: —

> "He who retires, as I have often done, on a bright summer evening, into the depth of one of our Hallamshire woods, while he saunters along in the dream-like repose of a brown study, or leans against an old oak in the fine abstraction of severer thought, might imagine himself alone and in silence, merely because his eye and his ear were *unobservant* of motions and murmurs perceptible on every hand. But were he to pause at one of those cheerful openings, where, from a small patch of ground, beneath a hand-breadth of blue sky, in a little amphitheatre of trees, the great world seems hermetically excluded, he would soon find himself in the very

midst of the joy and activity, the labour, fatigue, and anxiety of life. At first, the dazzling dance of insects in the sunshine, and their musical drone in the shade, might surprise him into a feeling of sympathetic delight; but the flitting forms and richer melody of birds would quickly charm away his attention, to hearken to the sweetest inarticulate tones in creation. If he were not startled from this entrancemont by a shrew-mouse suddenly running across his foot, or the glittering undulations of a snake among the withered leaves across his pathway, his eye would be unconsciously drawn off, and carried out of the forest, by discovering green glimpses of adjacent fields, and shining tracks of the river — here, a spire of one of the churches, there, the tower of another; clusters of house-tops; steam-engine chimneys, like obelisks; and distant hills, cultivated or barren, — through the loop-holes of intermingling boughs and broken foliage around him. Presently, voices and sounds of all kinds would assail him, rising in Babylonish confusion from the populous valleys and village-crowned eminences; but gradually distinguished, if his ear nicely perused them, through their innumerable varieties, harmonious and dissonant, loud and low, mournful and lively — the rustling of winds among the leaves, the gush of waters down the weir, the barking of dogs, the crowing of cocks, the cries of children, the chimes of the church clock, or the knell of a death-bell — a gun, a drum, a bugle-horn, a flourish of trumpets from the barracks, the whistling of carters, the rumbling of carriages, the ringing of anvils, the reverberating thumps of tilt-hammers — with an indistinct, but deep, perpetual, under-sound, like a running bass, composed of all those blended noises, covering the whole, and constituting the 'busy hum of men' thronging the streets of the town below, or travelling on the numerous high roads branching from it. These would form altogether a concert inexpressibly captivating, by the associations which they would awaken in the mind of him who could listen to them as *one of the millions of sentient beings,* whether brute or intelligent, that inhabit the little locality, exquisitely picturesque, and genuinely English, within the precincts of Sheffield. Though in solitude himself, his delight would not be solitary, but social in the highest and purest degree.

> Though not a living creature within the circuit of the horizon
> were thinking of him at that moment, he would be thinking of
> *them,* of them *all,* and *all together.* His joy would be a
> mysterious sympathy with all their joys, an ineffable interest
> in all their occupations, and a cordial good will to every thing
> that lived, and moved, and breathed within his *sensorium."*

Gentle reader, with whom, at this moment, "unseen, unknown", spirit
to spirit, I am colloquising, carest thou for the topic before us? —
lovest thou the country — the banks of the Don? Go forth on one of
these fine summer evenings, into the Old Park Wood, to which
reference has been repeatedly made, and there test the impressions,
and try the *locality* of the foregoing passage. It was published some
five years ago, and is introductory to a beautiful essay, entitled,
"Home, Country, all the World".

Although Mr. Montgomery has, with admirable judgment, forborne
generally to impress the imperishable productions of his muse with
the "image and superscription" of Hallamshire, there are numberless
spots in the neighbourhood of Sheffield, which his friends know to
be identified with his various compositions in prose and verse.
Several examples of the former have already been referred to the
banks of the Don: it will be appropriate now to mention one of the
latter. In the month of June, 1818, a party from Sheffield, including
Mr. Montgomery, the Rev. T. Best, the late Rev. T. Cotterill, and
others, "friends young and old, of either sex", made an excursion to
Wharncliffe. It was a glorious afternoon, long to be remembered, on
more accounts than one. Well, the nearer portions of the road having
been passed in company, it was deemed expedient to separate at
Oughtibridge: the ladies proceeded toward the Lodge by the regular
carriage road up the hill, while the gentlemen preferred to cross the
river by the *leapings* opposite to Wharncliffe Holme, formerly
described. It so happened that timidity, slipperiness, and the jolly
stream had met at the same spot, and exactly at the same moment
with the discreet personages aforesaid: the latter, however, after
mutual admonition, — in cautious and seemly file, proceeded to pass
the treacherous traject — presently, plump into the water stumbled in
succession, the two Clergymen! Anon, the poet, apparently not
deeming it decorous to start back from such orthodox example,
started beside it, and — plash! — there were all three sousing most
delightfully in the clear current of my companion river! —

Differing from the lad who, having swam to the middle of the mill-pond, swam back again, on account of the distance to the farther side – our plungers had the sagacity to emerge on the Wharncliffe side of the Don; their tempers, at all events, nothing ruffled by the intromersion of their legs — for, gentle reader, I must add, or at least intimate, that none of the party got overhead. Well, up the wood they clomb, and on gaining the summit, they soon forgot the trivial discomfiture of their persons, by witnessing from the "drive", one of the most gorgeous displays of many-coloured clouds which was perhaps ever noticed, even from this region of glorious sun-sets. — Once in an age, it may be, such colours and such combinations are seen and admired — not more than once in a thousand years (if we may judge from the lack of evidence), do such scenes find fitting record in song — the occasion here adverted to formed one of these instances; for in his exquisite lines entitled "The Little Cloud", Montgomery has depicted in glowing poesy the celestial beauty of that entrancing apparition.

> "The summer sun was in the west,
> Yet far above his evening rest;
> A thousand clouds in air display'd
> Their floating isles of light and shade,
> The sky, like ocean's channels, seen
> In long meand'ring streaks between.
> — One little cloud, and only one,
> Seemed the pure offspring of the sun,
> Flung from his orb to shew us here
> What clouds adorn *his* hemisphere;
> Unmoved, unchanging, in the gale,
> That bore the rest o'er hill and dale,
> Whose shadowy shapes, with lights around,
> Like living motions swept the ground.
> This little cloud, and this alone,
> Long in the highest ether shone;
> Gay as a warrior's banner spread,
> Its sunward margin ruby red,
> Green, purple, gold, and every hue,
> That glitters in the morning dew,
> Or glows along the rainbow's form,
> — The apparition of the storm.
> Deep in its bosom, diamond bright,

Behind a fleece of pearly white,
It seemed a secret glory dwelt,
Whose presence while unseen was felt;
Like Beauty's eye in slumber hid
Beneath a half-transparent lid,
From whence a sound, a touch, a breath,
Might startle it, — as life from death.
 — The day on which that cloud appear'd,
Exhilarating scenes endeared;
And made it in a thousand ways,
A day among a thousand days,
That share with clouds the common lot;
They come, — they go, — they are forgot:
This, like that plaything of the sun,
 — The little, lovely, lonely one,
This lives within me; — this shall be
A part of my eternity."

The foregoing are only detached lines of the exquisite poem in question — let the reader take down his own copy of the volume in which it occurs, and enjoy the piece in its integrity. And here I must conclude this rambling notice, congratulating the poet on his escape from the smoke, the din, the bustle, and the interruptions of a town residence, and wishing him health, happiness, and long life at his beautiful retreat at "The Mount" {Broomhill SK334867} — one of the most delightful of the numerous villas which gem the western precincts of the comfortable town of Sheffield.

No. XXX. — SHEFFIELD — RETROSPECT OF LOCAL CHANGES.

July 23rd, 1836.

"How many things hath time broke down to dust;
    How many piece-meal hath he swept away!
Age eats into the core of trees, and rust
    Gives brass and iron up to sure decay:
As men go to the grave, so surely must
    Their works — their very monuments have end:
But oft the tomb, the eulogy, the bust,
    Remain; while mansions go — while towers descend,
And ruins, heap with heap, half-buried blend."

ANON

THE changes alluded to in the foregoing lines, have largely taken place in and about Sheffield: perhaps the spot of all others in which a person finds himself surrounded with the most palpable evidences of the *genius loci* in connection with "the good old town", and times long gone by, is the chancel of the Parish Church. Here, the meddlesome hand of the utilitarian churchwarden, under the guise of "beautification" and "repairs", has not completed the list of ravages said to have taken place during the civil wars, when the church was gutted, and the painted windows demolished, by an insolent soldiery. Look at that gothic screen of heart of oak, enclosing the Shrewsbury Chapel — enter within the sanctuary, or peep through the rails — there lies, chisseled in alabaster, the effigy of the founder of this Chapel — George, the fourth Earl, between the full length figures of his two Countesses, each with clasped hands, "uplifted on the breast, in attitude of prayer —

    As though they did intend
    For past omissions to atone,
    By saying endless prayers in stone."

There too, under a most ample inscription, lies on a sarcophagus, the sculptured figure of another Shrewsbury — George, the sixth Earl, the whole recently painted and gilt anew; the features of that marble countenance are not ideal; doubtlessly they resemble those of the loyal subject to whom his sovereign, Elizabeth, entrusted the custody of a rival queen: —

> "When she by seventeen yeares abode with this great peer,
> Untill against her realme to worke she did conspire
> Great things; whereof by Lords thrice ten and six of name,
> She tainted was at last and suffered for the same.
> So great a trust as this so long was never seene,
> A subject for to be a keeper of a Queene :
> To scape out of his hands by divers waiss she sought;
> But still he did prevent the ways that she had wrought:
> For wisely he did see what perill might have been
> If she had scapt away, to realm or eke to Queene:
> Wherefore he showed himself most careful for to be
> So great a charge to keepe with all fidelity.
> Whereby he hath preserved his name's so great renowne;
> The Talbot ever true and faithful to the crowne.
> But yet for all his wealth his honour and his fame,
> See, where he lies in earth from whence at first he came!"

{Dodsworth, quoted in Hunter's 'Hallamshire' (1819), p149.}

Just cast your eyes over the floor: how impressive is that pavement of gravestones — their inlaid brasses, their deeply cut inscriptions — dates, names, and style, all reminding one of the generations gone by! To a contemplative looker on, there is something affecting in the contrast between these mortuary records, and some of those lively scenes which are constantly witnessed here: the gaiety with which almost every morning in the week, the individuals of a wedding party commonly trip over the graves to the altar — the bustle which is witnessed upon them every Sunday afternoon, in the crowds of Christenings that may be seen approaching the font, seem, at first right, to present jarring anomalies in our association of ideas: and yet who would be willing that these processions of life and love, of hope and infancy, should be withdrawn from the venerable chancel, and none but the feet of those who carry a corpse to the burial be allowed to walk upon the gravestone floor? There stands a memorial of the "old religion;" in that three-celled oak settle near the vestry door, formerly sat the priest and his two assistants during the performance of mass. It has indeed been said that a laudable disinclination on the part of our worthy Vicar, to consent to the removal of this ancient fixture, prevented the Chancel of our Church, from receiving, in addition to Chantrey's "first bust", some more ample and splendid work from his chisel: the report may be unfounded; but whether or not, I cannot but respect the unwillingness of the clerical head of this parish hastily to disturb the venerable heir-loom in question, glad as I should be to see in its vicinity some other of the precious efforts in marble of the sculptor whose genius was first developed in this town. In the church-yard, silently eloquent as are its memorials of past generations, we must not linger.

It has already been mentioned, as somewhat remarkable, that there is not known to exist any pictorial representation, either of Sheffield Castle or of the Manor-house in the Park, as both buildings stood two centuries ago {John Harrison, Survey of the Manor of Sheffield, 1637, mentions them}. About one hundred years later, a person of the name of Oughtibridge engraved a view of Sheffield, taken from Pyebank {Burngreave ~SK 357886} {Thomas Oughtibridge, 1737}, . This print, which gives us an interesting glimpse of the general appearance of the town at that time, having been re-engraved a few years back, has become common. It presents one droll peculiarity: the houses are nearly all represented in this curious picture as being without chimneys! Nor is the appearance of the windows less quaint either in arrangement or situation, being almost invariably in threes in the gables of the buildings, the uniformity suggesting the idea of their having been put into the plate with a three-pointed punch. Whether our forefathers confined the consumption of coal — or wood — to their smithies, none of which may be indicated in the plate, or whether the smoke of their household fires was left to find its way out of the door, or, at all events, by some aperture in the roof, less prominently featural than our present pot-surmounted stacks, might, so far as the artist is concerned, be matter of surmise. In the picture is included St. Paul's Church {SK353871}, then recently built, with the exception of the upper story of the tower and the dome which were not added until nearly fifty years afterward {St Paul's Church was largely completed 1721, though not opened until 1740, the dome was added 1769. Church was closed in 1937 and demolished in 1938 to be replaced by St. Paul's Gardens, nicknamed the "Peace Gardens", marking the signing of the Munich Agreement. In 1985, the space was formally renamed the "Peace Gardens"}. The absence of these portions gives a curious effect to the pile in Oughtibridge's view. A very superior view of the town, as taken from the Park-hill {~SK364872}, was published in 1746, by two brothers of the name of Buck {Samuel and Nathaniel Buck, East Prospect of Sheffield, 1745}: this print, although much less common than the former, can scarcely be said to be rare. So much for the elevation of old Sheffield; now for its nearly contemporary ichnography.

Gosling's coarsely-engraved plan, which was first published exactly a century ago, and with copies of which — impressions from the original plate — the public have recently been presented, shows us what the town was as to extent and arrangement in 1736. Indeed the change which has taken place in those respects, during the last one hundred years, and especially during the latter half of that time, cannot have resembled any like period in the previous history of the place. At the date above given, the town was defined northerly by Bower Spring {SK352879 – notable now as the site of the remnants of a cementation furnace}, West-bar {~SK354877}, and the Millsands Goit {~SK355878}; while on the east side it barely extended to the Sheaf, the entire space between the back of the old Shrewsbury Hospital {~Broad Street, SK358875} and Simon Wheel {SK359878} being laid out in gardens — building in that populous suburb now called "the Park" having little more than rudimentally commenced. Towards the south, Balm-green {~Barker's Pool, SK352872} and New Church-street {SK354872} formed the limit, except that Coalpit-lane {~Cambridge Street, SK352871} extended to nearly its present length; while the space included within the triangle formed by drawing a line from St. Paul's Church {Peace Gardens, SK353871} (then partly built) to Claywood {~Cholera Monument, ~SK361860} in one direction, and to Jehu-lane {~Commercial Street, SK358874} in another, and also between the two last-named points, was almost wholly unbuilt. What is now Norfolk Street {SK355872} was a road, having on the north-west pleasant gardens, amidst which stood the two old meeting-houses; on the opposite, or south-east side, an ample, open, tree-scattered plot called Alsop Fields {~Hallam University}, reached to Pond-lane {~Pond Street, SK357872}. But, within this limited extent, there were large plots unbuilt upon, and several cultivated spaces, which are now densely covered with houses. On both sides of Workhouse-lane {~Paradise Street, SK353876} there were openings of these kinds: gardens occupied much of the space between the Quakers' Meeting-house {Hartshead, SK355875} and Angel-street {SK356875} — also between the old Haymarket {SK357875} and

Shude-hill {SK358874}. It is remarkable that in Gosling's plan, laid down "from an actual survey", the word "street" occurs only six times, the thoroughfares being for the most part "lanes", a suburban appellation that finds much less favour with our present population than it did with their ancestors. The increase of the town in every direction within the last century, will be rendered strikingly apparent by tracing, on Tayler's recent map {1832}, the outline and open parts of the plan of 1736.

One hundred years ago the Parish Church was the only one to which the inhabitants could resort, — if we except the old Hospital Chapel; now the town includes six well-filled Churches. Little more than one hundred years ago, the Dissenters had a single Chapel in the town; they have now six. One hundred years ago, the Methodists had no Chapel in Sheffield — they have now, including those of seceders, twelve. To these places of worship we have to add the Quakers' Meeting House {Hartshead SK355875} and the Catholic Chapel {Norfolk Row, SK354872} – twenty six buildings in all, of which only three at the most were in existence a century ago: of their architectural character this is no place to speak in detail; some of them, however, have claims to admiration for exterior appearance; and taken collectively, they have not less altered the general aspect of the town in a pictorial point of view, than they must be supposed to indicate a greatly changed condition of population and opinion. Striking, as to an old Sheffielder, could we imagine him to rise from the grave to take a peep at the town, would be the vast extension of its streets, and what he would call the *grandeur* of its public edifices, it is probable the appearance of such a number of tall chimneys would strike him as by no means the least confounding objects — to say nothing of the works to which they are attached. It is exactly fifty years since the first steam-engine grinding-wheel was erected on the east side of the Sheaf; there are now at least fifty engines at work in the town, which, rating their average power very low, namely, 35 horses — and some of them are 50, 60 and even 80 horse power! — would give an increase to our effective manufacturing agencies of at least the effort of 1750 horses!

It is now fifty years since that abominable nuisance, the old slaughter-houses {later the Market Place, ~SK356875}, which used to stand in the centre of the town, were removed to the site of the demolished Castle {~Castlegate, SK358877}, and the present

commodious shambles erected. Previously to that time, meat was
sold in miserable wooden stalls; while

> "— at the market-place head,
> Were the broad shallow tubs to sell oat-meal for bread."

The foregoing lines are quoted from an amusing description in
rhyme, of the improvements in the town, printed a few years since.
In allusion to the old name of Castle-street, our poetaster has the
following laughable passage: —

> "You remember the sinks in the *midst* of the streets;
> When the rain pours in torrents, each passenger greets
> His fellow, with 'what a wide channel is here!
> We all shall be drowned, I am greatly in fear,
> For lately two lovers were sat on a rail,
> On the edge of the sink, fondly telling their tale,
> When the flood washed them down in each other's embrace,
> For no longer the lovers could sit in that place,
> And hence True-love's Gutter the name that was given,
> Because by the flood these two lovers were driven.' "

{by James Wills, ?1827, also quoted in R. E. Leader, Sheffield in the
Eighteenth Century, 1901, p151. Truelove's Gutter was actually
named after its occupiers, the Trulove family.}

Sheffield, at a very early period, included within the range of its
streets, as well as possessed in its vicinity, a considerable number of
public wells, for the conservation of which various sums of money
were at different times expended, as appears by old accounts of the
Town Trustees and others. No record exists to show that any of
these springs were surmounted with architectural or other devices so
as to be rendered ornamental as well as useful; unless we may
except Broomhall Spring {at the junction of Gell St. and Wilkinson
St. SK344870}, the site of which was, until the present year,
preserved in Gell street, by the following inscription which was cut
upon a stone placed over the trough: —

> "1791, November 26th. Spring Garden Well. To the Public
> use, by the Rev. James Wilkinson, and Philip Gell, Esq.
> Freely take — Freely communicate — Thank God."

Owing to neglect, or other causes, many of these wells had become
lost to the town; but within the last few years, they have, in several

instances, been restored to the inhabitants, and cast-iron pumps erected over them, so that water in those situations is placed within the reach of all who will fetch it. There is something refreshing to the mind, especially at this season, to imagine how delightful would be the effect of a fountain playing in the Market Place! And why not realize the conception? Water might surely be had in plenty, and at no great expense, while the height from which it would descend would be exactly suitable for a *jet d'eau.*

A signal era of alteration and improvement, was that which resulted from the operation of the Police Act obtained in 1818. How picturesquely, until that period, projected over the streets the iron brackets on which the sign-boards swung! How boldly broad piles of door steps usurped the causeway! while scrapers projected beside almost every threshold, pretty much like fixed bayonets! These, and sundry other antiquated obstacles, were at once swept away, giving quite a new internal aspect to the town; while the whole was illuminated by the brilliant gas light which was contemporaneously introduced, and the withdrawal of which would produce a greater alteration in the general appearance of our streets, than would the absence of any other improvement of the last fifty years.

No. XXXI. — SHEFFIELD — SAMUEL BAILEY

July 23rd, 1836.

"I look'd around, beheld unbounded wealth,
And ample skill to give the body health;
Recorded knowledge of all ages past;
Experience dearly earn'd by labours vast:
But yet, from all these rich materials, none
Th' inductive code of moral truths had won :
Disease and penury oppress'd mankind,
And folly triumph'd o'er the prostrate mind."

REPROOF OF BRUTUS. {John Minter Morgan, 1830}

THIS gentleman, without having given his name to a single work, enjoys the reputation of having been the author of several, any of which might well entitle him to rank with those who have cultivated one of the highest species of investigation known to our literature — the abstract — the intellectual. By the *Edinburgh Review,* — to say nothing of inferior authorities, — Mr. Bailey has been pointed out and commended as the man whom, of all others, Sheffield ought to delight to honour. To him, as "The Bentham of Hallamshire", Elliott has dedicated his poem entitled, "Withered Wild Flowers". And assuredly, for acuteness of mind, gentlemanly deportment, and honourable character, the individual before us belongs to the first rank of his townspeople. Mr. Bailey is of a local stock, his father having been a respectable and successful merchant in the town. Our author himself, who has long been disengaged from mercantile pursuits, resides at Burn Greave, a pleasant villa, standing on a gentle rise north of Sheffield, and about a mile out of the town.

The works attributed to Mr. Bailey are: — "Essays, on the Formation and Publication of Opinions"; — on "Truth, Knowledge, Evidence, and Expectation"; — on "The Nature, Measure, and Causes of Value"; and "The Rationale of Political Representation"; with two or three more. As might be expected, the works bearing the foregoing titles are mainly devoted to discussions in the severer style of thought, on topics moral, political, and religious. The writer of this passing notice would have been happy could he have exonerated the character of these works from the charge of militation against sound doctrine. This, he is afraid, cannot be done. Previously to reading certain of these books, he was assured that, however pure the intentions of their author, the tendency of his sentiments must, if carried out, inevitably be to unsettle the foundations of social order, and to cut up divine revelation by the roots. It is neither possible nor desirable in this place to go largely into the merits of these questions, transcendantly important as they are. The transcription, however, of a few passages, will enable the reader to judge, with slight risk of mistake, whether our author's sentiments are to be regarded as falling within or without the bounds of orthodoxy. Perhaps the work that has obtained the largest measure of notice is that named first in the above enumeration. It is, indeed, most beautifully, tastefully, and ably written.

From his premises therein laid down, our author has deduced this startling doctrine — for startling surely it will appear to every Christian reader — namely,

> "that those states of the understanding which we term belief, doubt, and disbelief, inasmuch as they are not voluntary, nor the result of any exertion of the will, imply neither merit nor demerit in him who is the subject of them. Whatever be the state of a man's understanding with regard *to any possible proposition,* it is in a state of affection devoid equally of desert and culpability. The nature of an opinion cannot make it criminal. In relation to the same subject, one may believe, another doubt, and a third disbelieve, and all *with equal innocence.*"

> "If belief, doubt and disbelief are involuntary states of the understanding, which cannot be affected by the application of motives, and which can involve no moral merit or demerit, it follows, as a necessary consequence, that they do not fall within the province of legislation: that they are not proper subjects of rewards and punishments."

> "In contending that neither merit nor demerit can be imputed to any one for his opinions — we are advocating the innocence of the man, not the harmlessness of his views. Errors are by their nature injurious to society; and while he who really believes them ought to be regarded as perfectly free from culpability, every one who sees them in a different light is justified in endeavouring, by proper means, to lessen

> their influence; which is to be effected, not by the application of obloquy and punishment, but by addressing arguments to the understanding."

This portentous hypothesis of man's irresponsibility for his belief, is built on the presumption that there is such an accordance between truth, i.e. a sufficient evidence of physical or moral fact, and the mind or faculties of man, that the understanding acts independently of the will as to the admission or repulsion of opinions. To a question that might here be expected to present itself, as connected with revelation more particularly, our author replies: —

> "Although we have no absolute test of truth, yet we have faculties to discern it, and it is only by the unrestrained exercise of those faculties that we can hope to attain correct opinions."

> "The way, then, to obtain this result is to permit all to be said on a subject that can be said."

To shew how little religion has to hope, in the opinion of our author, from this unbridled spirit of free discussion — take the following significant passage: —

> "Nothing more, it is manifest, would be required for the destruction of error, than some fixed and immutable standard of truth, which could be at once appealed to, and be decisive of every controversy to the satisfaction of all mankind; but that no such standard exists, the slightest consideration will be sufficient to evince. If it be asserted that on points of religion the sacred writings are such a standard, it may be urged in reply, that this is only an apparent exception; for in the first place, we have no standard by which the authenticity of those writings can be determined beyond all liability to dispute; and in the second place, supposing we had a test of this nature, or that the authenticity of the Scriptures was too evident to admit of the least doubt from the most perverse understanding, yet we have no decisive standard of interpretation."

Few persons will mistake the import of the foregoing passages: the following is not less clearly significant. "Men of vulgar creeds", will not mistake its object, namely, to palliate the reproach of the dying scenes of such persons as Voltaire, Paine, and other polite infidels.

"In religion, the strong power of associations, in opposition to the convictions of the understanding, is peculiarly worthy of notice, especially in the case of changes from a superstitious to a more rational and liberal creed. The force of a man's education has perhaps long held him in bondage, and his whole feelings have become interwoven with the tenets of his sect. By the enlargement of his knowledge, however, he discovers his early opinions to be erroneous; different conclusions force themselves on his understanding, and his faith undergoes a radical alteration. Yet his former feelings still cling to his mind. A long time must often elapse before he can cast off the authority of his old prepossessions. It is not always that the mind can keep itself at a proper elevation for viewing such subjects in a clear light; and till it has acquired the power of retaining its vantage-ground, it may be reduced to its former state by the influences of vivid recollections, customary circumstances, general opinion, or any thing which may occasionally overpower its vigor, or dim its perspicuity. Thus men, who have rejected vulgar creeds in the days of health and prosperity, manfully opposing their clear and comprehensive views to prevailing superstitions, have sometimes exhibited the melancholy spectacle of again stooping to their shackles in the hour of sickness and at the approach of death; not because their understandings were convinced of error by any fresh light, but because they were unable to keep their rational conclusions steadily in view; because that intellectual strength, which repelled absurd dogmas, had sunk beneath the pressure of disease, or the fears of nature, and left the defenceless spirit to the predominance of early associations, and to the inroads of superstitious terror. Such men are re-plunged into their old prejudices, exactly in the same way as he, who has thrown off the superstitions of the nursery, is overpowered as he passes through a churchyard at midnight, by his infantile associations."

The last work attributed to Mr. Bailey's pen is entitled "The Rationale of Political Representation". Apart from the theories involved, this book may be praised as a model of purity of style, logical precision of argument, and a felicitous exhibition of views as clearly conceived in the mind as they are admirably pourtrayed with the pen. To this may be added the higher merit, that these pages may be read with profit and delight by all who wish to acquire distinct ideas on the important topic discussed, however they may dissent from the general political creed of the writer. The doctrines specifically advocated in this volume, are those generally understood among writers of a certain class by the term "Utilitarian": hence, Jeremy Bentham is the oracle most complacently quoted for authorities; the legislative arrangements of the United States most frequently adduced for illustration; while the subject of Religion is as carefully excluded from all interference or consideration *pro* or *con,* as if it had no existence. For the sake of those who may be uninitiated in the mysteries of what it has pleased a certain order of political economists to designate as "the greatest happiness theory", it may be added that the author of this "Rationale" would, in the first place, considerably diminish the number of members in the legislative body; — secondly, he advocates provincial legislatures, secret voting, and triennial elections; — thirdly, he would have Members of Parliament more advanced in life, than the law at present requires, as the earliest age at which they can be admitted; — in the fourth place, it is contended that representatives should be free from engagements of trade, business, or profession; — and lastly, he would resort to an ancient practice of making the office of Parliamentary representative a stipendiary one: this latter object, he supposes, might be attained at an expense not exceeding half a million sterling. Perhaps the feeblest and least becoming portion of the book is that in which the author affects jocularity on the subject of a property qualification being required in a member of Parliament; while the most amusing part is certainly one in which the essayist gravely sets forth and advocates the equality of female rights in the constitution of the electoral body!*

* The following passage, exhibiting as it does the staple of the advocacy alluded to in the text, is too curious to be omitted: —

"The specific ground urged in the case of women, is incompetency from ignorance. Though the female sex may be allowed, in all existing societies, to be on the whole inferior in intelligence to the men, yet the higher classes of females are superior in this respect to the lower classes of the males. Women, for instance, possessing £500 a-year, are generally superior in information to men of *£60* a-year, although not perhaps equal to men of £500. If this is a true statement, the obvious expedient is, not to exclude women, but to place their pecuniary qualification higher. Even the necessity of such a higher qualification may be doubted, inasmuch as in that peculiar intelligence which is requisite for a judicious choice of persons to fill public offices, females are in some respects greater proficients than men of the same station. Female tact, in the discrimination of at least certain qualities of character, is universally admitted: and it can scarcely be questioned, that such coadjutors would be highly useful in the selection of representatives, were their minds fully brought to bear on the merits of the candidates by their having a voice in the decision. With regard to any other disqualification under which the female sex may labour, if any exists, it has not hitherto been brought into discussion. The inconsistency of the exercise of a valuable political privilege with female delicacy will scarcely be alleged."

The quotation of half a dozen lines will let the reader at once and largely into Mr. Bailey's view of the object and province of Government: —

"When we recollect that in the main, the power of the State in its effects on human happiness is supplemental and preventive of evil, rather than primary and creative of good, we shall at once see, that nothing can be more unfounded than the large share which has been attributed to Governments in the prosperity of nations." —

The important question mooted in the foregoing lines, and upon which the dictum of our author is so strikingly at variance with general opinion and universal practice, is discussed in the work, but cannot be entered upon here.

When, after the passing of the Reform Bill, Sheffield became invested with the right of sending two Members to Parliament, one of the four banners that waved over the hustings, at the first general election, bore the name of Mr. Bailey. His political sentiments were cast in the most liberal mould; his partizans were many of them highly respectable, and for the most part ultra-Liberal; and yet, with these advantages, added to mental powers — not to say abstract senatorial qualifications — undoubtedly superior to any of his opponents, he was not only unsuccessful, but was perhaps the least popular candidate in the field.

His want of success was obviously ascribable to several causes: with a political creed so welcome and complacent towards the crowd, few persons appear less affable and approachable than Mr. Bailey. This peculiarity may be largely due to the logical severity of his studies; a circumstance in itself little calculated to render him a popular orator, or to allow him to assume those flexible attitudes, which may be right or wrong, but at all events are so important in electioneering strategies. Moreover, he derived no advantages from the reputation of piety, or the outpourings of benevolence. As a citizen, the character of Mr. Bailey is high and unsullied: and if we are to have legislation independent of religion, no man has a fairer claim to be safely entrusted with the representation of the borough in which he resides; and this admission is not flippantly but sincerely recorded: if, on the other hand, Christianity be, as an eminent jurist has affirmed that it is, part and parcel of the laws of England, and if, with especial reference to that glorious and distinguishing characteristic of our country, every religious individual is, as he should be, influenced by the sentiment, *nolumus leges Anglice mutare {"We do not wish the laws of England to be changed"},* — then have the electors of Sheffield hitherto acted wisely in refusing their Parliamentary influence to Mr. Bailey.

No. XXXII. — SHEFFIELD — POPULAR CHARACTERISTICS AND REMINISCENCES.

August 6th, 1836.

"Still on its march, unnoticed and unfelt.
Moves on our being: we do live and breathe
And we are gone. The spoiler heeds us not.
We have our spring-time and our rottenness;
And as we fall, another race succeeds,
To perish like ourselves. Meanwhile Nature smiles —
The seasons run their round — the sun fulfils
His annual course — and heaven and earth remain
Still changing, yet unchanged."

H. K. WHITE. {'Poem on Time'}

In the records of a town which has undergone the striking topographical and other local changes adverted to in preceding chapters, we should expect to find traces of social, moral, and intellectual vicissitude no less distinct, and, at the same time, still more interesting. And the fact is, Sheffield, on account of its inland situation, and perhaps equally so in consequence of the peculiarly localised nature of its manufactures, appears to have retained traces of primitive manners, habits, and dialect, much longer than many other large towns.

In the earliest periods of which history has preserved any notices, the inhabitants of that large undulating district now known as "Hallamshire", and of which, wherever may have stood the earliest "Aula", or residence of its Saxon lord, Sheffield has for centuries been the capital, — appear to have possessed, on the whole, characteristics in common with similar classes of the population in this part of the country generally. Rude, boisterous, athletic, and impatient of restraint, as the natives who dwelt on the banks of our picturesque rivers, must have been, from their earliest settlement, the spirit of the feudal system which so long and so influentially prevailed through all our institutions, social, civil, and religious, had no tendency to obliterate, however it might modify those traits in the ancestral character. And it is remarkable, how long the influence of hereditary habit survived, in many things the extinction of the causes in which it originated, or by which it was directly fostered. The greenwood exploits of Robin Hood and his band of outlaws, which tradition has identified with this neighbourhood, seemingly by the slender thread of coincident resemblance between the name of the river Loxley and one of the brave bowmen of the ballad, and the pranks of the avowedly fictitious characters in "Ivanhoe", which have given a character of romantic interest to the vicinity of the Rother, are at least in character with the men, and the circumstances of the ages to which the stories respectively belong; — as recreations, hawking, archery, and cudgel-playing, which occupied the leisure of our ancestors, were certainly more picturesque, and surely less brutal, though equally unprofitable pursuits, than the hare-hunting, pigeon-shooting, and pugilism which prevail in our own times. Of the predilections of the ancient inhabitants of this district for the royal pastime of falconry, we do not possess, that I am aware of, any specific records; though the state of the country and the tastes of the people leave little room for doubt as to its prevalence here, as well as elsewhere: of the early indulgence of a passion for bow-shooting the evidence is strikingly explicit. The level space, now called the Wicker {SK358879}, was the scene of the exercises of the local archers: here they were regularly and authoritatively trained — here stood the public butts upon which were fixed the targets: these trainings were, in part at least, maintained at the cost of the town trustees, they setting up, in 1571, the "nare butt and far butt".

The fair authoress of the "Royal Exile", has adverted to this spot, and its appropriation in former times to gymnastic exercises, in the following lines: — north of the castle,

> "The waters of the Don,
> To meet the humble Sheaf delighted run;
> Beyond the stream a wide spread level green,
> The mart of mirth and revelry is seen;
> There, from their neighbouring homes, with joy resort
> Old age and youth, to view or join the sport;
> And ere the twilight draws its curtain round
> The weary tribes are in the Wicker found.
> See, by the river side where willows grow,
> The archer train, with quiver, dart, and bow;
> There, fixed and silent, as each breath were fate,

The anxious candidates the signal wait;
Till one, advancing from the crowd apart,
To the strong bowstring fits the feathered dart, —
Upraises, points it to the mark, and then
Darts down its shaft his keen experienced ken;
Swift flies the arrow, as the voices swell,
The target pierces and dissolves the spell:
By turns advancing from the anxious band,
Another, and another, takes his stand,
Till each in turn his skill and prowess tries, —
All strive, but one alone receives the prize."

On the same ground also, during the sixteenth and part of the seventeenth centuries, the freeholders of Hallamshire were accustomed to assemble with horse and arms at the annual muster. Playing with the quarter-staff, a species of gruff exercise of which the author of Ivanhoe has exhibited a lively example in one of his scenes, when —

"With many a stiff thwack, many a bang,
Hard crabtree and old iron rang",

was early and long popular with a certain class of rustic bravos; indeed, some degree of proficiency in breaking heads, according to the rules of the game, was at one time deemed an accomplishment, entitling the possessor to something above what was regarded as mere vulgar distinction: so long did this hard-headed, hard-handed fancy exist, that persons are living who will recollect seeing a pair of cudgels lying outside the doors of certain houses or shops in this town, as an intimation that, if any passer by having mettle in him and disposed to make play, choose to take up one of the sticks, the owner, who was at hand, would be found free, able, and willing to assume the other!

Dodsworth has recorded a custom, the annual recurrence of which must have been hailed with no little delight by the sport-loving Sheffielders of the latter part of the sixteenth century. In the palmy state of Sheffield Park, its open glades and umbrageous coverts were enlivened by the presence of great herds of "deer of antler"; and, says our authority, the Earls of Shrewsbury,

"were wont on every yeare, on a certaine day, to have many bucks lodged in a meadow neare the towne side, about a mile in compass, to which place repaired almost all the apron-men of the parish, and had liberty to kill and carry away as many as they could with their hands."

A bustling scene this same buck catching would be, no doubt — one would like to see the subject happily illustrated by the pencil or the graver.

Let it not be imagined, however, that the Hallamshire Lords during the reigns of the Tudors, left the people who dwelt within the shadow of their castle to have it all their own way, and that the capture, incarceration, and execution of offenders, are modern innovations on the rights of society. In the olden time, Sheffield, in common with many other towns, could boast of a ducking-stool, pillory, public stocks, and, if we would believe tradition, a gallows also. The former instrument, a sort of chair, used for the ducking of scolding women, is frequently mentioned in the old town accounts; but where it stood does not appear, nor whether the discipline was administered in "*stinking water*", though this was the case in Saxon times; hence the chair was called *cathedra stercoris* {a "dung chair", which exposed the sitter's buttocks to onlookers}. Of the pillory, I know nothing: the stocks, that "wooden Bastile", were in existence, if not in use, until lately: this engine symbolised a state of society when vice, not having become quite insensible to shame, was sometimes capable of being looked out of countenance: ten to one, to place a modern drunkard or sabbath-breaker in the stocks, would be to make a sort of hero of him, in the estimation of lookers-on. An elevated situation, called "Gibbet-hill" {#}, a little west of the town, is the only ground * for a supposition that capital punishment was, at one time, inflicted here: relative to this locality, there exists a picturesque tradition — a culprit was suspended on the gibbet *alive,* and with a loaf just out of reach of his mouth; the man lived some time, and on inquiring the cause, it was found that a little girl — his own child perhaps — was in the habit of stealing off to the fatal tree, with a part of her meals, which she contrived to give to the malefactor, and by this means sustaining his life. Such is the story; it is sufficiently improbable; but one wonders it is not more so, considering how long it must have floated in the popular breath. Having alluded to engines of punishment, it may be added that Sheffield stands happily free from any very signal notice in the annals of crime, as well in ancient as in modern times. — I am sorry to be compelled to explain that this remark does not reach to murder, ordinarily considered.

{# Gibbet Hill is mentioned in Hunter's Hallamshire (1819), p196, but the location is unclear. R.E.Leader (in a lecture to Sheffield Lit. and Phil. Soc. in Feb 1906) suggests that it was at the highest point of the packhorse road over Lydgate (~SK324872).}

* It seems, however, there is good evidence to substantiate the claim of Sheffield to the distinction mooted in the text. In a communication to the Sheffield Mercury of August 13, signed "Antiquarius", but which betrays the discriminating hand of the author of "An Essay on the History of the Burgery of Sheffield", one of the most interesting local documents ever read before the Literary and Philosophical Society of this town {by Samuel Mitchell, 10th Oct 1828}, the friendly writer observes that the fact of a gallows having existed at Sheffield,

> "does NOT depend solely on tradition. The following translated extracts from the Court Rolls of Sheffield, will shew, that the Lords of the Manor claimed the right of gallows, and that there is little doubt of their having exercised that right. I give two instances, and probably others might be found on a more careful examination of the Rolls. The Lords certainly claimed this privilege before the reign of Edward I.

>> '8th July, 6 Henry VI. — John Kay, alias Botelar, of Shenston, Co. Stafford, was arrested at Sheffield, on suspicion of having stolen a mare, then in his possession. He, being brought before this Court, and having pleaded not guilty of the felony, the Bailiff proceeded to impanel twenty-four men of the Liberty, who, upon their oaths, found the said John Kay guilty of the said felony, The Bailiff, therefore ordered, that the said John Kay should be taken to the Gallows of the Liberty, (ad furcas libertatis) and should be hung by the neck; and that his goods should be forfeited to the Lord of the Manor.'

>> '10 Hen. VII. — John Dore being put on his trial, for the robbery and murder of one Fidler, was condemned to be hung by the neck until he should he dead.'

I can throw no light on the other 'picturesque tradition' about this gibbet, which your Correspondent mentions; I believe it

could scarcely have had other existence than in the glowing
imaginations of painters or poets.

I feel some doubt also, as to the Sheffield gallows having
ever been placed on Gibbet Hill; the fact of the site, as now
pointed out, being within the independent manor of Ecclesall,
seems to militate against such an opinion."

One of the most striking changes which time and circumstances have
effected in Sheffield, even within a century, is in the increase of
population: in 1736, the town contained 2,695 inhabitants; at
present {1836}, the number is estimated at little short of 100,000.
The extension of the town has already been noticed; connected with
this multiplication of houses, there is one peculiarity which must
materially and favourably affect the domestic character of the
inhabitants: every family, or nearly so, occupies a separate dwelling-
house — at all events, we have none of those vast tenemented piles,
imposing enough outside, but too frequently characterised by filth
and squalor within; it might, perhaps, be possible to find a miserable
family dwelling in a garret, but not in a cellar, I believe. Such an
arrangement as that which gives to every married man a house of his
own, must obviously be of immense advantage on the score of
comfort, cleanliness and health — and certainly I never saw the town
where these commendable traits are conspicuous in the labouring
classes to the same extent as in Sheffield.

The dialect of this place, whatever may be its claims to be considered
as distinct from that of the northern parts of the county generally, has
had the luck to receive the attention of three very independent
elucidators. The base or foundation of "this goodly column of our
local speech", is undoubtedly Hunter's "Hallamshire Glossary", a
learned and curious book, containing not the colloquial and vulgar
terms formerly in use, but such archaic words — venerable at least
from their antiquity, and often also for their authority — as were in
good use between the years 1790 and 1810, and many of which may
even still be heard occasionally. The shaft of this rich pillar of words
was carried up to a proportional height by the Rev. H. H. Piper, in a
most ingenious essay on the peculiarities of our pronunciation and
dialect, read before the Literary and Philosophical Society, in 1824:
it would be pleasant, had we space, to give a specimen or two from
the pages of this essay, as it would present the colloquial phraseology
of the bulk of our townspeople in its attic purity. The finishing work

of this dialectic pile — the elaborate corinthian capital of the column — consists of a series of conversations assumed to have taken place amongst certain grinders in "the wheel" or mill where they work. The "Shevvild Chap", who, during the last five years, has at intervals amused himself and others — and, perhaps, also *profited* one party — by the publication of these "Conversations "has often happily caught the idioms and the pronunciation of the least refined portion of the population — perhaps, however, he has, in some cases, for the sake of effect, Tim-Bobbinized the dialect into an exuberance of vulgarity, scarcely classical even "Uppa are Hull Arston". Assuredly a stranger, having only these printed evidences before him — namely, the archaisms of Hunter, the colloquialisms of Piper, and the vulgarisms of Bywater, might well anticipate the need of an interpreter, should his way lie through Sheffield; yet the fact is, we continue to make ourselves understood; nor, with the exception, perhaps, of the veriest Cockney, have visitors much reason to complain of our clipping or sweating the "King's English", beyond the general privilege of "Broad Yorkshire".

"A Shefeld thwytel bore he in his hose", says the father of English poetry, describing the Miller of Trompington. Whatever may have been the description of knife here designated by Chaucer a *whittle,* it probably differed no less in form and finish from the cutlery of the present day, than the dress and manners of the reign of Edward III. differed from those of William IV. The staple wares of Sheffield have attained to an extraordinary degree of perfection; nor is the variety of articles and patterns less surprising, especially to an old manufacturer who has watched the advance. Perhaps, however, no circumstance — not even the appearance of our immense manufactories — would so much astonish an old master cutler of the seventeenth century, could he revisit the banks of the Don, as the rapidity and extent of our travelling in search of orders. A tradesman, at the period alluded to, would probably have deemed it necessary to have made his will, pending a journey to London: his successor of the present day visits the metropolis with almost as little of anxious forethought as he goes to his warehouse; while a voyage to America, or a residence there, are undertakings talked of almost with indifference — one misses, or perhaps hardly misses, for a few weeks, some familiar face — again we recognise our acquaintance — he has just been across the vast Atlantic — spirit of Columbus! to interchange the courtesies of trade in New York, shake hands with the President of the United States, see the falls of Niagara; and here he is walking the streets again, as if merely to or from his dinner!

This is truly a locomotive, as well as a manufacturing age; and whereas, formerly, the man who travelled, was the wonder of his compeers, astonishment is now transferred to him who stays at home — and sometimes not without reason.

Remarkable as may be considered the stationary life of many whose want of means, or whose unremitted local avocations preclude their frequent or even occasional migration, this peculiarity of disposition is perhaps more striking, as one sometimes meets with it exemplified in persons who are not thus compulsorily tethered to the spot. I encountered a case the other day: an excellent individual, engaged in one of the most exquisite of the mechanical arts, had resolved to pay a visit to London: this journey, to one whose life had been so sedentary, was a matter of importance, and looking forward to it and contrasting therewith his past immobility, my friend remarked —

> "here have I been for years, quietly seated on this chair, while all has been in motion around me — persons have come in to say good-bye — they have gone to America — to the East Indies — to the South Seas — they have returned, and have found me still seated in the same spot: while I have sat here, Captain Ross has gone out to explore the arctic regions — been unheard of for years — and safely returned again — kings have died, and the bells of the church have rung their mournful peal — kings have been crowned and merry music has flowed from the same steeple; I still sat as at this moment: yea, the Catholic Emancipation Bill has passed — the Reform Bill has passed — France has been twice yea thrice revolutionized: some, whom I knew as children, when I first sat down here, I now meet as fathers and mothers — others, who at that time appeared comparatively young persons, now see their childrens' children, while here I am, unaffected, as a mere looker on might suppose, equally by the lapse of time and the flux of events."

The late Miss Jane Taylor {1783-1824, the author of 'Twinkle, Twinkle Little Star'!} — the most *Cowper-like* of poetesses, has admirably delineated a similar character, so far as the generic peculiarity goes —

> "There he sits at work, —
> A man might see him so, then bid adieu, —
> Make a long voyage to China or Peru;
> There traffic, settle, build; at length might come,
> Alter'd, and old, and weather-beaten, home,
> And find him on the same square foot of floor
> On which he left him twenty years before."

{From 'Essays in Rhyme on Morals and Manners'}

Gone with the Castle and the Crosses is the old Grammar School — a charity, the original foundation of which dates from the reign of James the First. How many are there now in the prosperous ranks of our mercantile population who well remember the low building at the top of School croft {School Croft ran from Tenter Street. Opposite White Croft, to the top of Townhead Street, SK351874}, as it lay ensconced below

> "The high raised wall, that half-shut out the day.
> And fixed attention while it bounded play;
> The gloomy entrance with its double door,
> The scooped threshhold and the deep-worn floor."

Many will remember too, that on the said floor there was a mysterious mark, not worn by boyish feet, but left there by the "hoofed tread "of a nameless personage who, saith the story, made his appearance once on a time to a boy who had traced there a certain mystical circle! The notion that the school had been favoured by the presence of such a visitor was calculated to make an awful impression on the uninitiated "greenies" — and to this end it was used by the leering rogues who understood the trick. Nor were notions of this kind confined to that spot and the youngsters in it; "children of larger growth", had their fears of the supernatural. — In by-gone days, simplicity, even when allied to piety, was liable to run into superstition: the danger is now, on the other hand, rather that of superficial knowledge leading to scepticism: fifty years ago, the tendency of the popular mind was to a painful apprehension of ghosts; at present, the danger is of doubting the existence of spiritual beings altogether; then, a man would have run off with his hair on end, had he but seen a cat in the church-yard, or an *ignis fatuus* on a bog — now, were he to meet a blue vapour or a green, "Billy-with-wisp and Peggy-with-lanthorn", his only anxiety would be to bottle up the vagrants, and carry them to be analysed at the Mechanics' Institution.

To the old Boys' and Girls' Charity Schools, modern benevolence has added numerous free work-day and Sunday Schools: that these must render current generations more keenly intelligent, no one can doubt; let us hope they will be found more strictly moral also. The great danger in these days, even of those who inculcate religious knowledge, seems to be lest more attention be paid to doctrines than to duties — to the theoretical than to the preceptive character of the Gospel. The important duty of *subordination,* if one may name so obsolete a virtue — which may have been largely overdrawn in a past generation, is now by far too generally despised, neglected, or dishonoured.

At every period a most important relation must have subsisted between the character of the resident Clergy, and the moral condition of the inhabitants: formerly, indeed, the prevalence of a sort of dogmatic theology, connected, on the part of the laity, with ideas of implicit obedience, gendering, at all events largely fostering a practical indifference to religious truth, left the chances of clerical consistency almost wholly at the mercy of the patrons of the Church: in our times, the case is somewhat altered, the character of the Clergyman and that of the people reacting upon each other to a considerable extent for good or evil. The universal circulation of the Holy Scriptures in this country, on the one hand, has placed the unerring standard of religious truth conspicuously before the public; while, on the other hand, a style of preaching, avowedly in conformity with the spirit and the letter of that standard, has been so long familiar to the people, that a Minister of the Gospel, whose faith and practice were not in some degree conformable to Scripture, would be likely to possess comparatively little influence through the medium of his clerical character. These remarks apply, of course, most directly, though by no means exclusively, to the Clergy of the Established Church.

Before the Reformation, the ecclesiastical state of Sheffield appears not to have presented any features to distinguish it particularly from other places. At all events, neither of patrons nor priests, have contemporary writers left, or succeeding ones alleged, anything to disparage their claims to rank with the best portions of their respective classes. During the earlier period of the Protestant era, the same general praise, enhanced as it is by more ennobling considerations, must be allowed to be due to the administration of religious duties. — When Charles the Second passed that memorable Act, which it would be difficult, if not unjust, to characterise by any single term, but of which the immediate result was, undoubtedly, the infliction of a tremendous mass of inconvenience, suffering, and persecution upon the non-conforming clergy, Sheffield, in common with so many other places, witnessed in one of its ministers the deliberate sacrifice of his pulpit and his freedom, as the painful alternative to trammelling his conscience. With this good man commenced, that Dissenting race of "godly preachers of Christ's holy Gospel", who assuredly shone with distinguished lustre for the next century at least. The next great religious era in Sheffield was the introduction of Methodism — that all-pervading, spirit-stirring system, to which indisputably the "march of intellect", no less than the prevalence of that style of preaching designated *par excellence,* "evangelical", are mainly, if not wholly, attributable. A fundamental peculiarity in the system referred to, was the investing human character with its awful amount of responsibility and importance in the *individual* as well as *species*: and although the primary tendency, indeed the direct intention of this was to arrest attention to spiritual things, the necessary result was at the same time, and no less, to elevate man in the scale of mental and social importance, by transferring him from a general to a particular position; in short, by rendering his character as a unit in society subsidiary to the claims of his independent relation to God as a being destined to immortality. Those who are curious to know what was the state of manners, of morals, and of religion in this town, during the period just referred to, will be gratified with a perusal of Everett's "Methodism in Sheffield" {1823, by James Everett (1784-1872)}, — suffice it to say here, that in matters of mobbing and abusing the preachers, demolishing chapels, and performing other infamous exploits, the Sheffielders showed themselves not a whit behind the chiefest desperadoes in the kingdom; nor, let it be added, have the inhabitants of this place in later years shown themselves less zealous in the adoption and support of sentiments to which a previous generation had been so violently opposed.

To a race of preachers, of whom the praise was more frequently couched in social or political than religious epithets, and in which the gentlemanly may be said to have too generally predominated over the Christian characteristics, has happily succeeded (I speak of the Established Church) a body of clergy, no less zealous in duty than sound in doctrine, no less unwearied in pastoral attentions than irreproachable in private life, no less gentle in demeanour than firm in discipline. Of the Sheffield clergy, it may truly be affirmed that, whatever others may do, *they* preach the Gospel; that, whatever others may be, *they* are benevolent; that, whatever others may do, *they* do not seek to interrupt the usefulness of their fellow-Christians of other denominations; that, whoever are ready for every good work, local or national, *they* are ready; that, whoever else may do it, *they* make everything beside subservient to the Christian character. Such is the popular estimate of the Sheffield clergy as a body. May I be permitted to speak of the vicar in particular? To the Rev. Thos. Sutton {Vicar of Sheffield 1805-1851, died 1851 aged 73}, this parish owes, under God, a weight of obligation which assuredly it never lay under in respect to any other clerical person. The name of this good man ought ever to be associated with prayers, that blessings may descend upon him, for the manner in which he has administered and does administer, the important trust devolved upon him, in caring and providing for the churches. An anonymous and disinterested writer may perhaps be allowed, without offence, thus to express himself.

References, Sources and Acknowledgements

The following is a small selection of the more general sources used in annotating this book, and other books mentioned in the text. They may be of interest for further reading. Many other sources, largely on the internet, have also been consulted on specific points.

Camden, William (1607). **Britannia**. A 'hypertext critical edition' by Dana F. Sutton of The University of California, Irvine, with an English translation by Philemon Holland, is available on-line at the 'Philological Museum' web-site at The University of Birmingham.

Coles, Graeme L.D. (2011). **The Story of South Yorkshire Botany, and the *Flora Sheffieldiensis* of Jonathan Salt**. Yorkshire Naturalists Union.

Hunter, Joseph (1819). **Hallamshire, The History and Topography of the Parish of Sheffield, in the County of York**. The version used in this work is available on Google Books, and the first 4 chapter are available on WikiSource. A second expanded edition was produced in 1869 by the Rev Alfred Gatty.

Hunter, Joseph (1828/1831). **South Yorkshire - a history of the Deanery of Doncaster**. A CD version is available from Yorkshire CD Books including both volumes.

Rhodes, Ebenezer (1818-1824). **Peak Scenery; or, The Derbyshire Tourist**. The first edition, published in 4 parts from 1818 to 1824 included engravings from drawings by Francis Chantrey. These were omitted from the second edition (1824) which is available on Internet Archive.

Acknowledgement is due to Graeme Coles for his help in correcting the botanical information, to the staff at Museums Sheffield for their encouragement and for their input, and to Hilary for putting up with 'The Tour' for so long!

Printed in Great Britain
by Amazon.co.uk, Ltd.,
Marston Gate.